ADVANCE PRAISE FOR

Bitches Unleashed: Performance and Embodied Politics in Favela Funk

"Centering the voices and performances of funkeiras—Black and Brown favela performers—to examine embodied gender politics in Brazil, *Bitches Unleashed: Performance and Embodied Politics in Favela Funk* offers fresh and insightful ways to engage with racialized performances of femininity from the perspective of the Global South. Theoretically rich and methodologically sensitive, Moreira decenters white, Western epistemological frameworks to provide an important contribution to Communication, Cultural Studies, and Gender Studies. This is a timely and significant book!"

Gust A. Yep, Professor, Communication Studies Department,
Graduate Faculty, Sexuality Studies Program,
Faculty, Ed. D. Program in Educational Leadership,
San Francisco State University

"*Bitches Unleashed: Performance and Embodied Politics in Favela Funk* represents truly cutting-edge, outstanding and groundbreaking scholarship in Critical Intercultural Communication Studies. Raquel Moreira demonstrates an intersectional, performative approach to study historically nuanced and culturally specific modes of gender, sexuality, and the body among Brazil's favela funk performers who are mostly Black and brown singers in the age of globalization. The most significant aspect of this book is to unapologetically showcase the paradox of desire in performing hypersexualized feminine genders which are often controlled, disciplined, and surveilled by patriarchy, sexism, and heteronormativity."

Shinsuke Eguchi, Associate Professor,
Department of Communication & Journalism, University of New Mexico

"I loved this book and could not put it down. While academic in tone, it is also conversational and interesting to read for any audience. Moreira's book is an astute look at intersectional feminine performances in the contexts of Brazil and Funkeiras. Her interviews demonstrate the power of qualitative methodologies to uproot long-held assumptions that femininity is anything other than strength and resilience. This text offers scholars of communication studies, femininity studies, and/or women, gender, and sexuality studies a brilliant take on a specific community, with lessons of feminine empowerment for us all."

Kathryn Hobson, Assistant Professor,
School of Communication Studies, James Madison University

"We want the (favela) funk! Gotta have that (favela) funk! Moreira, in *Bitches Unleashed*, dismantles Global North and White, U.S. centric perspectives of research by reconceptualizing systems of gender and sexuality through transfeminista formulations of agency. By focusing on structural change and decolonizing cisheteronormativity, the centering of people of color and travesti communication offers the reader powerful analyses of white feminist failures, coloniality, transgression, intersectionality, and critical qualitative methodologies."

Robert Gutierrez-Perez, Assistant Professor,
Editor, *Border-Lines: Journal of the Latino Research Center,*
Department of Communication Studies, University of Nevada, Reno

Bitches Unleashed

Critical
Intercultural
Communication
Studies

Thomas K. Nakayama and Bernadette Marie Calafell
General Editors

Vol. 27

The Critical Intercultural Communication Studies series
is part of the Peter Lang Media and Communication list.
Every volume is peer reviewed and meets
the highest quality standards for content and production.

PETER LANG
New York • Bern • Berlin
Brussels • Vienna • Oxford • Warsaw

Raquel Moreira

Bitches Unleashed

Performance and Embodied Politics in Favela Funk

PETER LANG

New York • Bern • Berlin
Brussels • Vienna • Oxford • Warsaw

Library of Congress Cataloging-in-Publication Data

Names: Moreira, Raquel, author.
Title: Bitches unleashed: performance and embodied politics
in favela funk / Raquel Moreira.
Description: New York: Peter Lang, 2021.
Series: Critical intercultural communication studies; vol 27 | ISSN 1528-6118
Includes bibliographical references and index.
Identifiers: LCCN 2021003706 (print) | LCCN 2021003707 (ebook) |
ISBN 978-1-4331-6956-4 (hardback) | ISBN 978-1-4331-6957-1 (paperback) |
ISBN 978-1-4331-6958-8 (ebook pdf) | ISBN 978-1-4331-6959-5 (epub) |
ISBN 978-1-4331-6960-1 (mobi)
Subjects: LCSH: Women—Political activity—Brazil. | Political
culture—Brazil. | Funk (Music)—Brazil—Rio de Janeiro—History and
criticism. | Marginality, Social—Brazil. | Resistance (Philosophy)
Classification: LCC HQ1236.5.B6 M675 2021 (print) |
LCC HQ1236.5.B6 (ebook) | DDC 320.082/0981—dc23
LC record available at https://lccn.loc.gov/2021003706
LC ebook record available at https://lccn.loc.gov/2021003707
DOI 10.3726/b18307

Bibliographic information published by **Die Deutsche Nationalbibliothek**.
Die Deutsche Nationalbibliothek lists this publication in the "Deutsche
Nationalbibliografie"; detailed bibliographic data are available
on the Internet at http://dnb.d-nb.de/.

© 2021 Peter Lang Publishing, Inc., New York
80 Broad Street, 5th floor, New York, NY 10004
www.peterlang.com

To Deize, Carol, Xuxú, Linn, and Dandara

Contents

Figures

Acknowledgements

I have been meaning to write this book for at least the past five years. Countless people have helped me find the courage and time to finally do it. The process of finding courage and time to do it has been influenced by countless people. I am grateful for their support during this demanding and all-consuming process.

First and foremost, I would like to thank my partner, Isaac Pressnell, who has been my emotional pillar during this taxing time. Thank you, my love, for caring for our daughter, Isadora, our dog, Gatolinos, our house, and my emotional needs—all while dealing with a global pandemic, a chronic illness diagnosis, and the death of my father. Thank you, Isaac, for giving me space to write this book during an impossible time in our lives. We both know I would still be procrastinating if not for your constant reminders that this was actually the right time to do it.

I want to thank Bernadette Marie Calafell for her intellectual generosity and mentorship. It has been an honor to learn from and with her. I remember the first time she told me to submit a book proposal. It was in Las Vegas, during the 2015 NCA, as we walked into an elevator. It *only* took me four years to follow through. Thank you, Bernadette, for encouraging me to write this book. Her request for a proposal made me feel accountable to finishing this work.

To Deize Tigrona, Dandara, MC Carol (and Ana Paula!), MC Xuxú, Linn da Quebrada (and Izabela!), MC Kátia and LD, MC Pink, and the Abysolutas: this work exists because of them. I am eternally grateful for all that I have learned during our time together. Meeting you has changed my life.

I am thankful for my Brazilian family, Carla Moreira, Luiz Carlos Moreira, Maria Martha Bruno and Carolina Damico for their support during and after my 2013 fieldwork. Every single one of you has lent me a car to go meet with an artist or attend a performance. Mom, thank you for coming to a not-so-safe party with me—and for not freaking out about it. Grandpa, thank you for your financial support during that summer. Even though you are not a big *funk carioca* fan, you are still a champion for social justice.

To my Cidade de Deus friends, Don and Mingau, thank you so much for spending time with and for introducing me to so many funkeiras. I will never forget the afternoon we spent at MC Mãe's (descanse em paz) rooftop in 2012—that was the first time I heard about MC Carol. Many thanks to Felícia Cristina, who took me to a baile in São Gonçalo and put me in touch with several artists.

Many thanks to my copy-editor, Kristen Foht, for her curiosity, competence, and thoroughness. I could not have done this without her help. I am thankful, too, for my Peter Lang editors, Erika Hendrix and Ashita Shah, who were patient and helpful throughout this process.

I am grateful for my friend, Jen Abraham, who joined our family pod during the Covid-19 pandemic to help us care for our baby. I did not think I would be able to have whole-day writing retreats! I would also like to thank my fierce academic friends for their support and encouragement over the years: Dr. Fatima Zahrae Chrifi Alaoui, Dr. Leslie Rossman, Dr. Shadee Abdi, Dr. Pavithra Prasad, Dr. Catherine Clifford, and Dr. Kristin Seemuth-Whaley. Your badassery inspires me. I am also grateful for my dear friend Paula Martin, who was my emotional rock during my DU years.

I would like to acknowledge Dr. Adriana Carvalho Lopes's indispensable favela funk book, *Funk-se Quem Quiser*. Her work has had a tremendous impact on this project. Thanks also to Dr. Adriana Facina, Dr. Carlos Palombini, Dr. Pâmella Passos, and Dr. Pablo Laignier for their contributions to favela funk research. A special thanks to Dr. Mariana Gomes for sharing her passion for funkeiras (and frustrations with feminism) with me.

I would like to thank my University of Denver's Department of Communication Studies professors for their intellectual support, especially my dissertation committee members, Dr. Richie Hao, Dr. Darrin Hicks, and Dr. Luis León (descansa en paz).

I am very grateful for the scholars whose work have impacted this book deeply: the late Dr. José Esteban Muñoz, Dr. D. Soyini Madison, Dr. Mariza Corrêa, Dr. Sueli Carneiro, Dr. Jaqueline Gomes de Jesus, Dr. Kimberlé Crenshaw, Dr. Chandra Mohanty, Viviane Vergueiro, Dr. Brittney Cooper, Dr. Aisha Durham, Dr. Gust Yep, Dr. Karma Chávez, Dr. Shinsuke Eguchi, Dr. Rhea Ashley Hoskin, and countless others.

Many thanks to my Graceland University friends, who have amazed me during our many hallway conversations: Dr. Tim Robbins, Dr. Dan Platt, Jessie Sherman, Karen Gergely, Dr. Jonathan Montalvo, Leslie and Nate Robinson, Dr. Brittany Lash, and Dr. Steve Glazer. Special thanks to Dr. Brian White and Dr. Jill Rhae for helping me fight for and receive institutional support for this book.

I am also thankful for my Latina/o Communication Studies friends/ colleagues, whose work and dedication to our field always amazes me: Dr. Michael Lechuga, Dr. Robert Gutierrez-Perez, Dr. Leandra Hernández, Dr. Sarah De Los Santos-Upton, Dr. José Ángel Maldonado, Oscar Alfonso Mejía, Dr. Sara Baugh, Dr. Sergio Juarez, and many others.

I would like to thank my friend, Dr. Pedro Curi, for sending me a Valesca Popozuda video back in 2009 that triggered many ideas for this work. I am also grateful for Dr. Marildo Nercolini and Dr. Alexandre Werneck, for having one of the first talks about the funkeiras with me in 2009 as well.

Many thanks to Vincent Rosenblatt for allowing me to have his beautiful work illustrating this book cover.

To everyone who has supported me through this journey, thank you with all my heart. It really *does* take a village.

Introducing Bitches Unleashed

In the music video for Linn da Quebrada's "Coytada" ("Poor Girl"),[1] she chops up dildos of different shades on a cutting board. The video mimics a cooking show in which Linn and fellow Black *travestis* Jup do Bairro and Slim Soledad sensually and frantically play with baking ingredients: swallowing and spitting back out eggs, blowing flour on each other, pouring milk in their own mouths, and using rolling pins on dildos. The lyrics suggest that Linn would rather have sex with the devil than with someone who only likes "gym rats" and "bulls" (muscular men) because, according to her, "I'm very effeminate."[2] Linn da Quebrada illustrates well why I have been obstinate in my interest in favela funk as a research topic for the last 10 years. When I first started to notice the movement for the purpose of studying it, a performance like hers—even her popularity—would have been unthinkable. This book is a result of my journey after a decade of dedication to, first, women in favela funk and, now, to all who perform femininities within the movement. They are known as the *funkeiras*.

Rio de Janeiro's favela funk is a musical genre and cultural movement developed by poor folks of color in the 1980s. The characteristic beats, lyrics, dance moves, and clothing suggest a "social practice that is historically situated:"[3] favela funk is the product of the continuous unequal and violent conditions poor people of color face inside Rio's favelas. There are robust studies about favela funk in Brazilian academia and globally.[4] Often, this research focuses on the movement's criminalization, its ties with drug trafficking, and its aesthetic dimensions. Very few of them, hence, concentrate on the funkeiras. Indeed, the scarce debates regarding funkeiras in Brazilian academia had a lot to do with why I became interested in them in the first place.

As a 1990s kid born in Rio, favela funk was regularly played on the radio and enjoyed at parties, even in middle-class parties like mine. By the time I became intrigued by funkeiras' performances in 2009, however, I had not attended a favela funk party—a *baile*—since 2001. The last bailes I had attended were dominated by artists from Cidade de Deus, or City of God, including a funkeira who is prominently featured in this work, Tati Quebra Barraco (Tati House/Shack Breaker). Years later, in 2008, while taking a class in women's history, occasionally one of us would bring up the funkeiras as an example of a "complicated" negotiation with femininity and sexuality. There was a tendency in most of us to understand favela funk, while acknowledging some of its nuances (such as race and class), as *machista* (sexist). But that was it. There was no further analysis. It was not until the last year of my masters, in 2009, that my scholarly interest in the funkeiras emerged with full force. I was teaching a course in gender and media at Federal Fluminense University, and toward the end of the semester, I decided to show and discuss Denise Garcia's 2005 documentary, *I'm Ugly but Trendy.*[5] The class was relatively small, about 16 people, and a lot of the students were actively involved with feminist and LGBTQIA+ movements. Hence, I was hoping to have a good debate on how gender intersects with race and class. To my surprise, a lot of my students who identified as feminists were appalled by the documentary—"this woman just said she's going to be somebody's dessert!" Some even thought that the documentary was degrading to funkeiras, who were openly talking and performing about sex to the cameras. I realized that the students' disturbance was connected to the manner in which funkeiras performed femininity: the direct ways in which they spoke about sex, the way they danced, and the way they dressed. These elements, together, seemed to offend white, middle-class, feminine sensibilities.

That was, perhaps, the first of many times yet to come that I became aware of what I now regard as feminist failures. Whatever I had learned about feminism up until that point, and whatever I was teaching about it, was insufficient for understanding the funkeiras' performances beyond my students' impression that the documentary was demeaning to them. More than ten years later, my curiosity about the funkeiras, their performances, and their professional paths still intrigue me beyond questions of whether or not they are feminists. I have learned that part of what I perceive to be a scholarly struggle to provide a nuanced understanding of the funkeiras stems from scholars' tendency to work deductively to "uncover" whether or not those artists are feminists. This book does the opposite of that. Over the next six chapters, I engage this analytical shortcoming as I offer my own consideration of diverse aspects of funkeiras' performances. A fundamental element of this book's inductive approach originates from my choice of method.

Critical Methods for the Study of the Funkeiras

I frequently reiterate throughout *Bitches Unleashed* how much I believe past analyses of funkeiras fall short methodologically. Choosing methods to study their performances was actually very challenging. No single methodology seemed enough, since aside from live and recorded performances, social media has recently become central to funkeiras' self- and collective expressions. I knew my selections had to be versatile, ethical, and critical, meaning that they had to challenge cartesian thought binaries, such as mind (superior) and body (inferior).[6] The considerations featured in this book are, in part, the result of the critical methodological approaches necessary to understand funkeiras in their multidimensionality. Below, I make brief notes about critical ethnography, including interviewing, as well as connective ethnography.

To Dwight Conquergood, "ethnography is *an embodied practice*" (emphasis in original).[7] This perspective calls for "the project of radical empiricism," in which there is a change in "ethnography's traditional approach from Other-as-theme to Other-as-interlocutor," which also represents "a shift from monologue to dialogue, from information to communication."[8] Conquergood suggests that our scholarly foci need to move from centers to "borderlands," "zones of difference," and "busy intersections" where many identities and interests are not compartmentalized but articulated in multiple ways.[9] These changes have been materialized via critical ethnography. Thomas defines critical ethnography as "the reflective process of choosing between conceptual alternatives and making value-laden judgments of meaning and method to challenge research, policy, and other forms of human activity."[10] In comparing critical ethnography to its traditional counterpart, Thomas asserts, "critical ethnography is conventional ethnography with a political purpose."[11]

Madison's critical ethnography builds on the ideas exposed in the previous paragraph through five central questions.[12] These inquiries revolve around issues such as the intentions, purposes, and frame of analysis of the researcher; the possible consequences of the researcher's work, including the potential to do harm; if the researcher maintains dialogue that enables collaboration between herself and others; how the local affects the broader context; and, finally, if the research is committed to social justice—critical ethnography must be committed to politics. The chapters in this book indirectly answer these questions. For instance, I understand the funkeiras as my co-creators and often feature their voices through direct quotes from interviews and song lyrics not simply to illustrate points but also to formulate new knowledge and draw conclusions. If there is something missing from the few studies done on funkeiras, it is certainly their voices.

There are multiple elements in critical ethnography's methodological sequences, from investigating the researcher's positionality to tips for preparing for the field.[13] I would like, however, to shed light on interviewing, as it is so central to this work. The critical ethnographic interview searches for meanings in ways that go beyond trivial information or "finding the 'truth of the matter.'"[14] Madison points out that the researcher must always keep in mind that interviewees are not "objects." On the contrary, they are subjects "with agency, history, and [...] [their] own idiosyncratic command of a story."[15] Consequently, the primary goal of interviewing in critical ethnography is not to find reliable and verifiable information but to illuminate the complexities of "individual subjectivity, memory, yearnings, polemics, and hope that are unveiled and inseparable from shared and inherited expressions of communal strivings, social history, and political possibility."[16] To interview the funkeiras featured in this book, I relied on all three types of critical ethnographic interviews Madison conceptualizes,[17] sometimes intentionally and other times as a simple result of where my conversation with a funkeira was headed: (1) oral history, for when an interview is focused on the recounting of events as they relate to the lives of the individuals who experienced them; (2) personal narrative, which deals with the subject's point-of-view of an event or experience; and (3) finally, the topical interview, which concentrates on individuals' perspectives on an issue, process, or phenomenon. These distinct approaches to interviewing were useful, as they enabled funkeiras to direct our conversations how they wanted—some funkeiras joined the movement five years ago, and some have had over two decades of experience in favela funk.

Critical ethnography presents a fruitful perspective through which to observe, experience, and write about performances—whether live or mediated. Moreman and MacIntosh's analysis of Latina drag performances,[18] for instance, utilizes Conquergood and Madison's points about researcher and interlocutor's co-performativity during fieldwork in order to bring critical ethnography to the page: "We aesthetically (re)present these ethnographic moments on the page not only through our fieldnote vignettes to offer expression to the embodied messages but also to critically evaluate and expose their political implications."[19] Similarly, I offer vivid, embodied descriptions of funkeiras' performances first as a means to "honor the power and beauty of cultural expression"[20] and second as a way to comprehend their political repercussions. Like Auslander, I reject the opposition between live and mediated performances, as well as the assumption that live performances are somewhat superior to mediated ones. Indeed, these categories "are not mutually exclusive."[21] Funkeiras rely heavily on YouTube, for instance, to promote their work. Excluding mediated performances from this research would rob funkeiras' work of their currency and transformations over the years.

Social media has become an extension of the public sphere, a space in which funkeiras not only promote their careers but also narrate their everyday lives. When I first started my fieldwork in June 2013, only very young funkeiras like Pocah had any significant social media presence. Over time, it has become clear that social media offer platforms for funkeiras to perform aspects of their identities that might not interest mainstream media. This book relies on social media to access the performances of funkeiras I was not able to witness in person. To emphasize other digital content from these artists as extensions of their professional and quotidian performances seems appropriate.[22] As such, I rely on connective ethnography's principle, which advocates for a "stance or orientation to internet-related research that considers connections and relations as normative social practices and internet social spaces as complexly connected to other spaces."[23] For that reason, I have been following these artists where they are the most active—on Twitter and Instagram—for at least two years, checking in on their profiles every couple of days to make sure I do not miss anything. Thus, funkeiras' social media engagement, specifically on those two platforms, are featured in this book as opportunities to further include their voices and perspectives on matters of femininities, race, sexuality, politics, and other topics as they intersect with other aspects of their personal and professional lives.

Who Are the Funkeiras?

Funkeiras are favela funk performers, mostly singers—known as MCs—but also dancers, who are predominantly Black and brown and whose ages vary between early 20s to mid-50s. That is the short answer. The long answer is featured in the six chapters of this book, and each one presents aspects of them as people and performers that hopefully provides a more complete response to the question of who they are. Specifically, I interviewed eight artists—in person, via phone, and over video chat—six of whom are prominently featured in this work: MC

Kátia, MC Dandara, Deize Tigrona, MC Carol, MC Xuxú, and Linn da Quebrada. Pocah, Valesca Popozuda, and Tati Quebra Barraco are also important for this book, even though I was not able to interview them. I mention other artists in my analyses, but these nine funkeiras persist throughout the following pages. My intention was to include as many artists as possible in a way that their idiosyncrasies did not get lost in the numbers. That means that I absolutely did not intend to include *all* funkeiras, as favela funk is a very dynamic movement with new artists joining in constantly.

MCs Dandara, Deize Tigrona, Tati Quebra Barraco, and Kátia all have been in favela funk for at least 15 years. These trailblazers are Black women who started performing more seriously about sex and relationships in the early 2000s, except for MC Dandara who has had a career since the 1990s. Although these women are more or less from the same favela funk generation, their performance styles and levels of success are distinct. Tati Quebra Barraco remains the most popular funkeira in this group, followed by her fellow City of God artist Deize Tigrona, MC Kátia, and MC Dandara. Deize, however, is the most globally known because of DJ Diplo's use of her song's "Injeção" ("Injection") sampler in M.I.A.'s "Bucky Done Gun." During our personal interview, she told me, "I was so famous in Europe, I didn't even know!" I would like to think that, like Tati and Deize, this work was born in City of God. My mother had a couple of good acquaintances living in the community who later became my bridge to most of the funkeiras I interviewed back in the summer of 2013, including those from outside City of God, like MC Pink, MC Kátia, and MC Dandara.

Like the funkeiras mentioned above, Valesca Popozuda has had a career since the early 2000s. Valesca, however, achieved a level of celebrity that no other funkeira had obtained until very recently. Back in 2013, I had several exchanges with her manager at the time, trying and failing to schedule an interview with Valesca. Finally, in July 2013, he stopped taking my calls. Since her time with the feminine *bonde** Gaiola das Popozudas (Big Trunk's Cage), Valesca has been performing songs

---

* Bonde is a slang for gang or squad. In the 2000s, bondes formed by either all men or all women became popular in Rio's funk.

with explicit sexual content that, for the most part, cannot be played on mainstream media.[24] Still, the funkeira has been able to navigate between mainstream acceptance and favela funk popularity for at least the past 13 years. Perhaps the biggest difference between Valesca and the trailblazers mentioned above is the fact that she is significantly lighter-skinned, than say Tati and Deize, which gives Valesca a kind of media access that is rarely granted to Black funkeiras.

Rio-based Pocah, formerly known as MC Pocahontas, is another up and coming celebrity funkeira. I met the MC back in 2013, when she was only 18 years old but already had a significantly large and young social media following from all over Brazil. Like Valesca, Pocah's physical traits approximate her to white femininity—Pocah is perhaps even more conventionally pretty than Valesca, given her young age and petite body size—which places her in a position of privilege in mainstream media. Also like Valesca, Pocah's recent work focuses on autonomy, be it bodily or financial. She is currently identified as one of the most popular favela funk artists on YouTube.[25]

The artistic legacy of Tati Quebra Barraco is evident through young Black funkeira MC Carol. Like her predecessor, MC Carol's performance style includes a very peculiar mixture of aggression and disdain. Both Tati and MC Carol participated in Fox Life Brasil's reality TV show *Lucky Ladies*, hosted by Tati who served as a mentor to younger funkeiras.[26] MC Carol publicly acknowledges the importance of Tati's mentorship and their connection since the show, which has generated other kinds of partnerships, such as the song and music video "Mamãe da Putaria" ("Mother of Hoeness"). MC Carol is an avid social media user and an outspoken activist against racism, sexism, and fatphobia. I contacted her manager in May 2019, and after two and a half months, I interviewed MC Carol in August 2019 over WhatsApp phone call.

MC Xuxú and Linn da Quebrada are the last two artists prominently featured in this book. Both are Black and identify as *travesti* (Brazilian-based nonbinary transfeminine identity). Both artists are also the only ones I interviewed who are not from the state of Rio de Janeiro and whose audiences are probably more so localized at the intersection of Black and LGBTQIA+ communities from all over Brazil. MC Xuxú is from Minas Gerais and has been active in favela funk since

2012, when she briefly lived in Rio de Janeiro and fell in love with the movement. She was the first favela funk artist to unequivocally identify as travesti in her first hit, "Um Beijo" ("A Kiss"). MC Xuxú was the last artist I interviewed, via a WhatsApp video call in June 2020, when she finally found time to talk to me after I had contacted her a year prior. I experienced a similar process with Linn da Quebrada. I first contacted the São Paulo-based travesti back in May 2019, but it was only in April 2020 that I was able to interview her. Both artists were isolated in their homes due to the Covid-19 global pandemic, when live performances with large audiences essentially ceased for several months. Linn started her career more prominently in 2016, when she released several music videos featuring Black travesti themes in favela funk style. Today, she is perhaps more accurately described as a performance artist, though I identify her as a funkeira in this work—a label with which she is comfortable, per our interview.

The participation of funkeiras as protagonists of favela funk has been contributing to problematizing an essentially masculine environment in which cisgender men were the ones speaking up about a variety of matters, including about women and transfeminine people. I focus on funkeiras' personal experiences and perspectives, first and foremost, to highlight their contributions to favela funk. The theoretical conclusions and implications are a consequence of this work. My hope is to redress both the unacceptable silence about and misreadings of funkeiras in academia.

Intercultural Communication, Intersectionality, and a *Transfeminista* Sensibility

As an ongoing phenomenon, globalization and its effects are not limited to the economic and political realms. Academia is part of this process, as an increasingly complex "migration" of theories displaces and appropriates, resists and transforms knowledge as part of the development of a global academic community. Because these flows of knowledge are unequal, with the North as the economic center and the South as its exploited periphery, they mimic economic relations of dominance-subordination between Global North and Global South.[27] Intercultural communication sometimes reproduces this problematic tendency.

Communication's foundation on white, Western epistemology[28] has limited its engagement with non-Western issues, which in turn has generated a series of critiques in its subfields. Scholars of color in intercultural communication, for instance, have made important efforts over the years to dislocate the discipline's "white problem," or the tendency to re-center, even if unconsciously, white Western knowledges and concerns.[29] Eguchi and Asante contest this dynamic by asserting that the "U.S. American capitalistic heteronormative circulations of power recurrently patrol and protect the boundaries of intercultural communication theory"[30] at the expense of marginalized folks of color from the Global South. Additionally, other scholars have interrogated intercultural communication's reliance on single-axis analyses while also calling for the subfield's critical engagement with race, queerness, and cisnormativity, among others.[31] Accordingly, accounts of power relations in intercultural contexts will not be comprehensive if scholars overlook how people's existence is shaped by intersecting systems of oppression, such as race, class, nation, location, ability, and immigration status in locations beyond the Global North.[32]

While rich analyses of power dynamics outside of Western contexts are necessary for critical intercultural communication, so are epistemological frameworks that dislocate white, U.S.-centric perspectives. Intersectionality is often used as a perspective that can counter these tendencies. Kimberlé Crenshaw coined the term in response to the inadequacy of feminist and antiracist initiatives that consistently framed gender and race oppression as mutually exclusive— or through single-axis analyses—and thus deemed the experiences of Black women unknowable to identity politics.[33] However, Black feminists have warned that white feminists' cooptation of the framework has resulted in problematic and erroneous reproductions that simultaneously deflate intersectionality of its original meaning and erase its Black feminist origins.[34] Intercultural communication has also been at fault for this. Yep has warned communication scholars against treating intersectionality as a decontextualized series of boxes to be ticked.[35]

Additionally, Eguchi, Calafell, and Abdi argue that intersectionality in communication studies is traversed by the "logics of whiteness."[36] As I have proposed before, Brazilian *transfeminismo* provides a fresh and exciting perspective against problematic, white-washed instances of intersectionality that could be useful for intercultural communication.[37]

Bitches Unleashed adopts a *transfeminista* perspective formulated by Brazilian Black *transfeministas*. Much of the epistemological and political framework *transfeminismo* champions was born out of struggles against Western, white feminist exclusions.[38] A *transfeminista* approach is intersectional and antiracist; because many trans*[†] people are impacted by poverty, *transfeminismo* is class-conscious.[39] *Transfeminismo* is also evidently an important tool against biological essentialism, which not only excludes trans*, intersex, and other people with nonconforming bodies from feminist frameworks but also hinders the coalitional possibility that might exist among those who are oppressed by cisnormativity.[40] Finally, *transfeminismo* is committed to decolonizing cisnormativity, which *transfeministas* argue is inevitably connected to other colonial structures, such as race, class, and sexuality.[41] This epistemological perspective is woven through the analyses in this book.

An Overview of *Bitches Unleashed*

Tati Quebra Barraco released "Cachorra Solta" ("Unleashed Bitch") in response to MC Taizinho's song "Cachorro Solto" ("Unleashed Dog"), in which a man claims that a woman is trying to "trap" him by getting pregnant. Tati's song was on my mind when I chose *Bitches Unleashed* as the title of this book. In her version, she plays with the common assumption that cisgender women are the ones interested in using pregnancy to deceive cisgender, heterosexual men: "you got me pregnant thinking you were gonna trap me/but you're the one who got fucked/you're the one who is trapped/I'm an unleashed bitch [...]/and you're gonna watch the baby!"[42] This may seem like a simple inversion of subject

---

† Trans* activists in Brazil use this prefix to indicate an umbrella term that is appropriate for the Brazilian context.

positions, but the social consequences for ciswomen, especially Black women, who snub motherhood can be severe.[43] This is also a representative example of how funkeiras transgress femininity's normative, white version, as I show in the next six chapters.

I begin my exploration of funkeiras' performances by analyzing what I term "white feminist failures." These failures, which originate in white feminism's supremacy in places like Brazil, have impacted previous analyses of the funkeiras, specifically in regards to questions around agency and possessing a "feminist agenda"—whatever that means. A central, taken-for-granted, aspect of white feminism is its relationship with normative white femininity. Like white feminism itself, which is often simply referred to as feminism in the singular form, normative white femininity is frequently apprehended simply as femininity. Next, I provide an overview of Other(ed) femininities relevant to the examination of the funkeiras and take into consideration the Brazilian context. Finally, I explore femininity vis-à-vis agency, white feminist blind spots, and Third World and postcolonial feminist reconceptualizations of it that are important for the comprehension of funkeiras' embodied politics.

Chapter Two provides the essential backdrop for funkeiras' performances. I begin with an overview of the development and current status of favela funk, both as a cultural movement and as an industry. This section underscores the material realities funkeiras face in the industry as poor people of color from the favelas. Additionally, I delve into the gendered aspects of favela funk as labor, according to funkeiras' own assessment. Aspects of gendered labor include issues of abuse from heterosexual cismen in the industry, professional and romantic relationships with managers, and professional autonomy. This unit is purposefully centered around funkeiras' voices, whose perspectives on favela funk contextualize the subsequent chapters.

I begin to address performances of femininities in favela funk more overtly in Chapter Three. In it, I outline the connections between performance and transgression with a concentration on marginalized femininities. In connection with this, I then expose funkeiras' reflections on how they negotiate the multiple personae they embody on stage. In fact, many funkeiras affirm that the stage, or the ability to perform, is a privilege they cherish; it provides them with a platform for artistic expression that is denied to many people who look like them. I end this section by examining the idiosyncrasies in funkeiras' transgressive performances of racialized femininities. The performances and interviews I present in this chapter serve as initial evidence against the dichotomous and homogenous apprehensions of the funkeiras.

Chapter Four continues the work of exploring funkeiras' multifaceted performances of racialized femininities through their relationships with other women and cismen. Often, the backlash against funkeiras stem precisely from the contentious gendered relationships they embody during performances.[44] I divide this unit in sections that first address the wife, mistress, and *recalcadas* (haters) trend in feminine favela funk. All of these themes are becoming less popular over the years, and Chapter Four makes an argument for why that is the case. Next, I analyze funkeiras' clashes with cismen, which are frequently belligerent but also scornful. Performances meant to challenge men tend to revolve around cheating, taking financial advantage of them, having sex on whose terms, and embracing marginalized femininities.

Even though race as an integral part of funkeiras' performances of femininities is present in the analyses throughout this book, Chapter Five more unequivocally explores funkeiras' relationship with whiteness and Blackness over the years. The discussion starts with a brief overview of race politics in Brazil, with emphasis on the colonial roots of anti-Blackness in the country as well as myths around racial democracy. As Lopes rightly asserts, funkeiras tended to evade overt references to race and specifically to Blackness in the early days of their success.[45] My interviews with Black funkeiras in 2013, however, show that they were very much aware of the material impact race had on their lives. Black funkeiras now not only include references to race in their performances, but they also use public forums like Twitter and Instagram to scorn and question whiteness, affirm Blackness, and in this process, create a defying version of Black femininity.

Chapter Six deals specifically with travesti femininity and identity in favela funk by focusing on the trajectory and performances of three artists: dancer Lacraia and MCs Xuxú and Linn da Quebrada. I provide an overview of travesti identity in Chapter One as part of my exploration of marginalized femininities. Given the particularities of travestis, I being Chapter Six by asking, "is travesti queer?" While concepts of queerness may be important to understanding travesti femininity, I contend that using queer to define non-Western categories of gender and/or sexuality erases the differences, nuances, and potentials of these identities. The diverse iterations of travesti in favela funk I examine suggest that context plays an important role in how much space and flexibility these artists have to perform. Lacraia, for instance, who was famous in the early 2000s, had her identity mocked and exploited in mainstream media multiple times. Differently, MC Xuxú and Linn da Quebrada, who did not quite achieve Lacraia's 2003–2004 mainstream popularity, clearly articulate in their interviews with me and in performance that their version of travesti identity, albeit different from one another, both engage in disidentificatory practices that aid them in working within and against dominant culture.

I end *Bitches Unleashed* with a conceptualization of embodied politics that recognizes racialized performances of femininity from the Global South and relies on Third World and postcolonial feminist formulations of agency. In connection with these concepts, I then provide insights that stem from the question of whether or not funkeiras are feminist. Admittedly, this question has damaged more complicated understandings of funkeiras. In the process of investigating this query, I offer further critiques to white feminism to then formulate an answer about feminine artists in favela funk. The end of the book looks at the current conservative landscape in Brazil, which certainly clashes with funkeiras' aspirations to live beyond survival. Because the livelihood of many funkeiras is precarious and bounded by context, scholars should continue listening to them and echoing their contributions to feminism in ways that help legitimatize their existences.

Notes

1 Linn da Quebrada, "Linn da Quebrada—Coytada (Clipe Oficial)," September 17, 2018, YouTube video, 3:01, https://www.youtube.com/watch?v=IUq4WWJRngE.
2 da Quebrada, "Coytada."

3 Adriana Lopes, *Funk-se Quem Quiser: No Batidão Negro da Cidade Carioca* (Rio de Janeiro: Bom Texto, 2011), 19.

4 For more on favela funk, see Pablo Laignier, "Towards a Political Economy of Funk Carioca: Notes on Postmodern Theory and Its Developments in Contemporary Popular Music," *Ciberlegenda* 2, no. 24 (2011): 61–76; Alexandra Lippman, "'Law for Whom?': Responding to Sonic Illegality in Brazil's Funk Carioca," *Sound Studies* 5, no 1 (2018): 22–36; James McNally, "Favela Chic: Diplo, Funk Carioca, and the Ethics and Aesthetics of the Global Remix," *Popular Music and Society* 40, no. 4 (2017): 434–52; Mylene Mizrahi, "Indumentária *Funk*: A Confrontação da Alteridade Colocando em Diálogo o Local e o Cosmopolita," *Horizontes Antropológicos* 13, no. 28 (2007): 232–62; Dennis Novaes, "Funk Proibidão: Música e Poder nas Favelas Cariocas," *Plataforma Sucupira*, 2006, https://sucupira.capes. gov.br/sucupira/public/consultas/coleta/trabalhoConclusao/viewTrabalhoC- onclusao.jsf?popup=true&id_trabalho=4374709; Carlos Palombini, "Proibidão em tempo de pacificação armada," in *Patrimônio Musical Na Atualidade: Tradição, Memória, Discurso e Poder*, ed. Maria Alice Volpe (Rio de Janeiro: Universidade Federal do Rio de Janeiro, 2013), 215–36; Pâmella Passos and Adriana Facina, "'Baile Modelo!': Reflexões Sobre Práticas Funkeiras em Contexto de Pacificação," *Proceedings from the VI Seminário Internacional de Políticas Culturais: Fundação Casa de Rui Barbosa* (Rio de Janeiro: RJ, Brazil, 2015).

5 Denise Garcia, *Sou Feia, Mas Tô na Moda* (São Paulo: Imovision, 2005), Film.

6 Dwight Conquergood, "Rethinking Ethnography: Towards a Critical Cultural Politics," *Communication Monographs* 58 (1991): 179–94.

7 Conquergood, "Rethinking Ethnography," 180.

8 Conquergood, "Rethinking Ethnography," 182.

9 Conquergood, "Rethinking Ethnography," 184.

10 Jim Thomas, *Doing Critical Ethnography* (Newbury Park: Sage, 1993): 4.

11 Thomas, *Doing*, 4.

12 D. Soyini Madison, *Critical Ethnography: Method, Ethics, and Performance* (Thousand Oaks: Sage, 2005).

13 Madison, *Critical Ethnography*.

14 Madison, *Critical Ethnography*, 25.

15 Madison, *Critical Ethnography*, 25.

16 Madison, *Critical Ethnography*, 26.

17 Madison, *Critical Ethnography*.

18 Shane Moreman and Dawn Marie McIntosh, "Brown Scriptings and Rescriptings: A Critical Performance Ethnography of Latina Drag Queens," *Communication and Critical/Cultural Studies* 7, no. 2 (2010): 115–35.

19 Moreman and MacIntosh, "Brown Scriptings," 117.

20 D. Soyini Madison, "Narrative Poetics and Performative Interventions," in *Handbook of Critical and Indigenous Methodologies*, eds. Norman Denzin, Yvonna Lincoln, and Linda Tuhiwai Smith (Los Angeles: Sage, 2008), 392.

21 Philip Auslander, "Live and Technologically Mediated Performance," in *The Cambridge Companion to Performance Studies*, ed. Tracy C. Davis (Cambridge: Cambridge University Press, 2008), 109.

22 Kevin M. Leander, "Toward a Connective Ethnography of Online/Offline Literacy Networks," in *Handbook of Research on New Literacies*, eds. Julie Coiro et al. (New York: Routledge, 2010).

23 Leander, "Toward a Connective," 35.

24 Lopes, *Funk-se*.

25 Rodrigo Ortega, "Kondzilla em Queda: Por Que o Canal de Funk Perdeu Audiência e a Liderança nas Paradas?" *G1*, June 4, 2019, https://g1.globo.com/pop-arte/musica/noticia/2019/06/04/kondzilla-em-queda-por-que-o-canal-de-funk-perdeu-audiencia-e-a-lideranca-nas-paradas.ghtml.

26 Márcia Pereira, "Funkeiras cantam, gritam e armam barracos em novo reality show," *UOL*, May 25, 2015, http://noticiasdatv.uol.com.br/noticia/televisao/funkeiras-cantam-gritam-e-armam-barracos-em-novo-reality-show-7993.

27 Claudia de Lima Costa, "Being Here and Writing There: Gender and the Politics of Translation in a Brazilian Landscape," *Signs* 25, no. 3 (2000): 727–60.

28 Rona Tamiko Halualani, Lily Mendoza, and Jolanta A. Drzewiecka, "'Critical' Junctures in Intercultural Communication Studies: A Review," *The Review of Communication* 9, no. 1 (2009):17–35; Tom Nakayama and Robert L. Krizek, "Whiteness: A Strategic Rhetoric," *Quarterly Journal of Speech* 81 (1995): 291–309.

29 Dreama G. Moon and Michelle A. Holling, "A Politic of Disruption: Race(ing) Intercultural Communication," *Journal of International and Intercultural Communication* 8, no. 1 (2015): 3; Dreama Moon, "Concepts of Culture: Implications for Intercultural Communication Research," *Communication Quarterly* 44 (1996): 70–84.

30 Shinsuke Eguchi and Godfried Asante, "Disidentifications Revisited: Queer(y)ing Intercultural Communication Theory," *Communication Theory* 26 (2016): 171–72.

31 Karma Chávez, "Pushing Boundaries: Queer Intercultural Communication," *Journal of International and Intercultural Communication* 6, no. 2 (2013): 83–95; Eguchi and Asante, "Disidentifications"; Shinsuke Eguchi, Bernadette M. Calafell, and Shadee Abdi, *De-Whitening Intersectionality: Race, Intercultural Communication, and Politics* (Lanham, MD: Rowman & Littlefield, 2020); Julia Johnson, "Cisgender Privilege, Intersectionality, and the Criminalization of CeCe McDonald: Why Intercultural Communication Needs Transgender Studies," *Journal of International and Intercultural Communication* 6, no. 2 (2013): 135–44; Gust Yep, "Toward the De-Subjugation of Racially Marked Knowledges in Communication," *Southern Communication Journal* 75, no. 2 (2010): 171–75.

32 Eguchi and Asante, "Disidentifications"; J. Johnson, "Cisgender Privilege"; Gust Yep, "Queering/Quaring/Kauering/Crippin'/Transing 'Other Bodies' in Intercultural Communication," *Journal of International and Intercultural Communication* 6, no. 2 (2013): 118–26.

33 Kimberlé Crenshaw, "Mapping the Margins: Intersectionality, Identity Politics, and Violence Against Women of Color," *Stanford Law Review* 43, no. 6 (1991): 1241–99.

34 Sirma Bilge, "Intersectionality Undone: Saving Intersectionality from Feminist Intersectionality Studies," *Du Bois Review* 10, no. 2 (2013): 405–24; Brittney Cooper, "Intersectionality," in *The Oxford Handbook of Feminist Theory*, eds. Lisa Disch and Mary Hawkesworth (New York, NY: Oxford University Press, 2016), 1–15.

35 Yep, "Toward De-Subjugation."

36 Eguchi, Calafell, and Abdi, *De-Whitening Intersectionality*, xix.

37 Raquel Moreira, "De-Whitening Intersectionality Through *Transfeminismo*," in *De-Whitening Intersectionality: Race, Intercultural Communication, and Politics*, eds. Shinsuke Eguchi, Bernadette M. Calafell, and Shadee Abdi (Lanham, MD: Rowman & Littlefield, 2020), 203–22.

38 Thiago Coacci, "Finding Brazilian Transfeminism: A Preliminary Mapping of a Rising Branch," *História Agora* 15 (2014): 134–61.

39 Jaqueline Gomes de Jesus, "Gender Without Essentialism: Transgender Feminism as a Critique of Sex," *Universitas Humanística* 78 (June 2014): 241–57; Jaqueline Gomes Jesus and Haley Alves, "Transgender Feminism and Movements of Transsexual Women," *Cronos* 11, no. 2 (2012): 8–19.

40 Jesus, "Gender Without Essentialism."

41 Jesus, "Gender Without Essentialism"; Viviane Vergueiro, "Por Inflexões Decoloniais de Corpos e Identidades de Gênero Inconformes: Uma Análise Autoetnográfica da Cisgeneridade como Normatividade" (Unpublished master's thesis, Bahia: Universidade Federal da Bahia, 2015).

42 Diogo Santos Maxi, "Cachorra solta—Tati Quebra Barraco," April 15, 2012, YouTube video, 2:22, https://www.youtube.com/watch?v=B1rL8OOSv4c&list=RDLj6Mk_1KHFQ&index=19.

43 Cathy Cohen, "Punks, Bulldaggers, and Welfare Queens: The Radical Potential of Queer Politics?" *GLQ: A Journal of Lesbian and Gay Studies* 3, no. 4 (1997): 437–65.

44 Mariana Gomes, "My Pussy é o Poder. Representação Feminina Através do Funk: Identidade, Feminismo e Indústria Cultural" (Unpublished thesis, Federal Fluminense University, 2015); Lopes, *Funk-se*.

45 Lopes, *Funk-se*.

Chapter One

Femininities, Agency, and White Feminist Failures

"I'm not a feminist, and I don't even have power to be that," said Deize Tigrona, who is featured on the cover of this book, in reply to the "feminist question" at the height of the funkeira's mainstream media popularity, in 2006.[1] Deize's answer illustrates what is at the core of this chapter, namely that: (1) the funkeira associated feminism with power—she was likely referring to class and racial power—and, consequently, (2) the perception that, as a poor Black woman, feminism was not for her. In a way, Deize was correct: much of the feminist theory and movements that had reached Brazil at the time of the interview, in 2006, either ignored favela funk in general and funkeiras in particular or vehemently criticized both.[2] That was a symptom of the overreliance on white and middle-class feminist perspectives (many of which originated in the Global North) and their focus on "gender first" analyses, which then tended to generally understand femininity homogenously, as a de-racialized patriarchal device.[3] Feminist theory and movements' tendency to devaluate all femininity through the unexamined focus on its white, normative version, have positioned femininity in opposition to masculine agency. As a result, they have also disregarded agentic and transgressive potential of marginalized femininities for political change.

White feminist approaches to agency tend to take for granted ideas of liberal Western agency and its analytical dichotomy—subordination and resistance. Whether for praise or critique, this focus seems reliant on a concept of universal "womanhood."[4] These takes fail in several forms. When treated as a choice, the contingency and constraints of agency, as well as the motivations, restrictions, and potentials of marginalized bodies to perform femininity, are often glossed over. When treated as ineffective to change patriarchal structures, it dismisses the ways in which poor women and feminine folks of color use their bodily performances not as mechanisms of resistance but as tactics of survival. I start this chapter by tracing key ideas in the understanding of normative white femininity as the analytical norm in white, Western feminist theory. Because funkeiras are pushed to negotiate with this ideological construction, I found it important to expose its mechanisms. Next, I shed light on the specific ways in which femininity—associated with race, class, and gender identity—is constructed in Brazil through key identities and representations. Finally, I delve into concepts of feminist agency in connection with and disconnected from normative white femininity. Once again, I find this move necessary since researchers tend to use this analytical device to explain funkeiras' experiences in relationship to feminism. Ultimately, this chapter lays the groundwork for the subsequent analyses of funkeiras' quotidian and staged performances of subaltern femininities in ways that can broaden current understandings of embodied politics and agency.

Whose Femininity?: The Essentializing of Normative White Femininity

Valesca Popozuda reached considerable mainstream success in 2013 with her first solo hit, "Beijinho no Ombro" (Kiss on the Shoulder).[5] The popularity of the song was partly driven by the pompous music video, which had over 100 million views as of April 2020. In it, Valesca wears a series of "sexy queen" outfits while moving and dancing around a mansion that is made to look like a castle.[6] Before flying solo, Valesca was known as the lead singer of funk group Gaiola das Popozudas (Big Trunk's Cage). She was also famous for embodying one of favela funk's most visible trends among ciswomen: a combination of voluptuous, muscular bodies and obscene, in-your-face stage performances.[7] However, once Valesca rose to mainstream fame with the aforementioned "Beijinho no Ombro," her body and embodiment of femininity changed significantly. She lost a substantial amount of weight; her legs and arms became noticeably less muscular; her wardrobe went from small, glittery one-piece bodysuits to more modest and less sparkly clothes. Not coincidently, celebrity media discourse around Valesca changed drastically. From being mocked for having buttocks that were "huge" and "creepy"[8] and for thinking she was "fashionable,"[9] Valesca became the sophisticated and feminist face of favela funk. In a 2014 interview to Grupo Globo's weekly magazine, *Época*, Valesca was compared to other notable (white) feminists. The introductory paragraph states:

> After Simone de Beauvoir, Betty Friedan, and Naomi Wolf, Valesca Popozuda. Since "Beijinho no Ombro," her big early 2014 hit, the funkeira from Rio started to talk about feminism in her interviews and has embraced a campaign on sexual violence against women … the feminist phase is also a "slimmer" phase—considering her tights used to be bigger than Giselle Bündchen's waist.[10]

The suggestion that Valesca's improved physical image aligns with her new feminist persona illustrates two issues I would like to address in this chapter—normative white femininity's claim to universal femininity and its relationship with (white) feminism. While there is robust feminist discussion surrounding the way femininity operates and its value in feminist politics,[11] I am more interested in the classed, racialized, and cisnormative demarcations of femininity.

Because there is a tendency in feminist analyses to treat femininity as monolithic, little consideration is given to how socioeconomic class, race, and cisgender normativity intersect to create different challenges and possibilities for femininity.[12] Contemporary feminist analyses that consider class usually do so in relationship to neoliberal notions of self-discipline and control.[13] In neoliberal contexts, valuable individuals are those who know how to self-govern according to rules of the market.[14] Those who either ignore or misinterpret these rules are potentially deemed morally flawed[15] or are considered "subjectivities out of control, beyond propriety, excessive."[16] Hence, to properly perform femininity entails having control over one's body and bodily impulses, as well as over one's language and posture, especially in public.

Performances of femininity under neoliberalism are also accompanied by the idea that femininity is a condition that needs constant management.[17] This is currently realized through the "relentless drive for physical perfectibility."[18] In this vision of normative femininity, cis-women are pushed to perpetually remake themselves in order to be normatively, and not *too*, feminine. Accordingly, so-called incompetent femininities marked by race, class, and transness are being countered with self-regulatory discursive appeals:

> Modes of regulation are shifting from practices of policing and external regulation to technologies of self-regulation in which subjects come to understand themselves as responsible for their own regulation, as "free" and individual agents in the management of themselves as autonomous beings, which is central to a neoliberal project.[19]

An example of a neoliberal discursive construction as it pertains to femininity is the idea of "natural beauty."[20] "Natural beauty" is the normative counterpart to performative excesses, which are often connected to lower classness and include too much makeup, stiletto heels, tight clothes, heavy drinking, loudness, and publicly discussing sexual desires.[21] This construction is present especially in the media, and it could be considered feminist since it implies that cis-women who avoid the hyper-feminine traits listed above are "naturally" beautiful. Performative extravagances, on the other hand, expose the artificial nature of femininity. Failure to perform normative femininity can potentially challenge the artificial connections between sex and gender and enact a form of resistance to and transgression against normative femininity.[22] Funkeiras are constantly heralded as being excessive.[23] "Naturalness," then, constitutes the essentializing of (white, middle-class, cisgender) femininity, as if it did not entail any type of social location, performance, repetition, and practice.

While analyses of "failed" working-class femininity abound, the racialized nature of "failure" is usually pushed aside.[24] As much as class matters in constructions of femininity in favela funk, race plays perhaps an even more vital role in it. Indeed, normative femininity is not race neutral, as feminist analyses make it seem.[25] Deliovsky contends that white femininity is normative because it is perceived as *just* femininity or just gendered.[26] It is not unusual for feminist studies to treat femininity in this way.[27]

Normative white femininity is "the white capitalist patriarchal compulsion to adopt styles and attitudes consistent with an imposed white feminine aesthetic. This compulsion is a central element in the reproduction of whiteness and white femininity."[28] Not all of those who are white cisgender women are able to enact normative femininity. As Shome contends, "[White femininity] claims a universality of its position only through its gendering of very *particular* bodies—the white female upper-class heterosexual body, and that body's imagined relation to Anglo patriarchy."[29] The legacy of European colonialism and imperialism suggest that normative femininity was/is constituted within the framework of white supremacy and racial oppression.[30] In this context, white ciswomen, through their enactment of normative white femininity, have become the guardians of morality and virtuosity. As a matter of fact, "to be truly feminine is, in many ways, to be white."[31]

Normative white femininity is decidedly hetero- and cisnormative. Indeed, there is no white femininity without white heteropatriarchy. Shome argues that white femininity exists only in relationship to white patriarchy and has no meaning outside of that bond: "The subject of white femininity emerges in, and through, its subject/ification in white patriarchy."[32] As an ideological construction, white femininity is the glue that holds patriarchy together, and because of that, it needs to be firmly regulated. Specifically,

> As symbols of motherhood, as markers of feminine beauty (a marker denied
> to other women), as translators (and hence preservers) of bloodlines, as

signifiers of national domesticity, as sites for the reproduction of heterosexuality, as causes in the name of which narratives of national defense and
protection are launched, as symbols of national unity, and as sites through
which "otherness"—racial, sexual, classed, gendered, and nationalized—is
negotiated, white femininity constitutes the locus through which borders of
race, gender, sexuality, and nationality are guarded and secured.[33]

An essential part of the regulation white femininity endures is
through sexuality. The strict boundaries surrounding normative white
femininity include performative aspects that are inextricably related to
heteronormativity. These may involve "notions of female vulnerabil-
ity, sexual inaccessibility, and submissiveness," which "readily collude
with normative cultural versions of White, heterosexist femininity."[34]
Because normative white femininity is responsible for assuring racial
purity, the sexuality of the ciswomen who embody that kind of femininity is highly regulated in the service of white cisheterosexual men.
White patriarchy, hence, uses normative white femininity to regulate
boundaries of proper sexuality for everyone else.[35]

Since the ideological construction of normative white femininity
serves reproductive functions, cisnormativity, via biological essentialism, is a vital component of normative systems of gender. Cisgender
women are thought to have a feminine essence that is connected to
their bodies, especially their reproductive system.[36] Butler further prob-
lematizes some feminist theorists' tendency to look for a prehistorical,
prejuridical time before patriarchal law, which in turn suggests that
gender exists outside of culture, as though there exists an "authentic
feminine essence."[37] Particularly, Butler critiques the propensity among
certain second-wave feminists to place nature and culture into a binary
similar to sex/gender, a duality that is itself gendered. "This is yet
another instance in which reason and mind are associated with masculinity and agency, while the body and nature are considered to be the
mute facticity of the feminine, awaiting signification from an opposing
masculine subject."[38] The idea of a feminine nature is a sign of cisnormativity, even within some feminist studies. Likewise, cisnormativity's
focus on a "true," essential womanhood makes it integral to the reproduction of normative white femininity.

Cisnormativity and biological essentialism not only hurt transpeople but can also work against ciswomen. Black *transfeminista* Jesus[39] compares the personal account of a ciswoman's hysterectomy and the subsequent questions from others about her "womanhood" with the experiences of transwomen; "Mayer experienced an oppression that is daily imposed on transwomen: that they are … not women because they are missing a female *essence*," usually attributed to reproductive organs, such as a uterus.[40] Another relevant way in which cisnormativity and biological essentialism work together is through norms around body shape. Ciswomen who are perceived to be "too muscular" are often compared to cismen or are deemed not feminine enough.[41] Accusing ciswomen of "looking like men" is a known transphobic trope[42] and suggests that those ciswomen diverge from normative white femininity's beauty standards. When being muscular was a fitness trend in favela funk in the mid- to early 2010s, Valesca and other funkeiras who embraced this look had their bodies constantly mocked and scrutinized.[43] Part of Valesca's recent makeover, which concurrently led her to more modest performances of femininity and more openly feminist talking points, included slimming down her previously brawny body, per the news story highlighted above. In sum, normative white femininity plays a central role in the maintenance of white cisheteropatriarchy and, consequently, sets the standards against which all feminine people are evaluated.

Other(ed) Femininities

The place of femininity in feminism is historically contentious,[44] usually because femininity is approached as a patriarchal device used to control and discipline cisgender women.[45] Not only that, but femininity is also treated as naturally and culturally inferior within and outside of Western feminist studies.[46] Even though the narrative about femininity's inferiority is assumed, "current Western heteropatriarchal conceptualizations of femininity are not transhistorical but, rather, have been shaped by cultural, political and religious climates throughout history."[47] Hoskin argues that "little academic attention has been paid to the 'naturalized' subordination of femininity, which contributes to a striking pervasiveness of feminine devaluation ... Due to its ability to masquerade as other forms of oppression ... feminine devaluation remains obscure."[48] Hoskin supports this assertion by reviewing a series of (white) feminist work that demonizes femininity while ostracizing feminine people.[49] In fact, in her estimation, "Until a multifocal understanding of femininity and femme is developed, researchers cannot understand how deviations from hegemonic norms of femininity function as a source of oppression."[50] Performances of femininity that meet social expectations are not readily available to all who identify as women. Per the ideas exposed in this chapter so far, there are proper and correct ways to enact femininity. As the previous paragraph illustrates, Valesca Popozuda is perhaps a good example of how embracing marginal and normative versions of femininity generates diverse material and symbolic consequences.

The constraints of normative white femininity are well known to feminist scholars. After reviewing the normative boundaries of white femininity, I now delve into the oppressive constructions marginalized femininities endure in their comparison to the norm. In the subsequent chapters, I analyze how funkeiras negotiate with the norm via performances of peripheral femininities. Later, I explore the political possibilities in these performances of racialized, classed, gender nonconforming femininities. Even though the following subsections are divided into "racialized femininities" and "gender nonconforming femininities," a *transfeminista* approach affirms that these are not separate, but intersecting realms. My hope is to be able to shed light on the particular ways these systems subjugate feminine people in favela funk with the understanding that oppression cannot be compartmentalized.

Racialized Femininities

Western white feminism tends to treat femininity with the underlying assumption that it is "race neutral" or necessarily cisheteronormative, according to Deliovsky and Hoskin. It is unsurprising then that the particular violence perpetrated against other(ed) femininities is de-emphasized in this perspective.[51] Accordingly, "The exclusive critique and subordination of femininity within dominant feminist theories disregards the multiple ways in which femininity intersects with a racially marked subject."[52] The homogenization of femininity, thus, upholds "a normative feminist subject" that simultaneously deems other femininities, and the particular struggles associated with them, invisible.[53] Black and brown women have long endured regulation and disciplining "through the racialising and sexualising imperialist gaze."[54] Thus, unlike white ciswomen who epitomize beauty and innocence, Black and brown women "represent and signify the exotic/erotic but not the beautiful."[55] Black women especially have been targeted with limiting and damaging images.[56]

In Brazil, Black women's performances of gender and sexuality have been historically conceived of as improper, though at times, still desired.[57] Foundational discourses about race and gender in the country concomitantly celebrate and condemn women of color. On the one hand, the sexual violence that enslaved Black women endured at the hands of white masters in colonial times is romanticized as a necessary element of Brazilian *mestiçagem* (miscegenation). On the other hand, Black women were held morally responsible for the demise of the white family.[58] Consequently, Black women have become "anti-muses"[59] whose femininity is defined in contrast to and approximation with that of white women.[60]

Brazilian Black scholars suggest that representations of Black femininity and the Black feminine body are markedly present in aesthetics and medical discourse.[61] Corrêa argues that many of the supposedly positive accounts of the light-skinned Black woman (offensively known as "mulata") originated within aesthetics (music, literature, arts), in which artists seemed to be enticed by the "mystery" of her body.[62] The discursive construction of Black women as objects of desire includes certain natural elements, such as flowers, herbs, and enveloping scents. Through aesthetics, the desirable light-skinned Black woman became a national symbol of Brazil's sensuality and *mestiçagem*.[63] The "undesirable" Black woman, on the other hand, was established through a variety of discourses, from aesthetics to medicine and law, that were often referred to in the context of unrestrained sexual impulses and lack of morals.[64] The pathologized Black woman was apprehended, therefore, as pure corporeal sensations, as the one who caused the social descent of men, including men of color.[65] Even though Black women's existences were under constant scrutiny via social or legal constraints, Soihet notes that no matter how liberal or restrictive state policies were, their bodies were abundant in public spaces; Black women subverted and challenged prohibitions and racist/sexist laws while debunking the colonial idea that Black women were submissive and docile.[66]

In early twentieth century Brazil, the idea of different races peacefully coming together to form a national, unified Brazilian identity became particularly important for the still-pervasive notion that the country was a racial democracy.[67] The popular opinion that inequities stem from class, and not race, is a related development to this perception of Brazil as a racial paradise.[68] In this context, public mentions of racial oppression are somewhat uncommon—and frowned upon—compared to references to class. In fact, the intersection of race and class takes on a particular discursive shape in Brazil: even though race is mentioned infrequently, reference to it is common in discussions of the social and economic hierarchy of particular neighborhoods.[69] For instance, allusions to favelas, from those who live there to the cultural expressions—like favela funk—that come out of such areas, denote both classed and raced meanings. As a result, the gendered and classed violence against funkeiras is habitually wrapped in racism.

Research about women in favela funk usually centers on analysis of lyrics, with only a handful of studies exploring gender, race, class, and bodily performances.[70] Aragão, for instance, suggests that lyrics performed by and about funkeiras are decidedly sexist, because:

> The social context of ignorance, poverty, lack of culture, and education foregrounds principles and values that are not concerned with the fact that women are not only worthy as "mothers," "housewives" or sexual objects. People who enjoy singing and dancing funk, going to funk parties and exposing themselves sexually, have no awareness that there are more intelligent and productive roles women can partake in.[71]

The author assumes that funkeiras, as poor uneducated women, are pushed into foolishly perpetuating their own gender oppression. Race is never mentioned in Aragão's work, but when taking into consideration

Lopes's point about the coded language connecting race and class in Brazil,[72] it becomes clear that representing poor women who enjoy funk as over-sexualized people who "lack" culture is a prime example of the racial violence with which funkeiras are targeted in academia.

Even though funkeiras are very popular within favela funk, very few studies have been dedicated to them exclusively.[73] When research focuses on favela funk in general, women in favela funk—and consequently performances of racialized femininity—are usually left out.[74] Brazilian studies examining the movement from a gender perspective tend to concentrate on the idea that women in it are sexually objectified and are hence put in undignified positions that they embrace by naively taking part in male domination.[75] For instance, Oliveira (2007) states that, even though favela funk is composed by poor people of color looking for cultural legitimation, the sexism that traverses it is part of a "larger structure present in many societies" and even more so in economically disadvantaged groups.[76] This line of thinking also exposes the severe limitations of "gender first" analyses. Similarly, it reveals the problematic tendency to assume a cross-cultural feminist subject based on the omnipresence of Western patriarchy and gendered structures of domination. The same can be assumed about some feminists' uncritical use of femininity as a universally constituted category. The underlying assumption in Oliveira's and Aragão's work[77] is that femininity is equally performed by, and similarly impacts, all women.[78] At the same time, Oliveira and Aragão suggest that a feminist performance, though never defined, is not only incongruent with femininity in general but also with poverty and, given Brazil's racial context, brownness and Blackness.[79]

Gender Nonconforming Femininities

Gender normativity is a taken-for granted aspect of normative white femininity. Indeed, Hoskin asserts that "under patriarchal rule, femininity is only 'acceptable' (not to be confused with valued) in one mode: white, heterosexually available, DFAB, able-bodied, passive, self-sacrificing, thin, young, lacking self-actualization, and simultaneously negotiating Madonna/Whore constructs."[80] What happens, then, to people whose femininities challenge the fact that its normative equivalent is "reserved exclusively for those designated female at birth"?[81] While Hoskin focuses on the femme lesbian as a point of departure for the conceptualization of subaltern femininities,[82] I turn my attention to feminine transpeople, specifically those who identify as travesti, as their presence and popularity in favela funk continues to grow.[83]

The term travesti does not have a neat English translation. Largely used in Latin America, travesti has a few possible meanings, none of which is quite captured by the literal English version, "transvestite."[84] In Brazil, the word was more broadly adopted during the 1960s to refer to "homosexual 'female impersonators' (later known as *transformistas*) who had the opportunity to move from the Carnival—where they were accepted—to some of the most important theatre shows in the big cities as stars."[85] With the 1964 military-civilian coup in Brazil, travestis were accused of depravity and indecorum; their shows were often censored and criminalized.[86] The more feminine travestis were, the greater the persecution against them.[87] Travestis who were not able to leave Brazil during the 21 years of dictatorship found sex work a vehicle of survival, not just in terms of financial livelihood but also as the space in which they could express and embody femininities. Over the years, thus, travestis went from being recognized as artists to becoming associated with gender and sexual deviance and criminality, specifically sex work and drug addiction.[88]

Some scholars link travesti identity more to sexuality than to gender. Garcia,[89] for instance, partially agrees with Kulick's assessment that travestis "desire to embody homosexuality."[90] Garcia, however, understands travesti identity as a patchwork or a series of complex, at times contradictory, performances of traditional and peripheral femininities and masculinities, which include sexual practices.[91] Studies focusing on "homosexuality" in Brazil also suggest that travesti identity should not be used cross-culturally in uncritical manners—as a Western classification of sexual deviance—since Brazil has a culturally specific system of sexual practices and relationships.[92] Because these Brazilian categories are contingent upon cultural meanings that Western scholars at times miss, it is not uncommon for them to perceive travestis as "gays who cross-dress" with the understanding that it is their sexuality that determines their gender expression.[93] These assessments, as Vartabedian argues[94] and with which I agree, remove the idiosyncrasies of travesti identity while also reinforcing colonial, heteronormative understandings of gender and sexuality.[95] Similarly, the term "transgender" does not quite capture the particularities of travesti, and using it as an equivalent term further colonizes "trans experiences" while "overshadow[ing] local understandings of the travesti subculture."[96]

The term travesti evades the medicalization of gender nonconformity, unlike the monikers "transsexuality" and "transvestite." In fact, scholars contend that medical terms fail to capture the nuances present in travesti identity. As it is currently employed, the word:

> Refer[s] to people who want to look and feel, as they say, *like* women, without giving up some of their male characteristics, such as their genitals. Within this premise, they are aware that they do not want to *be* women, but they mainly seek to resemble women through the construction of a constantly negotiated femininity.[97]

Though Vartabedian's definition points to gender expression,[98] the focus on bodily alterations is still present. Belizario draws comparisons between scholarly versus self-identified definitions of travesti, and the differences are glaring.[99] While researchers focus on travestis' bodies as the starting point for their identities, travestis themselves focus on free gender expression and demands for human rights. Belizario highlights Brazilian Black trans scholar Jesus's definition of travesti as "people who experience feminine gender, but do not recognize themselves as either men or women, but as members of a third gender or of a non-gender."[100] Additionally, travestis understand their identities as political and as the result of colonial systems of race, class, and cisheteronormativity.[101]

Even though contemporary understandings of travesti identity are filled with contradictions, scholars agree that class and race are important markers of those who identify as such.[102] Garcia postulates that many travestis in his study located in the Brazilian southeast, where favela funk developed, come from poor migrant families who left the north and northeast regions "in search of economic opportunity, while also seeking some degree of sexual freedom."[103] While observing the racial composition of his interlocutors, Garcia further states that, among poor travestis, "the majority had common ethnic mixtures of indigenous or African origin."[104] Conversely, "those with higher incomes among the travestis had lighter skin.[105]" The most vulnerable travestis are, thus, feminine-presenting Black and indigenous people, which makes this identification classed and raced.

Ultimately, travesti identity challenges hetero- and cisnormative categories of gender and sexuality. Unlike other slightly more defined and accepted identities in the medical and LGBTQIA+ discourses, such as transgender and transsexual, travestis are regularly "constructed as the radical other."[106] The classed and raced nature of the travesti category means that folks who identify as such are often perceived as inferior, even by those who identify as transgender and transsexual in Brazil.[107] Consequently, the lived realities of travestis in the country are extremely hard. More than surviving discursive violence, travestis exist in a context that criminalizes and, most notably, violates them at very high rates. According to the organization Transgender Europe, with the support of Rede Trans Brasil (Brazilian Trans Network), the number of transpeople (mostly feminine-presenting) murdered in the country is two times higher than in Mexico and six times higher than in the United States.[108] A great majority of those murdered in Brazil are in fact travestis of color.[109] In this context of the dehumanization of travestis, it is important not to fetishize their complicated identities by understanding their performances of gender and sexuality solely in terms of transgression or "compulsory" subversion.[110] This fetichizing of travestis, which happens mostly in Western queer theory, ends up dematerializing their lived experiences. The analysis I propose later in this book is one grounded in the perspective of travesti artists, whose favela funk performances enable an embodied understanding of travesti femininity with material and political consequences and possibilities.

The presumed inferiority of feminized subjects means that feminist theory seems inclined to focus on normative femininity's agentic limitations.[111] The idea is that either a feminized subject, be them cis- or trans-, has limited power to act or that agency becomes part of the post-feminist narrative that turns everyday life's individualized performances into simple issues of choice. Funkeiras, their multifaceted enactments of femininities, and the context in which they perform challenge these established connections between feminized subjects and agency. In the next section, I briefly explore some of these conundrums and their limitations in feminist theory.

Femininity and Agency

In a fundamental work about favela funk, Lopes's reserves a section of her book to discuss gender and sexuality in the movement.[112] Unlike much of the previous research done on the funkeiras, Lopes argues that they indeed have agency. Basing her analysis on the work of Butler's gender performativity,[113] Lopes suggests that, though funkeiras have agency, they do not resist the oppressive gendered systems around them. In fact, they actually reproduce dominant gender relations in their songs. Furthermore, because the interviews she either performed herself or accessed through media funkeiras suggest that they perform about sex because "it sells,"[114] they are not engaged in a feminist project. Lopes never clarifies what feminism means in that context; it is merely assumed. What is more troubling is that the funkeiras became an addendum to a work that is otherwise focused on the oppressive junctures of race, class, and geographic location. Gender, thus, takes front and center in Lopes's analysis of the funkeiras, while other aspects of their material realities are acknowledged but not sufficiently engaged.

An equally problematic take comes from Lyra, who proclaims that funkeiras are in the vanguard of third-wave feminism.[115] The author explains that, in contrast to second wavers, third-wave feminists have a special concern with self-esteem and sexuality. Lyra proposes that funkeiras moved from the traditional place of passivity, usually conceived of as feminine, to the active role of the seducer—a conventionally masculine space. Hence, funkeiras, such as Deize Tigrona and Tati Quebra Barraco, invert gender roles with their daring songs. Though the focus is, again, more on what is being sung, Lyra, to some extent, recognizes that the subject position of the funkeiras as poor women of color from Rio's peripheries matters. That acknowledgment, however, does not address the problems with the conclusion that funkeiras engage in simple inversions of gender roles through the enunciation of lyrics. Research focus on whether or not funkeiras are feminists is troublesome for two reasons. First, these studies are inclined to privilege "gender first" analyses, which exclude raced and classed aspects of embodiment from notions of agency. Second, what feminism means is often taken-for-granted.

The discussion of agency in Western feminist theory is often tied to an essential, presumed category of woman. Because the subject of feminist politics has been unquestionably assumed to be ciswomen, Butler (2006) contends that "by conforming to a requirement of representational politics that feminism articulate a stable subject, feminism thus opens itself to charges of gross misrepresentation."[116] Because issues around the subject of feminism*, [117] have been well discussed, I would rather shift focus to the connection between agency and femininity. By problematizing assumptions about agency in white, Western feminist theory, I hope to lay groundwork for a discussion about embodied politics specifically as it pertains to marginalized femininities.

As previously mentioned in Lyra's analysis,[118] third-wave feminists regard embodied resistance to everyday sexism as a central feminist practice that is closely tied to the expression of sexuality.[119] Fixmer and Wood note that such resistance is a "personal and often physical, bodily action that aims to provoke change by exercising and resisting power in everyday life."[120] This definition of embodied politics may provide a starting point to understand the complicated public performances of funkeiras racialized femininities. It is not, however, sufficient, as the focus on "personal" acts and resistance does not fully encompass the funkeiras navigate marginalization. Each chapter in this book sheds light on specific aspects of funkeiras' embodied politics in ways that advance grounded, contingent understandings of the concept. Later in the conclusion, I lay out the characteristics and tenets of my approach to embodied politics.

While third-wave feminist theory claims to defy norms surrounding "correct" womanhood, "the acceptance of multiplicities and ambiguities has not been extended to femininity."[121] Ironically, the critiques

---

*   For more on the subject of feminism, see Butler (2006), Braidotti (2004), Mahmood (2001), and Mohanty (2003).

directed at second-wave feminists for essentializing the category "woman" is reproduced in much of third-wave feminism as "thinkers continue to participate in the homogenization, essentialization and white-washing of femininity."[122] Thus, even though there is a noticeable move in feminist theory to question the previously taken-for-granted idea of "difference from" white women, the same has not been the case in the analysis of femininity and feminine subjectivities.

In an analysis of Canadian women's and gender studies textbooks, Hoskin generated insights into how femininity is conceived in a dichotomous way that ultimately disables the agency of feminine subjectivities.[123] One prevailing contradiction in the evaluations of femininity and agency by feminists is that femininity is both deceptive and deceived. As deception, femininity is apprehended as a "mask":

> Women's use of cosmetics is described as a "desperate" "disguise" (Bartky, 2010; Weitz, 2010), a "masquerade" (Warnke, 2011, p. 67), a form of "concealment" (Rice, 2004), "tired decorations" (Forsyth, 2004, p. 13), and a "theatre of their enslavement" (Sontag, 2004, p. 278). While feminine adornments are described as protective in their utility of disguise, the authors argue that by "protecting themselves as women, they betray themselves as adults" (Sontag, 2004, p. 282). By [...] infantilizing femininity, the theories of feminine deception contribute to the objectification and ornamenting of that which is feminized.[124]

Whereas femininity is understood as a deceptive patriarchal device, "feminine subjects are simultaneously thought of as being 'duped' into practices and expressions of femininity—complacent in their own subordination."[125] According to this prevalent perspective in white feminist theory, even when ciswomen think they have free will, the choices they make are the result of sociocultural coercion. Hence, feminine folks naively subject themselves to the constraints of femininity. These limitations result in passive feminine subjects who are then devoid of agency.[126] Cisgender women, therefore, need to rid themselves of femininity in order to be free from the docile, non-agentic associations with it.

Perhaps the most troubling finding in Hoskin's analysis is that many of these conclusions about femininity are not connected to any other systemic markers or identities.[127] The rules and agentic restrictions of normative white femininity are reproduced with very little reflection on the raced, classed, and cisnormative aspects of that construction. Although passivity is one such characteristic that works as a roadblock to agency, "the conflation of femininity and passivity/subordination is challenged by the multiple manifestations of femme, whose lives and gender expressions do not reflect this naturalized equation."[128]

On the other hand, the neoliberal ideas surrounding choice that is found in some third-wave feminist work simplifies the particular contexts in which marginalized feminine subjects are inserted. This "postfeminist sensibility"[129] suggests that young women who selectively define feminism usually tie in personal choice as source of empowerment instead of advocating for feminist politics and structural change.[130] For Gill and Scharf, femininity plays a vital role in this shift[131]—one from objectification to supposed subjectification involving self-discipline and surveillance. Issues of race, class, body normativity, and more are either disregarded or are subsumed under what Puar calls "neoliberal pluralism" or the "absorption and accommodation of difference."[132] Puar further questions if current neoliberal accounts of difference in feminist theory serve to further reify white liberal feminism. Like Puar, I also believe that defenders and critics of agentic choice treat normative white femininity as the invisible center.

To move away from these shortcomings in the apprehension of agency, I use Mahmood's definition to demonstrate the complicated ways in which funkeiras engage in embodied politics.[133] Specifically, Mahmood argues that agency should be treated "not as a synonym for resistance to relations of domination, but as a capacity for action that historically specific relations of subordination enable and create."[134] In their everyday and artistic performances, funkeiras use embodied politics to publicly affirm and embrace their marginalized bodies in movement. Their performances of racialized, classed femininities challenge normative white femininity but provide diverse, contradictory practices for doing so. Furthermore, these transgressive performances of marginalized femininities from the Global South challenge second and third-wave feminist understandings of embodied politics through performances that do not clearly fit in dichotomous understandings of gender and oppression and that are not simple matters of choice.

As Dow and Wood point out, "[f]eminist activism, going back to the first wave, has been led mainly by privileged women who generally are more likely to have time and resources to devote to it."[135] For feminine folks with limited resources, embodied politics provides one avenue toward creating a sense of "communal agency" that can possibly drive structural change.[136] Embodied politics is simultaneously defiant and risky. It is risky because, as Durham, Cooper, and Morris remind us, feminine folks of color who publicly manifest their sexual agency and desire face "serious reprisals."[137] It is defiant because they confront systems that want to either demonize them or deem them invisible.

Feminist theory that proclaims to be concerned with the lives of marginalized people must pay attention to the different conditions under which embodied politics take place. These differences are integral to understanding how challenges to oppressive structures are possible. For marginalized people who have yet to experience significant structural changes, embodied politics serve to make their experiences visible in the fight against racist, classist, transphobic misogyny in media, politics, and in their communities—a struggle that has been historically perceived as belonging to cisgender middle-class white women. Embodied politics should not then be understood as just a matter of *choosing* to exercise one's individual agency. Funkeiras are people whose performances are not grounded in simple choices but shaped by oppressive structures.

Challenging White Feminist Failures

The two central themes in this chapter, femininity and agency, lay the theoretical ground against which the analyses about funkeiras will unfold. Funkeiras are forced to negotiate with normative white feminine standards in their everyday lives, and because so much of white feminist theory assumes white femininity to be the norm, agency is debated in relationship to that. As Alarcón poses, white feminism theorizes from the perspective of "an autonomous, self-making, self-determining subject who first proceeds according to the logic of *identification* with regard to the subject of consciousness" (emphasis in original),[138] a logic previously reserved only for white men. Not only that, but analyses that simplify funkeiras' lived experiences as producing either resistance or domination precipitously foreclose disparate conceptualizations of agency. Mahmood notes that "to analyze people's actions in terms of realized or frustrated attempts at social transformation is to necessarily reduce the heterogeneity of life to the rather flat narrative of succumbing to or resisting relations of domination."[139]

This project moves away from these assumptions and toward something like Anzaldúa's "mestiza consciousness,"[140] which works to disrupt dualistic thinking and structures of Western colonialism; it is grounded in the idea of contraction and ambiguity. Per Mohanty's assessment,

> Consciousness is thus simultaneously singular and plural, located in a theorization of being "on the border." Not any border, but a historically specific one: the United States-Mexican border. Thus, unlike a Western, postmodernist notion of agency and consciousness that often announces the splintering of the subject, and privileges multiplicity in the abstract, this is a notion of agency born of history and geography. It is a theorization of the materiality and politics of the everyday struggles of Chicanas.[141]

The task of understanding funkeiras' complicated and stirring performances of marginalized femininities functions in a similarly grounded and contingent manner. In this book, I specifically espouse Mohanty's conceptualization of Third World feminisms' dual, seemingly contradictory, intellectual and political projects. First, this book critiques "hegemonic 'western' feminism" and second, this book is invested in "the formulation of autonomous feminist concerns and strategies that are geographically, historically, and culturally grounded."[142] For people inserted in contexts of extreme systemic oppression, challenges to the status quo often do not come in the form of organized movements but as everyday practices, as in the lives of marginalized feminine subjects. Each chapter in this book provides thematic examinations of funkeiras as they relate to racialized femininities, embodied politics, and aspects of their personal and professional lives. My

analysis of varied aspects of funkeiras' quotidian and staged performances will hopefully illuminate the ways in which agency is not just
contradictory but also "anchored in the history of specific struggles."[143]

Embracing diverse and contradictory feminist identities is fundamental in the understanding of funkeiras. Because contradiction tran-
scends and disrupts false Western patriarchal dichotomies, it allows
for the emergence of complex alternatives outside of the limiting and
oppressive options available to women[144] and transfeminine folks.
Through contradiction, they "can negotiate social constraints to make
the best choices for that particular moment, recognizing the contingen-
cies of their historical contexts and material worlds as limitations, but
looking for ways to subvert those limitations if possible."[145] Although
there is a tendency among second-wave feminists to view the feminist
acts of the third-wave as individualized, Renegar and Sowards suggest
that contradictory acts that are repeatedly performed in public foster
"an understanding of agency as a communal effort that builds upon
itself."[146]

Funkeiras have very real material challenges that go beyond gender,
including race, class, and cisheteronormativity. Their use of embodied
politics seems to point to concurrent individual and collective survival.
The bonding aspect of funkeiras' experiences, aside from their connection to favela funk, is indeed their performances of subaltern femininities. As such, this project focuses on the particularities of cisgender
women and transfeminine people of color, as well as on their similarities, based both on their performances of femininity and the raced,
classed trans-misogyny they face.[147] Next, I delve into favela funk as an
industry and the labor relations in which funkeiras are inserted.

Notes

1 Nelito Fernandes and Alice Granato, "Mulherada de Respeito," *Época*, January 16,
  2006, http://revistaepoca.globo.com/Revista/Epoca/0,,EDR72874-6011,00.html.
2 Raquel Moreira, "Bitches Unleashed: Women in Rio's Funk Movement, Performances
  of Heterosexual Femininity, and Possibilities of Resistance" (PhD Thesis, University
  of Denver, 2014).

3 Rhea Ashley Hoskin, "Femme Interventions and the Proper Feminist Subject: Critical Approaches to Decolonizing Western Feminist Pedagogies," *Cogent Social Sciences* 3, no. 1276819 (January 2017): 1–16; Rhea Ashley Hoskin, "Femme Theory: Refocusing the Intersectional Lens," *Atlantis* 38, no. 1 (June 2017): 95–109; Lesa Lockford, *Performing Femininity: Rewriting Gender Identity* (Walnut Creek: Altamira Press, 2004).

4 Natalie Fixmer and Julia T. Wood, "The Personal is Still Political: Embodied Politics in Third Wave Feminism," *Women's Studies in Communication* 28, no. 2, (July 2005): 235–57; Saba Mahmood, "Feminist Theory, Embodiment, and the Docile Agent: Some Reflections on the Egyptian Islamic Revival," *Cultural Anthropology* 16, no. 2 (May 2001): 202–36; Chandra Mohanty, *Feminism Without Borders* (Durham, NC: Duke University Press, 2003).

5 "Popozuda Lança Música com Discurso Feminista e Ensaio Chique," *Ego*, October 31, 2013, http://ego.globo.com/famosos/noticia/2013/10/popozuda-lanca-musica-com-ensaio-chique-e-discurso-feminista.html.

6 Valesca Popozuda, "Valesca Popozuda—Beijinho no Ombro (official music video)," December 27, 2013, YouTube video, 7:34, https://www.youtube.com/watch?v=73sbW7gjBeo.

7 Raquel Moreira, "'Now that I'm a Whore, Nobody is Holding Me Back!': Women in Favela Funk and Embodied Politics," *Women's Studies in Communication* 40, no. 2 (April 2017): 172–89.

8 "Bizarrice Pouca é Bobagem! Relembre Algumas das Maiores Esquisitices das Celebridades em 2012," *Ego*, December 11, 2012, http://ego.globo.com/famosos/fotos/2012/12/bizarrice-pouca-e-bobagem-relembre-algumas-das-maiores-esquisitices-das-celebridades-em-2012.html.

9 Renata Mendonça, "Valeska Popozuda, Que Canta o Tema de Rakelli, Posa Vestida de Barbie," *Ego*, August 8, 2008, http://ego.globo.com/Gente/Noticias/0,,MUL716947-9798, 00-VALESKA+POPOZUDA+ QUE+CANTA+O+TEMA+DE+RAKELLI+POSA+VESTIDA+ DE+BARBIE.html.

10 Graziele Oliveira, "Valesca Popozuda: 'Ser Vadia é Ser Livre.'" *Época*, April 11, 2014, http://epoca.globo.com/ideias/noticia/2014/04/bvalesca-popozudab-ser-vadia-e-ser-livre.html.

11 Judith Butler, *Gender Trouble: Feminism and the Subversion of Identity.* (New York: Routledge, 2006); Lockford, *Performing Femininity.*

12 Kathy Deliovsky, "Normative White Femininity: Race, Gender and the Politics of Beauty," *Atlantis*, 33, no. 1 (January 2008): 49–59. Hoskin, "Femme Interventions"; Hoskin, "Femme Theory."

13 Jane Arthurs and Jean Grimshaw, *Women's Bodies: Discipline and Transgression* (London: Casell, 1999); Jessica Gerrard and Jo Ball, "From Fuck Marry Kill to Snog Marry Avoid: Feminisms and the Excesses of Femininity," *Feminist Review* 105 (November 1, 2013): 122–29; Estella Tincknell, "Scourging the Abject

Body: Ten Years Younger and Fragmented Femininity Under Neoliberalism," in *New Femininites: Postfeminism, Neoliberalism and Subjectivity*, eds. Rosalind Gill and Christina Scharff (New York: Palgrave Macmillan, 2011): 83–95; Milly Williamson, "Female Celebrities and the Media: The Gendered Denigration of the 'Ordinary' Celebrity," *Celebrity Studies* 1, no. 1 (March 17, 2010): 118–20.

14 Thomas Lemke, *Biopolitics: An Advanced Introduction* (New York: New York University Press, 2011).

15 Gerrard and Ball, "From Fuck."

16 Bev Skeggs, "The Making of Class and Gender through Visualizing Moral Subject Formation," *Sociology* 39, no. 5 (December 2005): 974.

17 Tincknell, "Scourging."

18 Tincknell, "Scourging," 83.

19 Jessica Ringrose and Valerie Walkerdine, "Regulating the Abject," *Feminist Media Studies* 8, no. 3 (September 2008): 229.

20 Gerrard and Ball, "From Fuck."

21 Gerrard and Ball, "From Fuck."

22 Gerrard and Ball, "From Fuck"; Lockford, *Performing Femininity.*

23 Moreira, "Women in Favela Funk"; "Veja o Resultado do Implante de Silicone No Bumbum de Valesca Popozuda," *Ego*, August 13, 2010, http://ego.globo. com/Gente/Noticias/   0,,MUL1613297-9798,   00-VEJA+O+RESULTADO+ DO+IMPLANTE+DE+SILICONE+ NO+BUMBUM+DE+VALESCA+ POPOZUDA. html; "Valesca Popozuda Exibe Bumbum Bizarro e Seios Nus na Sapucaí," *Ego*, February 21, 2012, http://ego.globo.com/carnaval/2012/noticia/2012/02/valesca-exibe-bumbum-bizarro.html.

24 Deliovsky, "Normative White Femininity"; Hoskin, "Femme Interventions"; Hoskin, "Femme Theory."

25 Deliovsky, "Normative White Femininity."

26 Deliovsky, "Normative White Femininity."

27 Rhea Ashley Hoskin and Allison Taylor, "Femme Resistance: The Fem(me)inine Art of Failure," *Psychology & Sexuality* (May 13, 2019): 1–20.

28 Deliovsky, "Normative White Femininity," 50.

29 Raka Shome, "White Femininity and the Discourse of the Nation: Re/membering Princess Diana," *Feminist Media Studies* 1, no. 3 (December 2, 2001): 328.

30 Patricia Hill Collins, *Black Sexual Politics: African-Americans, Gender and the New Racism* (New York: Routledge, 2004).

31 Sally Markowitz, "Pelvic Politics: Sexual Dimorphism and Racial Difference," *Signs* 26, no. 2 (Winter 2001): 390.

32 Shome, "White Femininity."

33 Shome, "White Femininity," 323.

34 Nicole Pietsch, "I'm Not That Kind of Girl": White Femininity, the Other, and the Legal/Social Sanctioning of Sexual Violence Against Racialized Women, *Canadian Woman Studies* 28, no. 1 (January 2010): 138.

35 Shome, "White Femininity."

36 Jaqueline Gomes de Jesus, "Gender Without Essentialism: Transgender Feminism as a Critique of Sex," *Universitas Humanística* 78 (June 2014): 241–57.

37 Butler, *Gender Trouble*, 50.

38 Butler, *Gender Trouble*, 50.

39 Jesus, "Gender Without Essentialism."

40 Jesus, "Gender Without Essentialism," 244.

41 Erica Nicole Kendall, "Female Athletes Often Face the Femininity Police—Especially Serena Williams," *The Guardian*, July 14, 2015, https://www.theguardian.com/commentisfree/2015/jul/14/serena-williams-female-athletes-femininity-police.

42 Joshua Gamson, "Talking Freaks: Lesbian, Gay, Bisexual and Transgendered Families on Day-Time Talk TV," in *Queer Families, Queer Politics: Challenging Culture and the State*, eds. Mary Bernstein and Renate Reimann (New York: Columbia University Press, May 2001), 68–86.

43 Moreira, "Bitches Unleashed"; *Ego*, "Valesca Popozuda Exibe."

44 Hoskin, "Femme Interventions."

45 Deliovsky, "Normative White Femininity"; Lockford, *Performing Femininity*.

46 Deliovsky, "Normative White Femininity."

47 Hoskin and Taylor, "Femme Resistance," 1.

48 Hoskin, "Femme Theory," 95.

49 Hoskin, "Femme Theory."

50 Hoskin, "Femme Theory," 96.

51 Deliovsky, "Normative White Femininity;" Hoskin, "Femme Theory."

52 Hoskin, "Femme Interventions," 11.

53 Hoskin, "Femme Interventions," 12.

54 Ringrose and Walkerdine, "Regulating the Abject."

55 Deliovsky, "Normative White Femininity," 55.

56 Patricia Hill Collins, *Black Feminist Thought: Knowledge, Consciousness, and the Politics of Empowerment* (New York: Routledge, 2009).

57 Mariza Corrêa, "Sobre a Invenção da Mulata," *Cadernos Pagu* vol. 6/7 (1996): 35–50.

58 Cláudia Barcellos Rezende and Márcia Lima, "Linking Gender, Class, and Race in Brazil," *Social Identities* 10, no. 6 (2004): 757–73.

59 Sueli Carneiro, "Enegracer o Feminismo: A Situação da Mulher Negra na América Latina a Partir de uma Perspectiva de Gênero," *Geledés*, June 3, 2011, http://www.geledes.org.br/enegrecer-o-feminismo-situacao-da-mulher-negra-na-america-latina-partir-de-uma-perspectiva-de-genero/#gs.hB=CYyY.

60 Côrrea, "Invenção da Mulata."

61 Carneiro, "Enegracer o Feminismo"; Corrêa, "Invenção da Mulata;" Mariza Corrêa, "Do Feminismo aos Estudos de Gênero no Brasil: Um Exemplo Pessoal," *Cadernos Pagu* 16 (2001): 13–30; Rachel Soihet, "A Sensualidade em Festa: Representações do

Corpo Feminino nas Festas Populares no Rio de Janeiro na Virada do Século XIX para o XX," in *O Corpo Feminino em Debate*, eds. Maria Izilda Matos and Rachel Soihet (São Paulo: Unesp, 2003): 177–97.

62 Côrrea, "Invenção da Mulata," 39.
63 Côrrea, "Invenção da Mulata."
64 Côrrea, "Invenção da Mulata."
65 Côrrea, "Invenção da Mulata."
66 Soihet, "Sensualidade em Festa."
67 Liliane Windsor, "Deconstructing Racial Democracy: A Personal Quest to Understand Social Conditioning About Race Relations in Brazil," *Social Identities* 13, no. 4 (July 2007): 495–520.
68 Rezende and Lima, "Linking Gender"; Windsor, "Deconstructing."
69 Adriana Lopes, *Funk-se Quem Quiser: No Batidão Negro da Cidade Carioca* (Rio de Janeiro: Bom Texto, 2011).
70 Lopes, *Funk-se*; Mariana Gomes, 2015, "My Pussy é o Poder. Representação Feminina Através do Funk: Identidade, Feminismo e Indústria Cultural" (Unpublished thesis, Federal Fluminense University); Moreira, "Women in Favela Funk."
71 Gabriel Adams Castelo Branco Aragão, "O Discurso e a Construção da Imagem Feminina No Funk," *Cadernos de Pesquisa na Graduação em Letras* 1, no. 1 (2011): 80.
72 Lopes, *Funk-se*.
73 Moreira, "Bitches Unleashed"; Gomes, "Pussy é o Poder."
74 Adriana Facina, "'Não Me Bate Doutor': Funk e Criminalização da Pobreza," *Encontro de Estudos Multidisciplinares em Cultura*, Salvador, May 27–29, 2009; Lopes, *Funk-se*.
75 Aragão, "Discurso"; Edinéia de Oliveira, "A Expressão da Identidade Feminina No Gênero Musical Funk," *VI Semana Integrada das Licenciaturas*, Tubarão, October 22–26, 2007.
76 Oliveira, "Expressão," 941.
77 Oliveira, "Expressãol"; Aragão, "Discurso."
78 Moreira, "Bitches Unleashed."
79 Oliveira, "Expressãol"; Aragão, "Discurso."
80 Hoskin, "Femme Theory," 98.
81 Hoskin, "Femme Theory," 98.
82 Hoskin, "Femme Theory."
83 Raquel Moreira, "Bicha Travesti Worldmaking: Linn da Quebrada's Disidentificatory Performances of Intersectional Queerness," *Queer Studies in Media & Popular Culture* 4, no. 3 (September 1, 2019): 303–18.
84 Julieta Vartabedian, *Brazilian Travesti Migrations* (New York: Palgrave Macmillan, 2018).
85 Vartabedian, *Travesti Migrations*, 5.

86 Jefferson Puff, "LBGTs sofriam torturas mais agressivas, diz CNV," *BBC*, December 10, 2014, https://www.bbc.com/portuguese/noticias/2014/12/141210_gays_perseguicao_ditadura_rb.

87 Vartabedian, *Travesti Migrations*.

88 Vartabedian, *Travesti Migrations*.

89 Marcos Roberto Garcia, "Identity as a 'Patchwork': Aspects of Identity Among Low-Income Brazilian Travestis," *Culture, Health & Sexuality* 11, no. 6 (July 2009): 611–23.

90 Don Kulick, *Travesti: Sex, Gender, and Culture Among Brazilian Transgendered Prostitutes*. (Chicago: The University of Chicago Press, 1998), 224.

91 Garcia, "Identity."

92 Richard Parker, "Masculinity, Femininity, and Homosexuality: On the Anthropological Interpretation of Sexual Meanings in Brazil," *Journal of Homosexuality* 11, no. 3–4 (1986): 155–63.

93 Vartabedian, *Travesti Migrations*, 2.

94 Vartabedian, *Travesti Migrations*.

95 Viviane Vergueiro, "Por Inflexões Decoloniais de Corpos e Identidades de Gênero Inconformes: Uma Análise Autoetnográfica da Cisgeneridade como Normatividade," *Repositório UFBA*, 2015, https://repositorio.ufba.br/ri/handle/ri/19685.

96 Vartabedian, *Travesti Migrations*, 6.

97 Vartabedian, *Travesti Migrations*, 3.

98 Vartabedian, *Travesti Migrations*.

99 Fernanda Belizario, "Gênero: Feminilidade Travesti," *Medium*, March 7, 2019, https://medium.com/@febelizario/g%C3%AAnero-feminilidade-travesti-aaffaf7fb386.

100 Belizario, "Gênero."

101 Belizario, "Gênero"; Jesus, "Gender Without Essentialism."

102 Garcia, "Identity"; Jesus, "Gender Without Essentialism."

103 Garcia, "Identity," 612.

104 Garcia, "Identity," 612.

105 Garcia, "Identity," 613.

106 Berenice Bento, *O Que é Transexualidade* (São Paulo: Editora Brasiliense, 2017), Location No. 524.

107 Bento, *Transexualidade*.

108 Sayonara Moreno, "Brasil É o País que Mais Mata Pessoas Trans no Mundo," *Brasil de Fato*, Janurary 30, 2018, https://www.brasildefato.com.br/2018/01/30/brasil-e-o-pais-que-mais-mata-pessoas-trans-no-mundo.

109 Rede Trans Brasil, "Diálogos Sobre Viver Trans—Monitoramento: Assassinatos e Violação de Direitos Humanos de Pessoas Trans no Brasil," *Brasil*, 2019, http://redetransbrasil.org.br/wp-content/uploads/2019/01/Dossi%C3%AA-Rede-Trans-Brasil-2018-Portugu%C3%AAs.pdf.

110 Vartabedian, *Travesti Migrations*, 7.

111 Hoskin, "Femme Interventions"; Hoskin, "Femme Theory."

112 Lopes, *Funk-se*.

113 Butler, *Gender Trouble*.

114 Lopes, *Funk-se*, 169.

115 Kate Lyra, "Eu Não Sou Cachorra Não. Não? Voz e Silêncio na Construção da Identidade Feminina no Rap e no Funk no Rio de Janeiro," in *Comunicação, Consumo e Espaço Urbano: Novas Sensibilidades nas Culturas Jovens*, eds. Everardo Rocha, Maria Isabel Mendes de Almeida and Fernanda Eugenio (Rio de Janeiro: Mauad Editora, 2006), 175–95.

116 Butler, *Gender Trouble*, 7.

117 For more on the subject of feminism, see Judith Butler, *Gender Trouble: Feminism and the Subversion of Identity* (New York: Routledge, 2006); Saba Mahmood, "Feminist Theory, Embodiment, and the Docile Agent: Some Reflections on the Egyptian Islamic Revival," *Cultural Anthropology* 16, no. 2 (May 2001): 202–36; Chandra Mohanty, *Feminism Without Borders* (Durham, NC: Duke University Press, 2003).

118 Lyra, "Voz e Silêncio."

119 R. Claire Snyder, "What is Third-Wave Feminism? A New Directions Essay," *Signs* 34, no. 1 (Autumn 2008): 175–96; Lyra, "Voz e Silêncio."

120 Fixmer and Wood, "Personal is Still Political," 237.

121 Hoskin, "Femme Interventions," 12.

122 Hoskin, "Femme Interventions," 12.

123 Hoskin, "Femme Interventions."

124 Hoskin, "Femme Interventions," 9.

125 Hoskin, "Femme Interventions," 9.

126 Hoskin, "Femme Interventions."

127 Hoskin, "Femme Interventions."

128 Hoskin, "Femme Interventions," 10.

129 Rosalind Gill, "Postfeminist Media Culture: Elements of a Sensibility," *European Journal of Cultural Studies* 10, no. 2 (2007): 147–66.

130 Rosalind Gill and Christina Scharff, eds. *New Femininites: Postfeminism, Neoliberalism and Subjectivity* (New York, Palgrave Macmillan, 2011).

131 Gill and Scharf, *New Femininites*.

132 Jaspir Puar, "I Would Rather Be a Cyborg Than a Goddess": Becoming Intersectional in Assemblage Theory. *PhiloSOPHIA* 2, no. 1 (2012): 53.

133 Mahmood, "Feminist Theory."

134 Mahmood, "Feminist Theory," 203.

135 Bonnie Dow and Julia T. Wood, "Repeating History and Learning From It: What Can SlutWalks Teach Us About Feminism?" *Women's Studies in Communication* 37, no. 1 (2014): 35.

136 Renegar and Sowards, "Contradiction," 9.

137 Aisha Durham, Brittney C. Cooper and Susana M. Morris, "The Stage Hip-Hop Feminism Built: A New Directions Essay," *Signs* 38, no. 3 (2013): 725.

138 Norma Alarcón, "The Theoretical Subject(s) of This Bridge Called My Back and Anglo-American Feminism," in *Criticism in the Borderlands: Studies in Chicano Literature, Culture, and Ideology*, 3rd ed., eds. Hector Calderón & José David Saldívar (Durham: Duke University Press, 1998): 29.

139 Mahmood, "Feminist Theory," 222.

140 Gloria Anzaldúa, *Borderlands/La Frontera: The New Mestiza*, 3rd ed. (San Francisco: Aunt Lute, 2007).

141 Mohanty, *Feminism*, 81.

142 Mohanty's, *Feminism*, 17.

143 Mohanty, *Feminism*, 82.

144 Renegar and Sowards, "Contradiction," 9.

145 Renegar and Sowards, "Contradiction," 9.

146 Renegar and Sowards, "Contradiction," 16.

147 Julia Serano, "Reclaiming femininity" in *Transfeminist Perspectives in and Beyond Transgender and Gender Studies*, ed. Anne Enke (Philadelphia: Temple University Press, 2012): 170–183; Jesus, "Gender Without Essentialism."

Chapter Two

"I Don't Depend on Men for Shit!": Favela Funk as Industry and Funkeiras' Autonomy

Maysa Abusada walks on stage and immediately turns her back to the audience in a July 2013 live performance. The stage lighting accentuates her curvy, muscular brown body. She slowly shakes her hips and butt back and forth, throwing her hair sideways, while her two female dancers, one on each side of the stage, also dance with their backs to the audience and vibrate their hips frantically. Maysa wears a small black outfit that resembles a bikini with shiny golden details in the front that exposes her light brown skin. The fringes along her bust and waistline riot with her movement. After one minute or so, she turns to the audience and asks "where are the independent women here tonight?" Running her fingers through her long hair extensions, she continues, "that woman who doesn't depend on men for anything, who doesn't need a man to pay for our hair, who doesn't depend on men to get our nails done ..." She finally proclaims: "Those independent women who proudly say: I don't depend on man for shit!"

In a December 2014 story in the now-deceased celebrity website *Ego*, Maysa Abusada tells the reporter that she is scheduled to remove her buttock silicone implants in January of the following year.[1] The funkeira provides troublesome details of the day-to-day struggles her implants have been impinging on her, including the inability to sit for more than 10 minutes and cutting the length of her shows in half. What is truly striking in Maysa's account is the funkeira's concern over her livelihood without the implants. She says,

> Before [the implants], I made R$ 1,500 per gig [around US$300]. Today, because of my enormous butt, I charge R$ 3,000 per concert. I'm very concerned because I still don't know if I'll be able to replace the implants and maintain the size of my buttocks.[2]

These two tales about Maysa Abusada illustrate the ambiguous themes of this chapter: on the one hand, favela funk provides an avenue for feminine folks to gain and perform financial autonomy. On the other hand, favela funk, though a marginalized movement, works much like any cultural industry inserted in capitalist relations; they impose tough conditions with which artists must negotiate, especially those who are Black and feminine. In this chapter, I focus on live performances and personal interviews in which funkeiras transact levels of autonomy either as a group—as women or feminine people—or as individual artists. Here, I expand on the argument that, in the process of using embodied politics to survive, funkeiras have the possibility of fracturing the structures that oppress them and, in turn, impacting their social and economic well-being.

This chapter is inspired, in part, by the recent tendency among feminine artists in favela funk to provoke cisgender men by flaunting their economic and social independence. These performances, however, are not just a provocation. Funkeiras have a very pragmatic reason to perform: they need the money. As favela funk scholar Lopes points out, funk artists are, above all, workers in the music industry, and favela funk is their job.[3] As they become financially independent, funkeiras not only tend to support their families and communities but also report having more autonomy over their performances and careers. The rise of funkeiras to the center of favela funk changes the movement itself and impacts its practices and norms. This represents an important shift for these folks, given that sexist, racist, and classist structures make them more susceptible to poverty.[4]

Favela Funk: A Movement and an Industry

Favela funk is a musical movement born in the outskirts of Rio de Janeiro, Brazil. As a musical genre, favela funk has been consistently popular in Brazil since the 1990s,[5] reaching global markets in the mid-2000s.[6] But its expressions go beyond music. From the movement's parties (*bailes*, from now on) and rich dialect to its particular dance moves and fashion,[7] favela funk is the embodiment of contemporary expressions of Rio de Janeiro's African diaspora: it is creative, resilient, and dynamic. Research about favela funk as an industry abound,[8] but little has been written about the way women and transfeminine folks negotiate with and survive it. Before turning my attention exclusively to funkeiras, I provide a brief overview of favela funk as a movement and an industry.

Favela funk is a uniquely hybrid genre. Since its emergence, DJs and MCs combined different aesthetic forms whose elements were already the result of other hybrid musical practices, such as U.S.-based Miami bass, samba, and the sounds and chants from Afro-Brazilian religion, *Candomblé*.[9] This sonic mixture, thus, is the result of funk's transnationalism,[10] specifically as an element of the African diaspora.[11] Favela funk's aesthetics value sonic impact, "be it through beats, or through the high volume in which it is executed."[12] Per Caceres, Ferrari, and Palombini's assessment, favela funk is a type of "spoken music or music that is spoken over a rhythmic base."[13] Those who speak in favela funk are poor folks from Rio's "sub-urbanized areas."[14] As funk artists attest themselves, funk is "favela's reality," in that these spaces do not work simply as a source of inspiration for the music produced; indeed, the sonic elements of favela funk are a form of discursive organization "*from* the favela *about* the favela *to* the favela" (emphasis in original).[15] Favela funk music is both a reflection and an ordering element of life in Rio's favelas.

It is not by chance, then, that cultural elites have framed favela funk as one of the most detestable genres in Brazilian popular culture, with its melodies and lyrics deemed "poor," its singers never on key, and artists who end up debasing too many pop and classic songs with their own versions.[16] This criticism is not surprising given that music and other artistic expressions from marginalized groups tend to be labeled "inferior" in comparison to other already validated genres, such as Brazilian popular music.[17] Favela funk scholars agree that the aesthetic elements that compose the genre reflect its socio-historical emergence, so it would be hard to divorce the music from the conditions in which the social movement emerged.[18] In addition, critics only validate cultural expressions from the African diaspora in Brazil once they have been appropriated by white elites—and samba is an example of that.[19]

In the 1990s, after bailes were popular in clubs all over the city for almost two decades, mainstream media more consistently picked up on the movement's popularity, which resulted in both praise and condemnation of favela funk.[20] Lopes calls attention to the fact that, in all of the reports glamourizing funk as the hottest beat in town, its marginalized origins were erased as much as possible.[21] This suggests that, in mainstream media, favela funk's supposed drawback was more about who produced it and where it came from rather than the genre itself.[22]

A few crucial events served to solidify mainstream culture's vilification of favela funk. According to Facina, the 1990s marked the rise of neoliberalism in Brazil and replaced the welfare state with a police state that greatly impacted Rio's favelas, which contributed simultaneously to their impoverishment and intense media scrutiny.[23] The idea that violence, along with poor people of color, would remain within the limits of the city's favelas changed in the early 1990s with the so-called *arrastões*.* [24] Those events were characterized by local media as mass robberies happening at the famous Ipanema beach and were supposedly perpetrated by favela funk fans. Facina clarifies that the so-called arrastões were, in fact, clashes between groups from "beyond the

---

* A literal translation would be "trawlers." The term was actually created by the local media (Facina, 2009).

tunnel"[†] (dark-skinned, favela youth).[25] The fact that poor youth were intoning battle cries using the name of favelas and the word *bonde*[‡] together made the media presume that there was an inevitable connection between the assumed criminals and favela funk. After those events, mainstream media seemed to make efforts to link all sorts of crimes to favela funk in general but bailes in particular. Favela funk artists and frequenters from Rio's poor neighborhoods were gradually portrayed as if they were "the cause of several social ills," while their voices were systematically erased from the media coverage that worked to criminalize the movement.[26]

Despite heavy stigmatization throughout the 1990s, favela funk was part of an alternative music industry by the end of the decade. Improvised recording studios and radio stations were flourishing across Rio de Janeiro's metro area.[27] If during the 1980s favela funk parties were seen solely as a form of entertainment, by the end of the 1990s the movement had gathered a significant number of successful MCs, DJs, sound systems, dancers, radio and TV hosts, and more.[28] Above all, favela funk became an aggressive shout for public visibility for the people living in Rio's poorer areas. Late in that decade, Rio's government was belligerently targeting successful bailes across the city with heavy regulations, which made the legal organization of parties really difficult.[29] As a result, many of them closed between the late 1900s and the early 2000s.[30] As the 2000s approached, media coverage of the movement remained paradoxically immersed in approval and condemnation.

Favela funk started the 2000s facing a series of violent charges, from child prostitution to involvement with drug trafficking.[31] At that point, many bailes that used to happen in clubs throughout the city were pushed into Rio's favelas.[32] The symbolic connection between favela funk and crime was then solidified. The most significant media event associating the two was the murder of one of Rede Globo's[§] reporters

---

[†] Rio's wealthy side, the South Zone, connects with the different parts of the cities through tunnels.

[‡] *Bonde* literally translates as "tram." It is a slang generally used in "funk-raps" to designate, among other things, territory.

[§] Broadcasting company belonging to Brazil's largest media oligopoly.

inside the favela Vila Cruzeiro in 2002. Lopes maintains that there was little factual evidence suggesting that the murder had happened after the reporter attended a baile in the favela,[33] but mainstream media discourse was unanimous in establishing that association. By the mid-2000s, local media once again accused a group of MCs of "crime propaganda" through the performance of *proibidões*.** [34] This time, however, media's campaign against those MCs led to several arrests.[35] But the highest point of criminalization came with a 2008 statutory law tightening the already harsh restrictions imposed on funk parties in the early 2000s. This law resulted in the total prohibition of bailes inside slums.[36] The move happened in articulation with an extensive government policy termed "pacification": central favelas in the city would be slowly occupied by the military police, which would in turn expel drug dealers while monitoring illegal (musical) activities.[37] Together, mainstream media and state-coagulated discourses about Rio's favelas and funk as expressions of "evil, danger, and barbarism" brought great financial despair and social stigma to those involved with the movement.[38] To this day, favela funk is treated as "a representation of poverty and trigger of violence, crime and transgressive sexualities."[39]

Part of government and corporate media persecution of funk stemmed from a fear of moral corruption fueled by popular songs about non-romantic sex. Freire Filho and Herschmann suggest that the presence of white, middle- and upper-class youth at funk parties in the late 1990s and early 2000s generated anxiety about the transgressive mix of different socioeconomic classes and races those spaces promoted.[40] The moral panic that permeated news coverage of funk parties contributed to the public demands for regulation mentioned above.[41] According to the media, the "good" young people of the city were witnessing fights between gangs, becoming familiar with the life of the "natives" and their promiscuity, and being lured by sensual music and dancing.[42] Corporate media did not consistently condemn the consumption of funk as a cultural product; nevertheless, to experience it

---

** The word stands for "forbidden" or those songs that are not played in mainstream media. These are usually raw descriptions of the violent realities in Rio's slums.

inside the favelas represented great physical and moral risks to white, middle- and upper-class habitués.[43]

Parallel to the movement's criminalization, the 2000s also marked a noticeable increase in favela funk's popularity. Imported samplers and romantic lyrics were replaced with a locally developed and hybrid beat, the *tamborzão,*[tt] and tunes that narrated the "neurotic reality of the favelas," be that gang and police violence or casual sex and conquest.[44] Caceres, Ferrari, and Palombini show that these sonic changes in favela funk are indeed intertwined with national and local politics, and the popularity of the tamborzão aligns with the eight years of Luiz Inácio Lula da Silva's presidency.[45] His years in government and his dubious public safety policies of favelas' development and military occupation are "co-responsible" for the most original creation in favela funk at that time—an invention that was then severely persecuted and proscribed because of such policies.[46]

The tamborzão's popularity brought in more women and travestis to the movement. At the same time, many of the media's moralistic outbursts targeted specifically funkeiras and their public performances.[47] After being consigned to the margins of favela funk for years, ciswomen first and travestis later had finally become protagonists of a section of the movement denominated *funk putaria*, or dirty funk.[48] What started as male-only monologue about sexual courtship and conquest became a sort of a "sex war" when funkeiras began to respond to the songs performed by men using similar aggressiveness and mockery.[49]

Rio held the monopoly on favela funk production for decades, but that is no longer the case. In the last few years, São Paulo and Belo Horizonte have become competitors in the creation and circulation of favela funk, which now happens via social media.[50] The tamborzão is slowly being replaced by the fast-paced 150 BPM base sampler.[51] Though favela funk scholars are still catching up on how these trends continue to transform the movement, mainstream media noticed the significant rise in popularity of production companies, such as Kondzilla, which

[tt] The beat is a combination of heavy bass lines with Brazilian sounds. There's contention over the origins of the beat, but many artists suggest it was created inside Rio de Janeiro's famous favela, City of God.

was in 2017 the largest YouTube channel in Brazil.[52] I will touch on the importance of social media for favela funk briefly in the analysis below, but researchers should follow the footsteps of others who have started to investigate the power of YouTube videos in influencing the favela funk industry.[53]

To this day, favela funk is concomitantly a popular genre and the target of news headlines that continue to link violence and promiscuity with it.[54] The growing conservative wave in Brazil right now, in which even traditional forms of art are being persecuted,[55] might be an indication of further, more ferocious institutional oppression favela funk is slotted to face. For instance, in May 2017, a "legislative idea" proposing that favela funk should be criminalized received over 20,000 supportive signatures.[56] The author of the proposal claims that favela funk is no more than a "recruitment tool for the organized crime on social media" while also calling the movement "fake culture."[57] There were enough endorsements to call for a public hearing on the matter, but the chair of the senate's human rights commission at the time demonstrated little interest in pursuing this call for criminalization. It might be worth noting that this happened in a pre-Bolsonaro Brazil, which makes it difficult to imagine any positive institutionalization of favela funk under the current political landscape, like the one that happened in 2009 and that I describe below. Favela funk is dynamic and accustomed to dire material circumstances. The movement is likely to continue to reinvent itself, despite the high financial and emotional cost artists and others who depend on favela funk to survive face each time reinvention needs to happen.[58]

Favela Funk as Industry

According to a 2019 report, a record 41% of Brazil's employed population is in the so-called informal labor market, which includes those who are self-employed, under-employed, and those working without formal contracts.[59] This, of course, is part of a global trend, which includes the flexibilization of labor and depreciation of wages.[60] Favela funk is, no doubt, part of Rio's, and recently São Paulo's, informal economy with MCs, DJs, dancers, agents, producers, and the like making a living off live shows, bailes, music videos, and other social media engagements.[61]

Rio's favela funk became a mass phenomenon, even though it developed on the fringes of the mainstream music industry.[62] This contradiction means that, as a cultural product, favela funk has been accepted by ample sections of Brazilian society, including middle and upper classes.[63] Lopes argues that a process of professionalization of favela funk has led to the development of a specific "chain of production and consumption, creating new opportunities particularly to impoverished young people" to become MCs, DJs, dancers, musicians, producers, sound operators, and more.[64] This happened especially in the 1990s, when DJs and MCs from Rio's favelas begun to produce the music themselves.[65] Since favela funk is structured in ways that are similar to the mainstream culture industry, few actors dominate the ownership of the production and marketing processes.

Many public discussions about favela funk tend to homogenize the movement's identity.[66] Lopes explains that even critical research that intends to "deconstruct prejudices that middle and upper classes have against funk"[67] are centered on how the movement is perceived by outsiders and not on its backstage and internal tensions. Thus, it is common for researchers to forget that favela funk is not uniform and that many of the tensions within it stem from the fact that these artists are workers whose lives either fully or partially depend on the movement. For instance, with the heavy regulation of bailes in Rio's favelas in 2008 via military police occupation, along with the monopolization of the other few available spaces to perform, many artists were then out of work.[68] In fact, the military occupation of favelas ended up strengthening the monopoly of the so-called sound systems—groups of managers and DJs who organize bailes.

With most bailes inside centrally located slums ultimately shut down, two noticeable moves happened within favela funk. First, a group of MCs, DJs, scholars, and politicians came together to create the 2008 APAFunk (Association of Professionals and Friends of Funk) manifesto in which they affirmed the collective character of favela funk struggles, as well as contested abusive practices, both from mainstream media and from those few producers who control the funk industry.

The text was the first major political act from APAFunk, which later showed its political force when its proposed bill to recognize favela funk as folk culture in the state of Rio was turned into a statutory law in 2009.[69] Passos and Facina have examined the troubles stemming from bringing the 2009 statutory law into fruition, including the frustration of favela funk party producers to throw bailes with proper permits.[70]

The second noticeable motion in favela funk was the relocation of bailes back to clubs within and beyond Rio's metro area.[71] These spaces are usually owned by big players within favela funk, which gives artists little with which to bargain.[72] In her interviews with mostly male DJs and MCs, Lopes describes a pervasive tension in favela funk, namely the exploitation of MCs and dancers that occurs on the part of agents, DJs, and owners of clubs.[73] Many of the funkeiras I interviewed also protested the lack of labor protections in favela funk, as I discuss in the next section. Copyright, for instance, is a complicated matter in the movement and impacts artists' abilities to perform and ultimately make money.[74]

Funkeiras have been able to grow as artists and become an integral part of favela funk, even under exploitative circumstances. They have achieved more space in the funk movement within the last ten years, not just in terms of actual visibility but especially in the way they relate to cismen—the ones still primarily controlling favela funk. While women and other feminine folks—mostly travestis—are generally not in powerful positions in favela funk vis-à-vis cismen, the analysis below challenges previous research suggesting that they have very little control and autonomy over their careers. In fact, funkeiras seem to embrace the potential to confront cismen's power in both their personal and professional lives while advocating on an individual and collective/performative level.

Favela Funk, Gender, and Labor

Like men in the movement, funkeiras tend to be women and transfeminine people in their 20s and up who are generally Black or *mestiças*.‡‡ They perform mostly about sex, relationships, and competition

---

‡‡ *Mestiça* stands for brown, mixed race people.

with men and other women. MCs such as Tati Quebra Barraco, Deize Tigrona, and Valesca Popozuda became popular during the mid-2000s with hits such as "Fama de Putona" ("Hoe's Reputation"), "Miniatura de Lulu" ("Lulu's Miniature"), and "Minha Buceta é o Poder" ("My Pussy is the Power").[75] The participation of women as central artists of favela funk has helped to problematize an essentially masculine movement. Funkeiras' visibility in mainstream media gave them the opportunity to assert themselves as artists. Simultaneously, they have attracted criticism regarding the way they dress and dance, the type of lyrics they perform, and their life "choices" (to be teenage and single mothers and have numerous cosmetic procedures). In this section, I rely on personal and news media interviews and performances to investigate financial independence and professional autonomy among funkeiras in order to establish where they stand in relation to men and to the movement in general. As Madison poses, the critical ethnographic interview helps give rise to, among others, "expressions of communal strivings [and] social history."[76] This context, provided by the funkeiras themselves, offers a fundamental backdrop for the analysis of their performances in the subsequent chapters. Here, I draw comparisons with Lopes's 2011 research, since it is a fairly thorough account of the movement in the mid- to the late 2000s. Many of the issues Lopes reports persist, while others, such as funkeiras' autonomy over their careers, seem to have changed over the years quite a bit.

Besides being artists who want visibility and have fun performing in favela funk, artists in the movement are also looking for a source of income.[77] During my interviews with funkeiras, they showed a very pragmatic reason to perform: they needed the money. Funk artists certainly work a lot, which is something that both Lopes and I agree on. For instance, some of the most popular funkeiras reported performing at as many as eight different venues per night, especially over the weekends.[78] A lot of women also have or had other day jobs in order to make ends meet. MC Dandara had a small kiosk in her community at the time of our interview; Deize Tigrona used to work as a maid, a factory worker, and a garbage collector; MC Paloma is also an esthetician.[79] Below, I delve into the tensions and challenges funkeiras face in the industry, some of which are intrinsically related to issues of race and gender.

Some of the matters funkeiras face are, in fact, shared struggles with artists of all genders and genres, such as tensions related to song copyrights. Favela funk is known for having a complicated relationship with intellectual property.[80] Often, MCs do not own the songs they wrote and, instead, sign them off to DJs and other big producers in the movement for a relatively small share of the profits, in case the song becomes a hit. At the time of my fieldwork in 2013, it was very common for one person to write the lyrics to a song and then have a DJ produce it. Then, a DJ, manager, or owner of a big company, such as Furacão 2000 and DJ Marlboro, actually registers the song under their names. Hence, owning the rights to a song does not mean being the actual author of the track.

In my conversation with Deize Tigrona on an August 2013 afternoon at her home in City of God, she reported that nobody registered their songs at the time when tamborzão from City of God received mainstream media attention. Instead, one would take a potential hit to a DJ, who would then produce it and likely own the copyrights to it. When I asked Deize why she also did that, she replied, as she was standing by the stove making dinner, "we thought we were gonna be famous," so DJs owning 25% of the profit made off songs seemed like a "good deal." DJs, thus, work as powerful gatekeepers in favela funk.

Similarly, MC Dandara told me that she could have been more successful if either she had recorded songs she authored herself or if the people who became popular performing them would have given her the credit for the authorship. MC Dandara has two notable cases of popular songs that were signed off to different artists without credit: Gaiola das Popozudas's "Agora tô Piranha" ("Now that I'm a Whore") and "Nossa Bandeira" ("Our Flag"), which she decided to let two male MCs record for the hit movie Elite Squad's soundtrack. When telling me about how she ended up not performing "Nossa Bandeira," Dandara started by singing it. With her toddler on her lap in a tight office space, Dandara performed under the flickering fluorescent lights:

Let's talk about social prejudice
What makes you a "docta"
And what makes you a thug
Let's talk about social prejudice
What makes a good man
And what makes you a bad man
In the South Side:
- Hey bro, check out the time, go home
In the favela:
- Hands up, take off your shoes

Dandara recalls the first time she performed this song for an *Elite Squad* producer who approached her after being recommended by famous favela funk DJ Marlboro. "This is the song!" she tells me the producer said. The male MCs then contacted her asking for the song. At the time, Dandara says, "I was blown up in the media with a song called 'Pode me Chamar de Boa' ("You Can Call me Hot" or "You Can Call a Whore" in its dirty version)", unlike the male MCs, who were going through financial difficulties. Dandara says she gave in for having a "big heart." These two male MCs, who were very popular in the early days of favela funk in 1990s, were also the face of APAFunk. Curiously, APAFunk was known for criticizing the type of dirty favela funk songs for which MC Dandara became famous.

Another related tension in favela funk is precisely the battle between MCs who stopped being popular in the mid-1990s through the mid-2000s and those who became famous from the late 2000s on. Lopes, for instance, reports that 1990s MCs who are no longer in the spotlight complain about the exploitation of favela funk monopolies, while those who are popular now, including DJs, defend the system by suggesting that those MCs are out of touch with what is in demand.[81] I noticed something similar in my conversations with funkeiras. MC Kátia, perhaps, encapsulates this conundrum better than any other funkeira featured in this book.

I visited MC Kátia in her home, in the Mandela favela, in July 2013. Kátia's home is modest and well-organized. The couch where I sat for the entire morning during our interview is adjacent to the front door, which is actually on the side of the house. Her husband, who was also her agent and DJ at the time, joins us, but stays mostly quiet. Kátia becomes animated from time to time, gets up from the couch, and walks around while telling me about her story and struggles in favela funk. One of the big favela funk monopolies in Rio had blacklisted her, she tells me, after her ex-husband scammed them: "Once they closed doors for me, I didn't have any friends in the business." She gave a detailed account of the roadblocks some MCs face in the industry while assuring me that "if DJs would play my song, the public would enjoy it, and they wouldn't be able to hold me back." I asked her, if a song becomes a hit on, say, YouTube, will the DJs have to play it? She replies, "Yes, they'll have to play it." The opportunity to perform in bailes inside favelas does not depend on this kind of politics, according to MC Kátia. That is why, according to her, the UPPs (military police occupation of favelas)

> have hit MCs who depend on the community to become somebody really hard … the government is wrong. I understand wanting to end drug trafficking, but putting other people out of work? I lost a place to perform. The DJ lost a place to play. The food truck guy lost a place to sell food to then feed his own family. The boy who used to collect cans for cash after bailes lost that, too … Meanwhile, the clubs became stronger, formed an alliance, and now they call the shots. For me to play my music at a famous club, I have to pay $500, $1,000 reais.

MC Kátia is referencing the fact that bailes inside favelas have either been completely outlawed or were imposed severe restrictions that made them virtually impossible to produce.[82] She continues, "I'm an MC; I don't sell drugs. Funk is my job." When I ask her about the association of favela funk and crime, she replies, "If funk was only for criminals, what is it doing in places like Via Show [major venue in Rio's metro area at the time]?" Of course, to assume that no connection exists between local drug trafficking and favela funk is naïve. Favela funk artists claim that it is precisely government belligerence toward the bailes that strengthens that complicated relationship. While other scholars have documented the association between favela funk and drug trafficking,[§§] I witnessed first-hand the peculiarities of bailes

---

§§ For more on proibidões, favela funk, and crime, see Carlos Palombini, "Proibidão em Tempo de Pacificação Armada," in Patrimônio Musical Na Atualidade: Tradição, Memória,

inside favelas. These parties are usually funded by the only possible sponsors in a situation of outlawed parties—local drug dealers—which means that they hire and pay for MCs, DJs, and dancers to perform. Later in this chapter, I briefly analyze the gendered aspects of performing at these parties.

In 2019, when I contacted MC Kátia's husband/agent/DJ, known as LD, to ask for permission to include her interview in the book, he was telling me about MC Kátia's new career. She was enjoying the success of her 2018 music video, "Vem 5 Minutinho" ("Come 5 Minute"), produced by the famous favela funk DJ Batata. While on the phone with him, I could hear Kátia speaking in the background, asking him to ask me questions about the interview she had given in 2013. Understandably, they were concerned with "disgruntled" comments about the favela funk industry Kátia may have made at the time, particularly naming other MCs and producers. LD told me about the importance of social media for MC Kátia's career, from music videos on YouTube to Instagram posts sponsored by local businesses. Indeed, the embryotic relationship between social media and favela funk of 2013 had developed into a burgeoning lifeline for artists in the movement in 2019. However, video production companies turned into monopolies via YouTube channels, notably the aforementioned Kondzilla and GR6. Both channels, together, are responsible for a lot of the current favela funk hits.[83] Once artists are well-established, such as Pocah, they no longer rely on these YouTube channels to reach their audience, as they are able to draw fans to their own pages.[84] More needs to be investigated on the role of social media in favela funk, but it is hard to dispute that artists have more autonomy over their careers now than they had back in 2013.

Women and travestis face particular challenges in favela funk that are generally imposed by cismen in power. Scholars have shown little interest in investigating these internal challenges that are most certainly gendered. I attempt to help correct this gap in the next section by addressing issues of gendered autonomy within favela funk. Specifically, I examine

Discurso e Poder, ed. M. Alice Volpe (Rio de Janeiro: Universidade Federal do Rio de Janeiro, 2013), 215–36.

matters related to sexual harassment and abuse, beauty standards and race, and the mixing of personal and business relationships.

Favela Funk and/as Gendered Labor

Even though favela funk works on the fringes of the culture industry, several of the internal issues in the movement mimic those found in the mainstream music industry. Many funkeiras report that it is very common for men in power to offer professional assistance in exchange for sexual favors. MC and dancer Andressa, from the all-female group Fetixe, states that funkeiras "are afraid of being abused."[85] Similarly, transwoman MC Paloma TransTornada claims that "There's something really bad that happens in funk with me and my female friends: people want to help you, but you know how? By taking you to bed. But they *can't* help you out. They try to fool you."[86] In a recent interview with *Universa*, funkeira-turned-celebrity Valesca Popozuda told the reporter that, when she was the lead singer of Gaiola das Popozudas, the owner of a venue who had booked her show attacked her in the dressing room.[87] Even though Valesca says she was able to react by burning the man's penis with a curling iron, she says that she felt like there was no way to report him: "I was afraid people would say I was asking for it. He was married. Who do you think people would believe?"[88] Some funkeiras contend that this may be a factor in pushing them out of the movement.

Lopes asserts that, in favela funk, artists in general "are vulnerable to the decisions of managers."[89] The same happens with funkeiras who are managed by men related to them (husbands, boyfriends, brothers, etc.). Consequently, because they are mostly MCs and dancers and rarely DJs, producers, and managers, funkeiras' performances are often the result of men's final decisions.[90] While, I tend to agree with Lopes, what I have witnessed of these relationships during fieldwork seems to challenge this narrative of funkeiras' complete lack of professional autonomy. In fact, I directly asked them about these power imbalances, specifically the artist-manager relationship, and their answers partially challenged Lopes's account. Managers and producers were sometimes present during interviews. Three of the funkeiras I spoke with in 2013 are/were also romantically involved with their managers. Generally, the relationships of power between men and women, manager and artist, seem to have changed since Lopes's research. This could be due to the advances funkeiras have made within the movement, such as becoming central pieces in funk's mainstream image.

When asked if they had autonomy over their careers, the seven funkeiras I spoke with were unanimous in saying that, yes, they do. This autonomy is mostly related to the manager/artist relationship, as well as to what sorts of sacrifices they are willing to make for their careers. This self-sufficiency could be partial or negotiated or could have been achieved over time. Pocah, formerly known as MC Pocahontas, who is now a signed artist with Warner Music, used to have her fiancé-turned-husband manage her career. She acknowledges that her now-much-older ex-husband used to pressure her into singing about themes with which she was not comfortable, but that as she became popular, she was able to have a say in what she did not want to do.[91] Similarly, MC Carol (Figure 1) told me in August 2019 about her struggle to attain the current level of autonomy she has. She said,

> I never wanted to have a manager. I've always been afraid of this .... I used to work with a guy who was a Jack-of-all-trades, you know? He used to book concerts, drive me around, and it was ...[MC Carol pauses and sighs] difficult. He used to take money from me. I actually had an all-male team, and they were all 30 years old and older ... and I was 16 years old. So, you can only imagine how tough it was. Being on the road with them .... I didn't have a voice. For instance, they would drink all night long, and they would then take the wheel .... Things got better in 2016. I started to work with a woman named Ana. I have autonomy, you know? If I say, I don't wanna talk about this or sing about that, today, I'm able to do so. But it took me a long time.

Older MCs, such as MC Kátia, MC Dandara, and Deize Tigrona, all of whom are in their 30s and 40s and with over 10 years in funk, say they have autonomy in their relationships with managers. At the time of our interview in 2013, MC Kátia's DJ and manager, for instance, was also her husband, as previously mentioned. He looks considerably younger than her. Observing their interactions, it is not hard to notice she, indeed, has the last word over her career: MC Kátia is assertive and commanding. In fact, being married to her manager in this case

Figure 1: MC Carol.
Credit: Fernando Schlaepfer/I Hate Flash

might actually be an advantage, as the relationship is not only based on financial interests. This complicates the manager/artist relationship, but it also makes it more negotiable for women like MC Kátia. They can bargain using emotional appeal and sex without feeling like their morality is compromised.

MC Dandara says she does not have a manager but a business partner, which ultimately gives her freedom to decide which way she wants to go; her manager at the time was present during our interview and nodded in agreement. Deize Tigrona confirms that, though she has had a rough path in favela funk, mostly because of health issues, she has always been the one deciding the future of her career. In 2013, Deize's husband and her sister managed contracts and other administrative aspects of her career, but she made it clear then that she was the one guiding them through the business aspect, since she had more experience. In 2019, Deize became part of a São Paulo-based production company focused on Black and LGBTQ+ artists named Batekoo.

Funkeiras whose managers or producers are not related to them in any way are also not always completely powerless. Again, these relationships are usually negotiated, even with power imbalances between the parts. In July 2013, I attended a baile inside a favela in Rio's metro area. I had agreed to attend the live performance of an MC and her dancers. At 3 a.m. on a relatively chilly Sunday morning, I met with the artists' producer outside the community, so we could go in together for safety purposes. This favela was ruled by local drug dealers. With my headlights off and my internal lights on and windows down, I could hear the engines of motorcycles riding by; I later learned that we were being escorted. It was possible to catch the powerful bassline of the tamborzão even before arriving at the dark alley where the party was happening. The crowd of mostly young Black and brown people danced to the beats among several men armed with AR-15s and AK-47s. As I waited by the DJ stand for the girls to perform, men occasionally would fire their guns into the air in honor of others who had been either killed or imprisoned. It is common for artists to stick around for a while after an early morning performance; it is a way to please the local drug dealers who are paying for the performance. In this case, they referred to themselves as a "board of directors." Immediately after they performed, however, a clearly drunk man fired an Ak-47 right behind the MC. She was visibly startled and upset; she was also eight months pregnant. She said to the producer, "it is time for us to go." He immediately accepted her emphatic suggestion.

Funkeiras who are in charge of their own careers might pay a high professional price. Favela funk is still male-dominated, and refusing to follow some of the rules established by powerful men and their companies means that funkeiras will not be as popular as other artists who choose to conform to specific trends. Andressa says she is not willing to compromise her morals in order to be more successful in funk.[92] MC Pink rejects the suggestion of male managers who keep trying to change her style from quirky to sexy, which ultimately affects her popularity within the movement. Consequently, she says that "I have to keep proving to others that I'm a funkeira because I look different from what's expected."

Often, when funkeiras must make concessions, it is because material circumstances reduce their ability to choose or that resisting these concessions might mean the end of their careers; in summary, it is a matter of survival. Maysa Abusada's implant story in the beginning of this chapter, for instance, demonstrates the gendered relationship between funkeiras' bodies and their professional success. Maysa's position is not unusual. Back in 2012, Valesca Popozuda declared to a reporter, "My buttocks are my instrument of work."[93] Maysa and Valesca's cases pose a challenge to white feminist analyses of plastic surgery: on the one hand, second-wave feminist scholars who condemn plastic surgery as tools of patriarchy suggest that women and transfeminine folks are duped into it.[94] On the other, third-wave feminists argue that this is simply a matter of choice; women and transfeminine folks should do as they please. The funkeiras, however, are neither duped into it nor do they freely choose these procedures; they do so because there are material consequences for opting out, as I discuss below.

Sometimes, funkeiras are not financially able to keep up with feminine trends in favela funk, and curiously, those who felt left out of this particular physical embodiment of femininity in favela funk were Black and/or older ciswomen. MC Dandara, who is a Black ciswoman, told me that she is

> an artist based on my talent, not my face. I don't have beauty, a nice butt, I have no pretty face, I have no big ass …. But now I'm gonna get pretty, I have a manager investing in me …. In a few more years, I'll put in breast and butt implants.

Similarly, MC Kátia, who is a light-skinned Black woman, passionately vented about the struggles associated with not having a particular type of body:

> The issue I face is the following: I'm there on stage, I'm an MC. So there's a lot of people, men, the male audience, who think that for me to be an MC I have to, how can I say this, put in breasts [implants], butt [implants]… No. I'm an MC, you know what I mean?… But if I get breast implants, do a liposuction, and wear skimpy shorts, I'm gonna perform all over, because men want to see "hot" women.

I will delve into the specificities of performances of femininity in favela funk in more detail in the next two chapters, but for now, I would like to briefly examine why it seems like Black women did not have access to "the look" and the popularity attached to it. Favela funk as an industry works within and against racist, classist, and heteronormative systems. It is no surprise, then, that like in Brazilian society at large, white and light-skinned brown women are favored over Black women—even within favela funk. As a result, the work of Black women and transfeminine folks who are MCs is markedly different from other non-Black folks, whose femininity seems to be more accepted within favela funk. Note, however, that this does not mean that the femininity of MCs like Valesca or Maysa, both light-skinned brown women, is simply embraced by Brazilian society at large; on the contrary, these women are still castigated by mainstream media for not subscribing to normative white femininity, as I demonstrate in the next chapter.

Despite the barriers a male-dominated favela funk imposes on women and transfeminine folks, they are still able to negotiate and/ or divert from those obstacles and achieve professional autonomy and some financial independence. Pocah states that she always signs her own contracts and always knows how much she is making per show. Being on top of the financial gains her career generates has allowed her to be independent since she was 16 years old.[95] Now, the MC supports many family members, something common among poor women of color in general.[96] Deize Tigrona says that funk helped her buy many of the small properties she owns inside City of God.[97] In a live radio interview I witnessed in Rio back in 2013, the women from feminine bonde Abysolutas also stated that they were able to live off of their careers.[98] This professional autonomy spills over onto the stage, where funkeiras have begun to proudly proclaim their financial independence from cismen.

When funkeiras first became popular in the early to the mid-2000s, the themes of their songs were mostly related to sex and relationships. At that time, it was unusual for them to perform about financial independence, per the separate works of Lopes, Lyra, Aragão, and de Oliveira.[99] From the late 2000s on, songs about financial independence became more common and are now a regular topic in feminine favela funk.

The growing popularity of songs about economic self-sufficiency can be connected to funkeiras' emerging importance within the movement. If their professional independence is often tied to personal autonomy, as established above, then it makes sense that this newfound financial liberation would spill over into stage performances. Moreover, since Lopes reported that relationships between funkeiras and managers are at times riddled with violent practices—personal and professional[100]— it seems likely that funkeiras' performances about autonomy, likewise, incorporate liberation from abusive relationships. It is also fair to say that some of these performances, perhaps the minority of them per my research, are indeed a kind of a performative autonomy; funkeiras may sing about it because it is currently popular and not an actual lived experience. Still, the material gains funkeiras have achieved, and their public performances about it, might work as a crucial discursive shift within male-dominated favela funk, as I show below.

Valesca Popozuda has used the stage to perform about romantic and financial liberation from an abusive relationship. In a 2009 live performance of the song "I Dumped My Husband/I Became a Whore" that took place in a small venue, Valesca wears a shiny silver outfit, sort of a very short dress, that hugs her curvy, muscular brown body. Her abs expose a belly button piercing. The performance unfolds in the form of a dialogue between Valesca and the audience. When she starts performing the lyrics, she maintains a conversational tone mixed with the usual favela funk assertive tone. Valesca simultaneously asks for the support of women in the audience and sending a message to the heterosexual men present: "You would only beat me up and go out to party/I would stay home, waiting for you/I used to scream and cry like a crazy woman ... Thanks a lot, but now I'm a whore!."[101]

The audience responds enthusiastically, as Valesca continues:

> Some men like to beat us up. Yet they mock us saying "a little slap doesn't hurt."*** Hey, you jerk [pointing to someone in the audience],

---

*** "A little slap doesn't hurt" is a reference to a popular favela funk song from the early 2000s in which a male MC suggests giving a woman a little slap during sex. The female MC in the song sings the chorus "a little slap doesn't hurt."

hear me out! If a little slap doesn't hurt, let me tell you: hold on to your horn[†††] and fuck off![102]

Valesca's performance is significant for a few reasons. First, turning into a "whore" was successful as her way out of the relationship and perhaps of achieving financial autonomy. It is unclear in the performance if she intends to just sleep with multiple partners or/and to charge for it, but the Portuguese word she uses—*puta*—connotes sex work. Moreover, instead of choosing to physically abuse her ex-partner back, like funkeiras such as Tati Quebra Barraco have suggested in their performances, Valesca takes revenge by having sex with multiple partners. On the other hand, Valesca could be less worried about revenge and more concerned about liberating herself from an oppressive relationship and/or to seek personal and financial autonomy through her sexuality.

Like many funkeiras, Valesca was married to her manager, Leandro Gomes de Castro, also known as Pardal. Their relationship was kept secret from the public, but multiple folks in the favela funk industry told me they were aware of their romantic connection. Pardal continued to manage Valesca's career long after the two divorced.[103] It is hard to tell if the song performed in 2009 was aimed at him; either way, part of my argument is that these performances may become part of funkeiras' off stage reality eventually. Valesca now says that she has full autonomy over her career, that "nobody tells me what to do," and refers to the relationship with Pardal as "toxic."[104]

Maysa's performance described in the opening paragraph of this chapter would have been unthinkable in the early to mid-2000s. Now, however, it is not rare for funkeiras to perform their autonomy from men. Pocah, for instance, released a music video for the 150 BPM funk song "Não sou Obrigada" ("I Don't Have To") in which she challenges a cisman who wants to control her while surrounded by transfeminine people of color.[105] The chorus, "nobody bosses this ass," is repeated with images of those folks and Pocah twerking to the camera.

[†††] In Brazil's folk culture, to cheat on someone is to figuratively "put a horn" on that person's head.

In the 2018 music video for "Boy Machista," ("Sexist Boy") beginner MC Jessi sings: "Keeps asking me not to put on lipstick/this abusive thing doesn't go with my beat …/I've never depended on you …/ likes to boss me around (boy machista)/don't come trying to rule the roost."[106] The transformation in the performances of the funkeiras and the changes that happened in funk's backstage are deeply related. It is hard to track what started first or what drove what. It is possible, however, to establish their relationship. Funkeiras have been performing more autonomy-focused songs; similarly, some of them have more say in the direction and future of their careers, which in turn manifests in their professional performances. Even though, individually, funkeiras might not always be able to act as "self-making, self-determining" subjects,[107] these changes in favela funk point to an expression of communal agency: together, these artists are able to build on each other's performances in order to drive significant changes in favela funk. This chapter exposed the specific material conditions funkeiras must navigate within favela funk, which serve as an important foundation for their embodied politics practices I examine in the following chapters.

In the case of funkeiras, agency is not a simple matter. This chapter illustrated the complex layers in which favela funk is inserted, which in turn complicates funkeiras' existence within the movement. In their quest for survival, funkeiras are able to "imperfectly" exercise their autonomy. When it comes to professional autonomy, they are seldom provided with multiple choices and paths to act freely; still, they are able to navigate oppressive systems that put pressure on favela funk as they simultaneously negotiate their position within a male-dominated environment. Funkeiras are changing the movement while fighting for survival.

Notes

1 Cristiane Rodrigues, "Maysa Abusada Vai Fazer Cirurgia em Janeiro para Retirar Prótese dos Glúteos," *Ego*, December 6, 2014, http://ego.globo.com/famosos/noticia/2014/12/maysa-abusada-vai-fazer-cirurgia-em-janeiro-para-retirar-protese-dos-gluteos.html.
2 Rodrigues, "Maysa Abusada."

3 Adriana Lopes, *Funk-se Quem Quiser: No Batidão Negro da Cidade Carioca* (Rio de Janeiro: Bom Texto, 2011).

4 Sumaia Villela, "Na Luta Contra a Pobreza, Mulheres Buscam Autonomia por Conta Própria," *Agência Brasil*, March 8, 2016, https://agenciabrasil.ebc.com.br/direitos-humanos/noticia/2016-03/na-luta-contra-pobreza-mulheres-buscam-autonomia-por-meio-do.

5 Simone Sá, "Funk Carioca: Música Electronica Popular Brasileira?" *E-Compós* 10, no. 3 (2007): 1–18.

6 James McNally, "Favela Chic: Diplo, *Funk Carioca*, and the Ethics and Aesthetics of the Global Remix," *Popular Music and Society* 40, no. 4 (2017): 434–52.

7 Mylene Mizrahi, "Indumentária *Funk*: A Confrontação da Alteridade Colocando em Diálogo o Local e o Cosmopolita," *Horizontes Antropológicos* 13, no. 28 (2007): 232–62.

8 Silvio Essinger, *Batidão: Uma História do Funk* (Rio de Janeiro: Record, 2005); Pablo Laignier, "Towards a Political Economy of Funk Carioca: Notes on Postmodern Theory and Its Developments in Contemporary Popular Music," *Ciberlegenda* 2, no. 24 (2011): 61–76; Lopes, *Funk-se*; Hermano Vianna, *O Mundo Funk Carioca* (Rio de Janeiro: Editora Jorge Zahar, 1998).

9 Laignier, "Political Economy."

10 Micael Herschmann, *O Funk e o Hip-Hop Invadem a Cena* (Rio de Janeiro: Editora UFRJ, 2005).

11 Lopes, *Funk-se*.

12 Laignier, "Political Economy," 72.

13 Guillermo Caceres, Lucas Ferrari, and Carlos Palombini, "The Age of Lula/Tamborzão: Politics and Sonority," *Revista do Instituto de Estudos Brasileiros* 58 (2014): 177.

14 Caceres, Ferrari, and Palombini's, "Age of Lula," 177.

15 Caceres, Ferrari, and Palombini's, "Age of Lula," 178.

16 Adriana Facina, "'Não Me Bate Doutor': Funk e Criminalização da Pobreza," *Encontro de Estudos Multidisciplinares em Cultura*, Salvador, May 27–29, 2009.

17 Laignier, "Political Economy."

18 Facina, "'Não Me Bate'"; Laignier, "Political Economy"; Lopes, *Funk-se*.

19 Lopes, *Funk-se*.

20 Lopes, *Funk-se*.

21 Lopes, *Funk-se*.

22 Lopes, *Funk-se*.

23 Facina, "'Não Me Bate.'"

24 Lopes, *Funk-se*.

25 Facina, "'Não Me Bate.'"

26 Lopes, *Funk-se*, 41.

27 Facina, "'Não Me Bate.'"

28 Lopes, *Funk-se*.

29 Facina, " 'Não Me Bate.' "

30 Reginaldo Aparecido Coutinho, "The Acknowledgment of Funk Carioca as 'Patrimônio Cultural': Daily Life and Social and Political Clashes around the Law 5543/2009," *Antíteses* 8, no. 15 (2015): 520–41.

31 Lopes, *Funk-se*.

32 Facina, " 'Não Me Bate.' "

33 Lopes, *Funk-se*.

34 Lopes, *Funk-se*.

35 Facina, " 'Não Me Bate' "; Lopes, *Funk-se*.

36 Coutinho, "Acknowledgment"; Lopes, *Funk-se*.

37 Facina, " 'Não Me Bate.' "

38 Lopes, *Funk-se*, 63.

39 Alexandra Lippman, " 'Law for Whom?': Responding to Sonic Illegality in Brazil's Funk Carioca," *Sound Studies* 5, no 1 (2018): 3–4.

40 João Freire Filho and Micael Herschmann, "Funk Carioca," *Eco-Pós* 6, no. 2 (2003): 63.

41 Lopes, *Funk-se*.

42 Freire Filho and Herschmann, "Funk Carioca," 63.

43 Freire Filho and Herschmann, "Funk Carioca."

44 Facina, " 'Não Me Bate.' "

45 Caceres, Ferrari, and Palombini, "Age of Lula."

46 Caceres, Ferrari, & Palombini, "Age of Lula," 206.

47 Marcia Tiburi, "A Nova Moral do Funk," *Cult*, no. 163, November 2011, ^{revistacult}.uol.com.br/home/2011/11/moral-funk.

48 Lopes, *Funk-se*.

49 Freire Filho and Herschmann, "Funk Carioca"; Lopes, *Funk-se*.

50 Rodrigo Ortega, "Kondzilla Vira Maior Canal do YouTube no Brasil e Quer Dominar Funk Além de Clips," *G1*, April 11, 2017, https://g1.globo.com/musica/noticia/kondzilla-vira-maior-canal-do-youtube-no-brasil-e-quer-dominar-funk-alem-de-clips.ghtml; Rodrigo Ortega, "Kondzilla em Queda: Por Que o Canal de Funk Perdeu Audiência e a Liderança nas Paradas?" *G1*, June 4, 2019, https://g1.globo.com/pop-arte/musica/noticia/2019/06/04/kondzilla-em-queda-por-que-o-canal-de-funk-perdeu-audiencia-e-a-lideranca-nas-paradas.ghtml?fbclid=IwAR0KNfExZ1GQOcvm3hcboJglkOJ_aKYzSwk-1vlZf9vUSBhjLHpv0jCbL3A.

51 Vice Brasil, "Por Dentro do Funk 150 BPM," December 3, 2018, YouTube video, 21:19, https://www.youtube.com/watch?v=1T7-6aWp7Hs.

52 Ortega, "Kondzilla Vira."

53 Adriana Facina, Renan Moutinho, Dennis Novaes, and Carlos Palombini, "O Errado Que Deu Certo: *Deu Onda*, o Debate da Harmonia e a Construção da Batida Numa Produção Paulistana de Funk Carioca," *Opus* 24, no. 1 (2018): 222–63.

54 Bernardo Barbosa and Cleber Souza, "Antes de Pisoteio e Mortes, PM Cercou Baile, Dizem Frequentadores," *UOL Cotidiano*, December 1, 2019. https://noticias. uol.com.br/cotidiano/ultimas-noticias/2019/12/01/antes-de-pisoteio-e-mortes-pm-cercou-baile-funk-dizem-frequentadores.htm; Livia Torres, "Duas Pessoas Morrem em Tiroteio na Saída de Baile Funk na Zona Norte do Rio," *G1*, July 15, 2019, https://g1.globo.com/rj/rio-de-janeiro/noticia/2019/07/15/duas-pessoas-morrem-em-tiroteio-na-saida-de-baile-funk-na-zona-norte-do-rio.ghtml.

55 Dom Phillips, "Brazilian Queer Art Exhibition Cancelled After Campaign by Rightwing Protesters," *The Guardian*, September 12, 2017, https://www. theguardian.com/world/2017/sep/12/brazil-queer-art-show-cancelled-protest?C-MP=share_btn_tw.

56 e-Cidadania, "Criminalização do Funk Como Crime de Saúde Pública a Criança aos Adolescentes e a Família [sic]," *Senado Federal*, May 2017, https://www12. senado.leg.br/ecidadania/visualizacaoideia?id=65513.

57 e-Cidadania, "Criminalização."

58 Facina, "'Não Me Bate'"; Lopes, *Funk-se*.

59 Daniel Silveira, and Darlan Alvarenga, "Trabalho Informal Avança para 41,3% da População Ocupada e Atinge Nível Recorde, diz IBGE," *G1*, August 30, 2019, https://g1.globo.com/economia/noticia/2019/08/30/trabalho-informal-avanca-para-413percent-da-populacao-ocupada-e-atinge-nivel-recorde-diz-ibge.ghtml.

60 Evert-jan Quak and Annemarie Vijsel, "Low Wages and Job Insecurity as a Destructive Global Standard," *The Broker*, November 26, 2014, https://www.the-brokeronline.eu/low-wages-and-job-insecurity-as-a-destructive-global-standard-d46/.

61 Lopes, *Funk-se*; Raquel Moreira, "Bitches Unleashed: Women in Rio's Funk Movement, Performances of Heterosexual Femininity, and Possibilities of Resistance" (PhD Thesis, University of Denver, 2014).

62 Sá, "Funk Carioca."

63 Lopes, *Funk-se*.

64 Lopes, *Funk-se*, 102–3.

65 Sá, "Funk Carioca."

66 Lopes, *Funk-se*.

67 Lopes, *Funk-se*, 100.

68 Facina, "'Não Me Bate'"; Lopes, *Funk-se*.

69 Pablo Laignier, "Rodas de Funk: Remixando Música e Política com Alegria," in *Proceedings from XXXV Congresso Brasileiro de Ciências da Comunicação: Intercom— Sociedade Brasileira de Estudos Interdisciplinares da Comunicação* (Fortaleza: CE, Brazil, 2012); Lopes, *Funk-se*.

70 Pâmella Passos and Adriana Facina, "'Baile Modelo!': Reflexões Sobre Práticas Funkeiras em Contexto de Pacificação," *Proceedings from the VI Seminário Internacional de Políticas Culturais: Fundação Casa de Rui Barbosa* (Rio de Janeiro: RJ, Brazil, 2015).

71 Moreira, "Bitches Unleashed"; Haline Santiago, "A Adoção do Funk Como Expressão de Subversão da Sexualidade na Cena Gay da Zona Sul Carioca," in *Proceedings from VI CONECO: Congresso de Estudantes de Pós-Graduação em Comunicação* (Rio de Janeiro: RJ, Brazil, 2013).
72 Lopes, *Funk-se.*
73 Lopes, *Funk-se.*
74 Lopes, *Funk-se.*
75 Denise Garcia, *Sou Feia, Mas Tô na Moda* (São Paulo: Imovision, 2005), Film; Lopes, *Funk-se.*
76 D. Soyini Madison, *Critical Ethnography: Method, Ethics, and Performance* (Thousand Oaks: Sage, 2005), 26.
77 Lopes, *Funk-se.*
78 Lopes, *Funk-se*; Moreira, "Bitches Unleashed."
79 Moreira, "Bitches Unleashed."
80 Laignier, "Political Economy"; Lopes, *Funk-se.*
81 Lopes, *Funk-se.*
82 Passos and Facina, " 'Baile Modelo!' "
83 Ortega, "Kondzilla Vira"; Ortega, "Kondzilla em Queda."
84 Ortega, "Kondzilla em Queda."
85 Moreira, "Bitches Unleashed."
86 Moreira, "Bitches Unleashed."
87 Universa, "Valesca Popozuda: 'Fico no Baile até às 9h da Manhã,' " October 5, 2018. YouTube video, https://www.youtube.com/watch?v=BeuKVWsZulI.
88 Universa, "Valesca Popozuda."
89 Lopes, *Funk-se.*
90 Lopes, *Funk-se.*
91 Moreira, "Bitches Unleashed"; Marcela Ribeiro, "Pocah Fala de Namoro com Ex de Anitta e Suposta Rixa: 'Tudo Certo,' " *Famosos UOL*, September 25, 2019, https://tvefamosos.uol.com.br/noticias/redacao/2019/09/25/pocah-fala-de-namoro-com-ex-de-anitta-e-rixa-com-a-cantora-tudo-certo.htm.
92 Moreira, "Bitches Unleashed."
93 Marcelle Carvalho, "Valesca Popozuda: 'Bumbum Está no Seguro Porque É Meu Instrumento de Trabalho,' " *Extra*, February 2, 2012, https://extra.globo.com/tv-e-lazer/valesca-popozuda-bumbum-esta-no-seguro-porque-meu-instrumento-de-trabalho-3857097.html.
94 Patricia Gagné and Deanna McGaughey, "Designing Women: Cultural Hegemony and the Exercise of Power Among Women Who Have Undergone Elective Mammoplasty," in *The Politics of Women's Bodies: Sexuality, Appearance and Behavior*, 3rd ed., ed. Rose Weitz (New York: Oxford UP, 2010), 192–213.
95 Moreira, "Bitches Unleashed."
96 Villela, "Na Luta."

97 Moreira, "Bitches Unleashed."

98 Sábado Show. "As Abysolutas Interview." *Estilo Livre FM* 102,5 MHz, Rio de Janeiro, Brazil (2013, July 27).

99 Lopes, *Funk-se*; Kate Lyra, "Eu Não Sou Cachorra Não. Não? Voz e Silêncio na Construção da Identidade Feminina no Rap e no Funk no Rio de Janeiro," *Comunicação, Consumo e Espaço Urbano: Novas Sensibilidades nas Culturas Jovens,* ed. Everardo Rocha et al. (Rio de Janeiro: PUC-Rio/Mauad, 2006), 175–95; Gabriel Aragão, "O Discurso e a Construção da Imagem Feminina No Funk," *Cadernos de Pesquisana Graduação em Letras* 1, no. 1 (2011): 7–85; Edineia Aparecida Chaves de Oliveira, "A Expressão da Identidade Feminina no Gênero Musical Funk," *VI Semana Integrada das Licenciaturas*, Tubarão (2007), 933–47.

100 Lopes, *Funk-se.*

101 Anderson Oliveira, "Gaiola das Popozudas Agora Virei Puta Larguei Meu Marido," January 19, 2009, YouTube video, 4:15, http://www.youtube.com/watch?v=u1XLxXNhgFo.

102 Oliveira, "Gaiola das Popozudas."

103 Universa, "Valesca Popozuda."

104 Universa, "Valesca Popozuda."

105 Pocah, "Pocah—Não sou obrigada (clipe official)," March 29, 2019, YouTube video, 2:51, https://www.youtube.com/watch?v=HutLSVbLWHM.

106 Detona Funk, "Jessi—Boy machista (DJ Chileno)," June 5, 2018, YouTube, 3:00, https://www.youtube.com/watch?v=9SaOIZO7-gc.

107 Norma Alarcón, "The Theoretical Subject(s) of This Bridge Called My Back and Anglo-American Feminism," in *Criticism in the Borderlands: Studies in Chicano Literature, Culture, and Ideology*, 3rd ed., eds. Hector Calderón & José David Saldívar (Durham: Duke University Press, 1998), 28–39.

Chapter Three

Femininities on Display: Transgression and the Body in Performance

Even though funkeiras face similar systemic barriers as a group, they are not a monolithic unit. Mainstream media, governments, and academia insist on constructing funkeiras homogeneously, but their performative styles are actually diverse. The many ways funkeiras perform femininities are not only affirming of their positions as marginal artists, as women and travestis of color, and as poor individuals but are also in constant negotiation with normative white femininity and white cisheteropatriarchy, and differences in race and gender identity play an important part in the level of conformity funkeiras might try to enact. In this chapter, I discuss how the intersections of gender, race, and class shape funkeiras' transgressive embodiments of femininities. First, I make a brief note on the concepts of performance and transgression this analysis espouses. Then, I shed light on funkeiras' reflections on the material and symbolic aspects of their performances of racialized femininities on and off stage, such as clothing, body shape, and occupation in the movement (MC, dancer, or both) in connection with issues of morality. I end this chapter with further illustrations of funkeiras' varied ways of transgressing normative white femininity in performance.

A Brief Note on Performance and Transgression

The study of performance (and of identity as performance) is central to marginalized communities, as it offers an alternative to other ways of thinking that position identity and representation as exclusively symbolic and fixed.[1] Madison and Hamera add that, more than referring exclusively to theatrics, performance is conceptualized as "ways of comprehending how human beings fundamentally make culture, affect power, and reinvent their ways of being in the world."[2] Along with this understanding came the idea that the purpose of performance is not only to entertain but also "a way of *creation* and *being*" (emphasis in original).[3] This definition of performance is useful to examine the possible ways in which funkeiras' embodied enactments interrogate symbolic practices for transgressive purposes.

Performance scholars highlight the power of the moving body in escaping prescribed identities and hegemonic representations while potentially destabilizing them. Holling and Calafell understand performance "as an embodied practice," which "advances a narrative that is both personal and cultural."[4] They note that performances have the potential to be emancipatory and empowering practices that enable the re-centering of marginalized discourses "through a politics of embodiment and visual imagery."[5] Hence, performances generate opportunities to both expose the simulated nature of, say, normative white femininity while also becoming a site of transgression against those oppressive structures. According to Fenske, "[P]erformance calls identity into question ... while simultaneously reaffirming the force of the body's materiality."[6] Highlighting the performative aspect of identities not only questions the fantasy of stable and coherent identities but also enables new ways of thinking about the possible transgressive elements of performance.[7] Accordingly, Hill stresses that the " 'energizing voltage of performance' facilitate[s] the transgression of idealized myths,"[8] especially those related to normative white femininity. Performance becomes a vehicle through which funkeiras "intervene in the layers of inherited representations of femininity to corporeally challenge and remake them."[9] Furthermore, "performance artists can play with staging the [feminine]-marked body as producing excess meaning, which 'blurs the boundaries between inner and outer, depth and surface, truth and falsehood, that consolidates identity for the Western subject.'"[10] Excess meaning that distorts foundational binaries enables marginalized bodies to transgress strict identity categories.

The funkeiras' performances are not always in direct violation and disruption of normative white femininity. Part of the reason funkeiras' performances are often misunderstood by both Brazilian academia and corporate media is the contradictions that traverse their enactments of femininity, which cannot be explained with binaries like active/passive and oppression/resistance. In the same live show, they may perform about being faithful wives confronting their partners' lovers and then enact the role of single people demanding sex on their own terms. That is why the idea of transgression, as conceptualized by Jenks,[11] encompasses well funkeiras' embodied politics. In this case, transgression

is not simply a reversal, a mechanical inversion of an existing order it opposes. Transgression, unlike opposition or reversal, involves hybridization, the mixing of categories and the questioning of the boundaries that separate categories. It is not, in itself, subversion; it is not an overt and deliberate challenge to the status quo.[12]

The transgressive potential of embodied performances is less about "appearing" or representing the underrepresented and more about calling "attention to the very real transgressions bodies may perform."[13] Accordingly, performance defined as a way of creating and being does not prioritize aesthetics over the everyday. This perspective is appropriate for analyzing the performances of funkeiras, whose artistic enactments are constantly informed by everyday issues. It is imperative to examine how funkeiras negotiate with intersecting issues of gender, race, class, and sexuality off stage in order to understand how these may impact their artistic performances. Below, I offer funkeiras' reflections surrounding their identities as artists in relationship to favela funk's convoluted context. The analysis shows that while funkeiras have individual careers and assorted performance styles, their ability to perform often depends on how their identity as a group is represented within and outside of favela funk. Funkeiras' need to engage in embodied politics is propelled by their struggle for survival as individual artists and as a group of women and travestis of color.

Negotiating Artistic Personae and Performance in Favela Funk

"When I'm on stage, I have a power that I've never thought I would have, you know?" MC Carol tells me during our August 2019 interview. Many funkeiras report similar feelings about the stage being a place of visibility, for better or worse. Performance, whether live or recorded, presents a space of possibility in which funkeiras can enact various femininities, such as independent, assertive women and travestis, wives who cheat on their husbands, mistresses who make fun of faithful wives, and people searching for casual sex, among others. Funkeiras perceive the ability to perform in public as a privilege that allows them to experiment with different femininities. These embodied performances make funkeiras' transgressions against normative white femininity public and visible, which turns them into acts of courage. MC Carol talks about the power of this visibility:

> The first time I went on stage, I went on to dance. It was a dance competition. I won and then people started to chant my name—"Bandida! [Bad Bitch] Bandida!" I mean, my nickname [Carol laughs]. This happened in my hood. The feeling was just …[Carol pauses] I was like, dude, I want this feeling for the rest of my life! And that's what attracted me [to favela funk]. Being seen, being heard, you know? Being seen feels really good, you know? Because I used to feel invisible, get it? I was a teenage girl who lived on her own, you know? Who had to survive alone …. I was invisible. Then I went up on stage, and everybody was looking at me, chanting my name …. On stage, I'm seen; I'm heard. People are paying attention to what I'm saying; people are *repeating* what I'm saying. (emphasis added)

Deize Tigrona likewise asserts, "I can do whatever I want to on stage." The funkeira from City of God is one of the founders of dirty funk.[14] During our conversation in 2013, she protested mainstream media's hypocrisy for the constant moralistic criticism directed at favela funk's dirtiness, as it results in limited space for favela funk artists to perform. Even though Deize understands the risks that come with publicly performing about sex as a poor Black woman, she enjoys the sense of freedom public performances provide and recognizes that openly singing it on stage shows that she has "courage." Funkeiras understand the risks associated with their performances, but these negotiations related to morality are more complicated than simple acknowledgment.

Some of the funkeiras I interviewed stated that women in favela funk have a "bad image" in Brazilian culture, especially because of certain bodily and performative markers like silicone implants, "exaggerated" muscular and other nonconforming body types, provocative clothes, and overly sensual dance moves and lyrics. Frequently, these performative markers are associated with their raced and classed enactments of femininities. For instance, MC Kátia, MC Dandara, and Deize Tigrona—all MCs with more than a decade in favela funk—suggest that the way favela funk approaches sex is not necessarily different from other Brazilian popular genres, such as *axé* and *forró*, which are both popular Brazilian musical genres known for their employment of sexual metaphors and double entendre. What is different is the makeup of favela funk—people of color from the favelas—which is why the MCs think funkeiras face greater scrutiny in comparison to other artists who perform songs about sex. Funkeiras understand that being from favelas means they are judged more harshly than others because they are poor and are often women and travestis of color. This point suggests that transgressing normative femininity is riskier for them.

There are different outcomes and consequences for feminine folks who publicly use their bodies to transgress normative white femininity.[15] Cohen contends that the *choice* to perform gender and sexuality in nonconforming ways carries an inevitable dimension of privilege, especially related to class and race.[16] Consequently, transgression against normative femininity "functions differently across bodies according to markers of race"[17] and class. These identity categories are deeply intertwined in the context in which the funkeiras perform. In Brazil, poor women of color's performances of femininities, especially those of Black women, have long been deemed improper.[18] Given funkeiras' gendered, classed, and raced bodies, performative and bodily excess is always already present in a culture that values whiteness, middle class-ness, and proper femininity.

Funkeiras consciously negotiate their performances of feminin-ity in relation to what is considered morally acceptable versus what is vulgar. Often during interviews, some funkeiras frame what *other* funkeiras do on stage as "vulgar" and "obscene" (MC Kátia; MC Pink). Thus, even though certain funkeiras I spoke with use profanity and sing about sexual activities and desires, they do not consider their per-formances vulgar because they are neither dressed in skimpy clothes nor are dancing in an overly sexual way. MC Kátia and MC Pink, for instance, associate vulgarity and obscenity with how some funkei-ras present themselves on stage, such as when they flaunt muscular bodies while also wearing tight booty shorts and bra-like tops. Other artists see these condemnations of funkeiras' performances as prej-udiced reactions to favela funk's origins. For instance, MC Dandara points out that even though sex and "obscenities" can be found in different elements of Brazilian mainstream culture, funk is judged more harshly because "it comes from the favelas." Even MC Kátia, who openly condemns some funkeiras' dirtiness, recognizes that not all women from the favelas can get away with acting in an excessively sensual manner:

> These women with their bare breasts and shorts that look like underwear, this contributes to what? To more people saying funk is all about obscenities. But if you go to a rock concert you see the same thing ... or in *axé* ..."Oh, because women in funk go on stage naked." What about the ones who dance *axé* who put a bottle between their legs and go down shaking their hips?

MC Kátia's last sentence refers to the popular *axé* song "Na Boquinha da Garrafa" ("Top of the Bottle") in which female dancers thrust around the top of a bottle in staged performances. Kátia insinuates that women in *axé*, a popular musical genre with Afro-Brazilian roots that has been part of mainstream Brazilian culture since the late 1980s, can get away with performances for which funkeiras are criticized. When I asked MC Kátia why she thought there was prejudice against funk she did not think twice: "Oh, because it comes from the favela ... because real funk was born in favelas."

Another related dispute that exists in favela funk among funkeiras is the difference in performance styles. In Chapter Two, I mentioned certain funkeiras' criticisms of favela funk's particular beauty standards, which in turn hurts their ability to be popular. What I would like to examine here is how this is actually tied to a tension between funkeiras who are part of *bondes* and tend to embrace favela funk beauty standards and MCs who either cannot or do not want to embody that look. Drawing from the popular Rio slang, bondes, which can be roughly translated as "crew" or "squad," were musical groups formed at first by young men who would not only sing but also dance in very sexualized ways, with hip and buttocks moves.[19] Using similar performative tactics, women and transfeminine people later on formed their own bondes, such as Gaiola das Popozudas, Maysa e as Abusadas, Abysolutas, Fetixe, and many others. These were especially popular in the late 2000s and early 2010s and often included one lead MC/artist (such as funkeiras Valesca Popozuda, Maysa Abusada, Josy Abysoluta, and Andressa Fetixe, respectively). MC Kátia, who was never part of a bonde and who has more of an in-your-face performative style, attacked these feminine groups back in 2013 for using "their bodies" during performances in a way she deemed hyper-sexual. I ask her how these bondes impact her or why she thinks that is a problem. She replies, "Because then they [mainstream media] can say [funk] is denigrating women's image. How can it not be said that funk is all about indecencies?" I press her on it by saying, "Ok, but these things happen in clubs outside of favelas, too, and people seem fine with it." MC Kátia agrees, but adds, "But then someone films a girl in the favela doing the same, and she's called a whore, a slut ... but the bonde is up there [on stage] doing worse than the girl in the favela." Again, MC Kátia's position against feminine bondes is reactive, as she seems to be concerned about protecting funkeiras' (and her own) reputation from outsiders' scrutiny. Her reference to filming "a girl in the favela" doing something considered immoral by Rio's middle and upper classes is relevant. In the recent past, news media use of hidden cameras inside favelas to "denounce" what happens in bailes has generated a series of responses from local governments, which have led to tight regulations related to bailes that have, in turn, hurt some funkeiras' ability to perform.[20]

MC Kátia's stance on what she terms "indecencies" on stage is complicated by the fact that she has songs with overt and suggestive sexual content. In "Bota em Mim Pirocão" ("Put It on Me Big Dick"), for instance, she repeats the line " come small, big, thick/come fuck your queen/put it on me, big dick."[21] In aesthetic terms, this type of song is commonly known in the funk movement as an "assembly"—when the tamborzão is accompanied by the MC's rapping in loops. "Olha a Malandragem" ("Check Out the Trickery") is another example of a sexually suggestive song by MC Kátia. She sings that "The DJ here in the baile only plays dirty things … here I sit and shake my hips and then I do a massage!"[22] "To sit" and "to shake the hips" are popularly used in favela funk as double entendre. They concurrently signify dance moves and references to sexual positions. If we were to analyze MC Kátia's lyrics alone, detached from her reflections on singing versus performing those words, we would miss out on the ambiguous ways this funkeira transgresses normative white femininity. It is clear that MC Kátia's contentious position is a tactic of survival.

MC Pink, who is white and performs a pinup-like femininity—she is full figured but is neither muscular nor does she have silicone implants—agrees with MC Kátia: "they [mainstream media and people outside of the movement] think funkeiras all walk around wearing tiny shorts and cropped tops … they think that to be a funkeira, we have to walk around half-naked." MC Pink thinks the tamborzão phase of favela funk, in which lyrics have strong sexual connotation, is to blame for this. Also similar to MC Kátia, who says she has enough talent and hence does not need to rely on her body, MC Pink distinguishes between those two as well: "I want to be an artist, I don't want to be a 'popozuda.'*…[Being an artist] is different from seeing a bunch of women [on stage] with their butts up in the air." MC Pink objects to the fact that she has been approached by DJs and managers a few times before with the same specific request: to be "sexier," which means

---

* Popozuda is a slang in reference to the bonde Gaiola das Popozudas, who are the trailblazers in the kind of performance MC Pink disapproves.

wearing certain clothes, working out, and performing in a more explic-itly sexual manner. In my conversation with her, MC Pink reiterated her frustration over being thought of as an "illiterate," vulgar person and wants to distance herself from a certain kind of woman. MC Pink is the only funkeira to frame this issue in terms of perceived education and class—unlike MC Kátia, who understands that she needs to fight for favela funk's reputation in order to survive. Perhaps affirming this difference and separation from other funkeiras relates to the fact that MC Pink is white and does not live in a favela. In Chapter Five, I further examine the subtle ways in which whiteness manifests itself through classism in Brazilian culture.

Not surprisingly, being a dancer or an MC who relies on more phys-ical and sensual performances carries a stigma among some funkeiras, as the previous paragraphs show. In the case of dancers, one possible reason for the prejudice against them is the fact that some in favela funk, especially men, still think that women and feminine folks in general are meant to stay in the background as side entertainers.[23] The issue with MCs seems to be specifically tied to three things: (1) the way a funkeira dresses for artistic performances, (2) the body type of the funkeira, and (3) how they use their bodies in the process of enunciat-ing sexually suggestive lyrics. According to this logic adopted by MCs Kátia and Pink, the combination of having large breasts and buttocks, wearing very little clothes, and using the body to enact what is sug-gested in favela funk lyrics is morally degrading to *all* funkeiras.

Many funkeiras are concerned that negative perceptions about favela funk, grounded in sexism, racism, and classism, stigmatize all of them and ultimately affects their reputations and possibly their live-lihoods. The concurrent condemnation and justification of perceived hypersexualized performances by other funkeiras serves as a mecha-nism that possibly protects them from public scrutiny, while it acknowl-edges such judgment as sexist, classist, and racist. These contradictory positions also shed light on the tensions that surround some funkei-ras' relationship with normative white femininity. If normative white femininity sets the moral standards for all other women and feminine people, then it makes sense that some of them might want to emu-late it, especially those who might be closer to it—namely white and light-skinned cis and even some transwomen.[24] In this case, it seems that funkeiras apply those moral standards mostly to "inappropriate" *embodied* performances of femininity. This incongruity expresses both fear of stigma and a protective tactic to avoid further marginalization.

Other funkeiras see the use of the body on stage as an opportunity. Black travesti Linn da Quebrada, who is a performance artist in addition to being a funkeira, claims that bodies are so prevalent in favela funk performances because the genre "produces desires." During our interview in April 2020, she provides a beautiful reflection on the role of embodied performances in her career:

> The stage is a place of experimentation because it's the present; it's the here and now. It doesn't have an afterwards. To me, for instance, it's hard to think about recording my music because that's going to stay forever; it's the crystallization of my work. Being an artist for me is about creating about my existence. The stage gives me freedom to keep experimenting with all of my existences and transformations. It's the (a)live process .... The stage allows me to utilize my mistakes. The stage allows me to fail .... The stage for me *is* the process.

It is understandable that Linn approaches the stage in such a different way from MC Kátia. First, Linn is from a favela in São Paulo, which in general has experienced slightly less state-sponsored restrictions on favela funk and bailes. Second, and most importantly, Linn is Black, travesti, and from the favela. Because travestis are already perceived as the "radical other,"[25] Linn is very much aware of the many intersections of her marginalization. As I show in Chapter Six, travestis do not have as much room as cisgender funkeiras to try to avoid stigmatization—existing is already a major risk.

Funkeiras' performances are potentially threatening to the mainstream image of favela funk; they have become one of the central reasons why the movement is considered obscene and morally condemnable.[26] It is not surprising, then, that their reflections about performances of femininity are contradictory. However, I would like to reaffirm that funkeiras understand that the visibility they gain by performing publicly is a potent way to reverberate their voices—be them artistic and/or political.

In the next section, I continue to illustrate the multiplicity of racialized femininities funkeiras enact in performance. As I shift the focus to their artistic performances, I would like to highlight the power the moving body has to escape regulating representations, as well as destabilize them.[27] Thus, the power of funkeiras' embodied performances is not that of *representing* femininity in non-traditional ways but that of shedding light on the actual, material transgressions their bodies may perform. Ultimately, an "out-of-control" performing body, like the bodies of feminine MCs and dancers in favela funk, is threatening because it has the potential to transgress "idealized myths" of normative white femininity.[28]

Performing Transgressive Femininities

Funkeiras' performances, including the ways they embody lyrics and beats on stage, are marked by contradictions that seemingly conform to and defy normative white femininity. These moves, together, form the complicated ways funkeiras engage in transgression via embodied politics. Conquergood argues that the body is a central site of knowledge and resistance for marginalized folks.[29] While funkeiras do not or are not always able to engage in resistive embodied practices, they are keenly aware of the social and economic ramifications of their embodied performances. Maysa Abusada is one MC and dancer who employs such convoluted tactics. In June 2013, I was able to witness first-hand Maysa's performance with her bonde, Maysa e as Abusadas. I am in the crowd of her live show at a small club in the upper-class, new-money neighborhood, Barra da Tijuca, in the west side of Rio. The audience is very heterogeneous: white, brown, and Black folks from seemingly diverse social classes dance together to samba and favela funk. After the first minutes on stage, Maysa shouts to the audience with a deep, husky voice: "Who likes obscenities? Raise your hands! Who likes orgy? Raise your hands!" The dancer on the left, a curvy brown woman with long dark hair raises both her arms. "Because now it will begin … let the orgy begin!" The beat intensifies, and the tamborzão sounds almost like a human voice performing beatboxing. Maysa announces

"Vai Começar a Putaria" ("Let the Orgy Begin"), a cover of a song by male MC Mr. Catra. At this point, Maysa and her dancers synchronously move their hips back and forth. With knees bent and shoulders forward, their hands rest on their thighs. They move ferociously in perfect coordination with the roaring music.

Maysa's curvaceous body shape, along with her tiny outfit and thrusting dance moves, suggest an excessively feminine stage persona. Her brawny ties and throaty, booming voice contrast with her overly feminine characteristics and aggressive bodily performance. Normative femininity is implicitly cissexist, so it depends on a correspondence of sex and gender that seems "natural" and coherent. This funkeira's excessive expression of undue sexual energy breaks with proper bodily decorum and transgresses normative white femininity's ideals that suggest *all* women should correctly manage their public image—even if brown and Black women are held to different criteria.

Valesca Popozuda, former lead singer of bonde Gaiola das Popozudas, is known for having started those exaggerated and contradictory performances of femininity in the favela funk scene during the mid-2000s. "I go to the baile without panties! Now that I'm a whore, nobody is holding me back!" In a provocative bodysuit, Valesca Popozuda performs during a 2013 live show I attended, shouting the lyrics for MC Dandara's "Agora Eu Tô Piranha," ("Now That I'm a Whore"). An aggressive tamborzão bass line mixed with beatboxing accompanies the MC, who is performing in one of Rio's largest west side venues. At the time, Valesca was still cultivating a voluptuous, muscular body. Her deep, rasping voice echoes in the large gym-like setting amid shouts of "I go to the baile!" while her two dancers twerk to the beats, one on each side of Valesca. Before leaving the Gaiola das Popozudas to invest in her now-successful solo career, Valesca performed with the group at a spot known for having diverse audiences. The audience around me, mostly of brown and Black people, is an interesting assortment of cisheterosexual men, who seem focused solely on Valesca's body, as well as ciswomen and other feminine folks who are there to sing and dance along with Valesca. As I move toward the stage, I hear the audience cheering and singing along—their energy is electrifying. Valesca continues: "I go to the baile without panties/I've always been a whore and nobody is holding me back!" These lines are different from the lyrics of the original song, and Valesca almost yells them. In the original version, the verse reads, "Now that I'm a whore, nobody is holding me back." Valesca's version is unapologetically transgressive. There is no recent transformation in her sexuality; she has always been sexually active and out of others' control.

When analyzing the lyrics of "Agora Eu Tô Piranha" ("Now that I'm a Whore"), along with others of similar style, Lopes asserts that "women in funk carnivalize and cite an inside out logic of the 'active' and the 'passive,' once they implement the 'active' logic for women."[30] She continues to explain that, like in other Brazilian genres, in favela funk "men and women are signified in an antagonist way by a vernacular that is highly sexist, in which masculinity is always valued, and women are portrayed through the 'saint *versus* whore' dichotomy."[31] The supposedly empowering vocabulary funkeiras use then is the result of the same dualist process, Lopes concludes. Thus, even though funkeiras have agency for asserting themselves as women who like sex, they are not resisting traditional gender roles. While there is merit in Lopes's arguments, I disagree that the way funkeiras perform is grounded in, or results in, the reproduction of dichotomies. It would be extremely difficult, however, to disagree with Lopes without analyzing different dimensions of funkeiras' performances. By focusing on the symbolic aspect of their performances, as well as on binaries as an interpretive tool, it becomes hard to recognize the tensions, contradictions, and diversity of ways they negotiate race, gender, class, and sexuality—all categories that are not monolithic.

Visual and bodily elements are crucial to understand funkeiras such as Valesca as performers who transgress normative white femininity. Valesca's blonde hair extensions and green contacts that attempt to embody whiteness, as well as her hyper-feminine clothes, are juxtaposed with her deep voice and brown, excessively muscular body. This contrast highlights the artificiality of fixed notions of gender expression while also suggesting a racially ambiguous body.[32] Like Maysa, Valesca challenges normative notions of femininity because she blurs the lines between supposedly opposite poles, such as femininity/masculinity and Black/white. Both Valesca and Maysa embody a form of transgression that is simultaneously excessive and nebulous. Both performers are also light brown. Their ability to be racially ambiguous by whitening some of their physical traits, admittedly a strategy of survival,[33] hinges on their light-skinned privilege. Black funkeiras cannot get away with that kind of haziness.

Valesca and Maysa are not representative of all funkeiras' performances of racialized femininities. In fact, the point of this work is precisely to challenge homogenous readings of funkeiras' enactments of femininities. Pocah's performances, for instance, look very different from Valesca's. Early in her career, in 2013, Pocah invited me to attend one of her live shows in the same small venue Maysa had performed. I was in the VIP area, next to her mother, when Pocah started to talk to the audience about the favela funk beauty standard:

When I went on Super Pop [TV Show], Luciana Gimenez [the host] told me, "Wow, Pocah, you're so pretty, but you're so skinny! When they told me [your name was] Pocahontas, I was expecting a muscular woman with silicone implants." I thought to myself, "Is she trying to say I'm not hot?" I stopped and thought, fuck, there's only muscular women in funk, only women with silicone implants. If I was also like that, I would be just another [funkeira], isn't that true [asking the audience, who cheers]? And people want new stuff, do you know what I mean? I'm not belittling anyone, it's like my dream [to be muscular], but it doesn't fit me. I can work out for a whole year straight, I don't get muscular, I just don't. Congrats to all who work out and are hot, congrats to you all who are skinny. By the way, "a hot woman" is not just one with big boobs, a big butt, or the one with a curvy body. A hot woman is one who does it good [shaking the hips all the way down to the floor. Audience cheers loudly].

Pocah is a relatively tall and fit brown woman. She has green eyes and waist-length straight black hair, which at the time is comprised of extensions. In the performance I describe above, the MC wears a black cap with yellow brim; her hair is tied on the right side, falls over her shoulder, and goes all the way down to her waist. Her denim shorts are long enough to cover the very top of her thighs, and the black and silver cropped top barely covers her upper stomach. On her feet she wears a pair of black high-top sneakers with gold studs, which were uncommon among funkeiras at the time. Pocah's dancing style involves the usual favela funk hips and buttocks moves but with less twerking. Her teenage-like appearance—Pocah was 19 years old in this performance—and savvy use of social media attracted the attention of many teens outside of Rio.[34] Even though her body did not fit the particular beauty standards for funkeiras at the time, she is conventionally pretty. Perhaps her approximation with normative white beauty—green eyes, straight hair, light brown skin, and slim body—allowed her to become one of the most popular funkeiras in Brazil years later.[35]

Black funkeira Deize Tigrona represents a kind of racialized performance of femininity that became common among other Black women, such as Tati Quebra Barraco and MC Carol. In a 2008 recorded performance at a Berlin music festival, a young Deize Tigrona performs the song "Bandida" ("Bad Woman").[36] Deize is shown from the waist up, with flickering, colorful lights reflecting on her dark skin. She wears a light-colored, short-sleeve t-shirt and a bandana that covers her shoulder-length curly hair. Nothing in her clothing suggests a strong feminine performance. "Bandida" is an aggressive song in which a woman narrates what she is going to do with her man's lover when she catches her. (I further explore the wife/mistress theme in favela funk in Chapter Four.) Deize enacts the lyrics through firm and animated hand and arm gestures. Several times, she shapes her hands in the form of a gun while making noises of shots with her mouth followed by the line "get the bitch!" Those movements actually resemble U.S. rapping style, an influence that would not be unlikely given City of God's tradition of U.S.-influenced Black culture.[37] Deize's face glows and exudes the intensity required to perform such a belligerent song. However, it is also possible to note a smirk in her facial expression—a perfect encapsulation of favela funk's mockery, humor, and bellicosity that is especially embraced by Black funkeiras. Deize and other Black women are already at a disadvantage in their ability to subscribe to normative white femininity, even if they wanted to. On top of that, Deize challenges important stereotypes of Brazilian Black women: she is in charge of the stage. She is the main act. There is no attempt on her part to embody the oversexualized, agency-deprived Black woman; even her aggressiveness, which at face value could perhaps play into stereotypes of angry Black women, has a particular energy that could be coded as "masculine."

Deize transgresses normative white femininity by simultaneously subscribing to patriarchal values that push heterosexual women to compete with one another for men while also refusing to perform propriety, decorum, and docility common to normative white femininity.

Another type of performance of racialized femininity in favela funk is that of travestis. Linn da Quebrada and MC Xuxú both embody this type of defiant femininity in their performances. In "Um Beijo" ("A Kiss"), MC Xuxú's first hit music video from 2013, she appears dancing sensually surrounded by several feminine-presenting folks in what looks like an empty strip club with poles and hoops.[38] A tall, slender, light-skinned Black travesti, MC Xuxú plays with diverse clothing, wigs, and makeup styles—all very feminine. The song's main line, "A Kiss to the Travestis," is enacted as MC Xuxú and other feminine folks around her blow kisses to the camera. MC Xuxú, who is originally from the neighboring state of Minas Gerais, uses the tamborzão to perform openly about her racialized, hyper-feminine travesti identity; her affirmation of that identity through bodily enactments and repeated enunciation of it ("A Kiss to the Travestis") makes her performance defiant and courageous. As mentioned in Chapter One, Brazil is an extremely violent place for travestis. Proudly asserting that subject position is still unusual. Like other funkeiras in favela funk, travestis are also known for mocking and defying cismen of all sexual orientations. The next chapter focuses precisely on the way funkeiras confront men and other women in their artistic performances.

This chapter challenges dichotomous and homogenous understandings of funkeiras by focusing on their personal reflections and fieldwork observations of their live shows and recorded performances, with special attention to diverse performative markers like their bodies, lyrics and beats, and the context of their performances. Through this methodological and theoretical approach, I hope to have shown how the contradictions in funkeiras' performances disrupt monolithic, flattened meanings imposed on them as group. These ambiguities, in turn, enable a reading of the funkeiras' performances as transgressions against normative white femininity. Funkeiras do not solely conform to or reject the norms guiding normative femininity; they are in constant negotiation with those rules, often in order to survive.

The exploration of the funkeiras' performances of racialized femininities contributes to an intersectional approach to feminist expression that goes beyond white feminism's problematic practice of simply checking identity boxes. Indeed, the transfeminista perspective this work endorses has been proven useful against the compartmentalizing tendency in (white) feminist studies. Even though the subject of feminism, "the category of 'women,' " has been repeatedly confronted by postcolonial and feminists of color in favor of "an intersectional and multiperspectival"[39] approach, feminism is still mostly centered on the experiences of Western women, as I showed in Chapter One.[40] Funkeiras' complex performances draw attention to some of the tactics that poor women and travestis of color from the Global South have used to navigate, transgress, and possibly fracture oppressive structures. By shedding light on those transgressive practices of racialized femininities by marginalized folks, this chapter invites scholars to consider the ways in which funkeiras' performances can broaden our understanding of embodied politics.

Notes

1 Michelle Holling and Bernadette Marie Calafell, "Tracing the Emergence of Latina/oVernaculars in Studies of Latin@ Communication," in *Latina/o Discourse in Vernacular Spaces: Somos de una Voz?* eds. Michelle Holling and Bernadette Marie Calafell (Lanham: Lexington Press, 2011), 17–29.

2 Soyini Madison and Judith Hamera, *Handbook of Performance Studies* (Thousand Oaks, CA: Sage, 2006), xii.

3 Madison and Hamera, *Handbook*, xii

4 Holling and Calafell, "Latina/o Vernaculars," 59.

5 Holling and Calafell, "Latina/o Vernaculars," 61.

6 Mindy Fenske, "The Aesthetic of the Unfinished: Ethics and Performance," *Text and Performance Quarterly* 24, no. 1 (2004): 4.

7 Helene Shugart, "Parody as Subversive Performance: Denaturalizing Gender and Reconstituting Desire in Ellen," *Text and Performance Quarterly* 21, no. 2 (2001): 95–113.

8 Shonagh Hill, "The Crossing of Boundaries: Transgression Enacted," *Theatre Research International* 36, no. 3 (2011): 280.

9 Hill, "Transgression Enacted," 280.

10 Elin Diamond, "Mimesis, Mimicry, and the 'True-Real,'" in *Acting Out: Feminist Performances*, eds. Lynda Hart and Peggy Phelan (Ann Arbor: University of Michigan Press, 1993), 363–82, quoted in Deanna Shoemaker, "Queers, Monsters, Drag Queens, and Whiteness: Unruly Femininities in Women's Staged Performances" (PhD diss., University of Texas at Austin, 2004), 26, https://repositories.lib.utexas.edu/handle/2152/2202.

11 Chris Jenks, *Transgression* (London: Routledge, 2003).

12 Jenks, *Transgression*, 9.

13 Christina Foust, *Transgression as a Mode of Resistance: Rethinking Social Movement in an Era of Corporate Globalization* (Plymouth: Lexington Books, 2010), 152.

14 Janaina Medeiros, *Funk Carioca: Crime ou Cultura? O Som Dá Medo. E Prazer* (São Paulo: Terceiro Nome, 2006).

15 Aisha Durham, Brittney C. Cooper, and Susana M. Morris, "The Stage Hip-Hop Feminism Built: A New Directions Essay," *Signs* 38, no. 3 (2013): 721–37; Deanna Shoemaker, "Queer Punk Macha Femme: Leslie Mah's Musical Performance in Tribe 8," *Cultural Studies* ↔ *Critical Methodologies* 10, no. 4 (2010): 295–306.

16 Cathy Cohen, "Punks, Bulldaggers, and Welfare Queens: The Radical Potential of Queer Politics?" *GLQ: A Journal of Lesbian and Gay Studies* 3, no. 4 (1997): 437–65.

17 Shoemaker, "Queer Punk," 296.

18 Mariza Côrrea, "Sobre a Invenção da Mulata," *Cadernos Pagu*, 6–7 (1996): 35–50.

19 Adriana Lopes, *Funk-se Quem Quiser: No Batidão Negro da Cidade Carioca* (Rio de Janeiro: Bom Texto, 2011).

20 Facina, Adriana. "'Não Me Bate Doutor': Funk e Criminalização da Pobreza." ["Don't Hit Me Sir": Funk and the Criminalization of Poverty]. Encontro de Estudos Multidisciplinares em Cultura, 27–29 May 2009, Salvador, Enecult, 2009; Lopes, *Funk-se*.

21 Radio Conexão Ultra Dgt, "MC Kátia—Mete Em Mim Piroção [Lançamento 2013] [Dj Ld De Realengo]," September 6, 2013, YouTube video, 3:04, https://www.youtube.com/watch?v=UX50w_PAgGU.

22 Radio Conexão Ultra Dgt, "MC Kátia Olha a Malandragem {Os Brabos Produções}," February 8, 2013, YouTube video, 2:27, https://www.youtube.com/watch?v=0P9P9MxF8Yo.

23 Raquel Moreira, "Bitches Unleashed: Women in Rio's Funk Movement, Performances of Heterosexual Femininity, and Possibilities of Resistance" (PhD Thesis, University of Denver, 2014).

24 Moreira, "Bitches Unleashed."

25 Berenice Bento, *O Que é Transexualidade* (São Paulo: Editora Brasiliense, 2017), Location No. 524.

26 Moreira, "Bitches Unleashed"; Raquel Moreira, "'Now that I'm a Whore, Nobody is Holding Me Back!': Women in Favela Funk and Embodied Politics," *Women's Studies in Communication* 40, no. 2 (April 2017): 172–89.

27 Hill, "Transgression Enacted."

28 Hill, "Transgression Enacted," 280.

29 Dwight Conquergood, "Rethinking Ethnography: Towards a Critical Cultural Politics," *Communication Monographs* 58 (1991): 179–94.

30 Lopes, *Funk-se*, 182.

31 Lopes, *Funk-se*, 182.

32 Jessica Gerrard and Jo Ball, "From Fuck Marry Kill to Snog Marry Avoid: Feminisms and the Excesses of Femininity," *Feminist Review* 105 (2013): 122–29; Shugart, "Parody."

33 Bernadette Marie Calafell, *Latina/o Communication Studies: Theorizing Performance* (New York: Peter Lang, 2007).

34 Moreira, "Bitches Unleashed."

35 Rodrigo Ortega, "Kondzilla em Queda: Por Que o Canal de Funk Perdeu Audiência e a Liderança nas Paradas?" *G1*, June 4, 2019, https://g1.globo.com/pop-arte/musica/noticia/2019/06/04/kondzilla-em-queda-por-que-o-canal-de-funk-perdeu-audiencia-e-a-lideranca-nas-paradas.ghtml?fbclid=IwAR0KNfExZ1GQOcvm3hcboJglkOJ_aKYzSwk-1vlZf9vUSBhjLHpv0jCbL3A; Leonardo Torres, "MC Pocahontas Assina Contrato com a Warner Music," *Terra Popline*, January 16, 2019, https://portalpopline.com.br/mc-pocahontas-assina-contrato-com-warner-music.

36 Man Recordings, "Deize Tigrona Bandida Live," October 2, 2008, YouTube video, 3:29, https://www.youtube.com/watch?v=aLCt_Mby324.

37 Silvio Essinger, *Batidão: Uma História do Funk do Funk*, (Rio de Janeiro: Record, 2005).

38 MC Xuxú, "Mc Xuxú—Um beijo (clipe official)," November 5, 2013, YouTube, 2:34, https://www.youtube.com/watch?v=TZbyVY9slRo

39 R. Claire Snyder, "What is Third-Wave Feminism? A New Directions Essay," *Signs* 34, no. 1 (Autumn 2008): 175.

40 Raj K Mishra, "Postcolonial Feminism: Looking into Within-Beyond-to Difference." *International Journal of English and Literature* 4, no. 4 (2013): 129–34.

Chapter Four

Negotiated Femininities: Relationships with Men and Other Funkeiras

The opening shots for Pocah's 2019 "Pode Chorar" ("You Can Cry") shows the funkeira out of focus, walking into a room with a picture frame under her right arm.[1] Her long dark brown hair is down, and she wears a green animal-print top, a green pencil skirt adorned with golden chains, and golden hoops in her ears. Pocah comes into focus when she places the picture on the wall, next to others. Later in the music video, it is revealed that the frames display photos of men who were Pocah's former lovers/partners. The funkeira's voice precedes the 150 BPM beat with the following lyrics: "Today I'm going to party/I'm going to wear everything that he hates/today I'll free myself/he can beg/but it's going to be much worse/I'm going to learn how to live on my own." Pocah utter these words while sitting on a chair, legs crossed, using her arms to caress her chest, hips, and tights. "Pode Chorar" is one example of many in which funkeiras show derision toward cismen.

After exploring the multiple forms in which funkeiras think about and perform racialized femininities, I now concentrate on how funkeiras navigate relationships with other women (trans and otherwise) and cismen in their performances. An important part of funkeiras' transgressive embodiments of femininities stem from the ambiguous manners in which they enact these relationships, including the various roles they play in this process. Previous research has suggested that funkeiras' songs relate to men and other women in sexist and decidedly non-feminist ways.[2] As I mentioned before, much of this research largely focuses on the evaluation of lyrics, which I believe to be simplistic and damaging to a deeper comprehension of the funkeiras. Therefore, instead of overemphasizing the analysis of lyrics, my goal is to understand what funkeiras sing in a contextually specific manner that also accounts for the embodiment of those lyrics via performances and interviews. The favela funk themes I discuss here stem from these methodological considerations, especially stemming from critical ethnography. Funkeiras' voices and performances traverse the findings in this chapter because, as critical ethnographic research poses, they are my co-creators.[3] Accordingly, Thomas argues that one of the goals of critical ethnography is precisely to challenge established research that might aid in the marginalization of vulnerable folks.[4] In the next section, I first delve into the way in which funkeiras relate to one another through the complex wife versus mistress rivalry. Then, I continue to investigate competition between funkeiras that does not necessarily revolve around men via the *recalcada* (envious woman) topic. Finally, I examine the bellicose and humorous ways funkeiras challenge men in their performances. The developments highlighted in the next sections provide complicated perspectives on competition and solidarity among funkeiras. Together, these relationships point to the subtle but noteworthy ways favela funk and funkeiras have changed over the years.

Wives and Mistresses: Competing for Respect and Solidarity

"To the mistresses, this is my message
The boyfriend is mine
When you really want it,
You'll find your own

And when you find yours
Everyone is gonna fuck him"
MC Kátia "The Wife"

Feminine competition among funkeiras has been a recurring theme in favela funk since the beginning of their participation in the movement. Specifically, songs about the relationship between wives versus mistresses became popular among ciswomen in the mid-2000s.[5] The MCs performing about this tense relationship rely on belligerent language and body movements, particularly when singing from the perspective of the wife, as well as scorn and playfulness when performing from both the wife and mistress standpoints. Many funkeiras, in fact, enact both characters. As my analysis shows, respect is central in these arrangements: funkeiras must both impose themselves on the rival while on stage and gain admiration from other women in the audience.

I am at a Pocah live show in July 2013 when she performs one of her hits, "Ah, Eu Mato" ("Oh, I'll Kill Her"). She sings the first line "Oh, I kill her" and lets the audience repeat the line. I can clearly hear feminine voices repeating the lyrics. In fact, several of them even raise their hands in the shape of guns following Pocah's lead. She continues, with the help from the spectators: "If I see any whore hitting on my man …" She turns around, does quick hip moves, then goes back to singing, and points to someone in the audience: "… beat the shit out of her!" The song, melody, beats, and lyrics have a belligerent tone—indeed, it is possible to hear gunshot sound effects in the chorus after the line "If I see any whore hitting on my man …" Curiously, the aggressiveness is, at times, mixed with sexy dance moves. At some point, Pocah sensually shakes her hips, coordinating the moves with the sound of gunshots. The song continues:

Pocahontas is speaking up, don't give me bullshit
Real women are happy with what they got
Messing with others' men,
This is fucked up
If you mess with mine, look what I'll do to you
Oh, I'll kill her
If I see any whore hitting on my man

Threatening the lives of other women because of men is not exclusive to Pocah's performance. Many other funkeiras have enacted the role of the "faithful" or the wife. In Deize Tigrona's performance of "Bandida" ("Bad Woman") mentioned in Chapter Three, she describes what she would do to a woman who sleeps with her man. While performing this song to a German crowd, at Berlin club NBI in 2008,[6] Deize sings:

> My husband is shameless
> Shameless is the mistress
> But I am faithful, working hard 24/7
> And the bitch still wants to mock me?
> I'll show her some disposition ...
> If I were a gangster and had a gun in my hand
> I would shoot the bitch several times with a G-3 toy
> Get the bitch, beat her up, make her run naked!

Deize Tigrona sings aggressively and enacts the actions suggested in the lyrics—gun-shaped hands, assertive arm gestures, and facial expressions that mix grin and anger. By noting that she is faithful and works hard, Deize implies that this should be more than enough to earn another woman's respect. Her anger seems to stem precisely from the fact that the other woman mocks her for being good. In the process of performing about a man's infidelity, Deize de-emphasizes the role of the man to focus on the mistress' lack of respect for her.

MC Kátia tells me that she has made a career out of calling out "mistresses" who "disregard" other women by dating married men. Unlike any other funkeira, MC Kátia's performances revolve around issues of respect between women. Her first hit, "O Marido é Meu" ("The Husband Is Mine"), indeed sets the tone for many of her future songs. In a 2005 show recorded as part of sound team Furacão 2000s DVD called *Twister*,[7] MC Kátia starts the performance with a rhyme saying that she does not "fight over men/I simply stand up for myself/I'm a hard worker who takes care of the house and the children/... And now she mocks me ...?"

MC Kátia's performance of femininity carries a distinct toughness that I have not encountered in any other funkeira. Many of her songs reference physical violence and public shaming as punishment for "mistresses." In our interview, MC Kátia tells me that the focus on the wife versus mistress theme is her brand: "It's like how I'm identified in funk, defending faithful women [or wives], so I make songs about that … it's my 'marketing.'" More than a cultural product, she reaffirms that she believes mistresses need that kind of public treatment for disrespecting wives. Even though her style is simultaneously a brand and a moral stance that persists off stage, MC Kátia's position is not as morally stiff as it may seem. Perhaps if she were so personally invested in the "anti-mistress" position off stage as well, she would have not mentioned that one of the funkeiras she respects the most is MC Tati Quebra Barraco, who performs songs from the standpoint of the mistress ("If you can't handle him/I'll kiss your husband").[8]

Along with performances from the perspective of wives, songs from the point of view of mistresses were also fairly popular from the mid-2000s until the early 2010s.[9] MC Kátia "The Wife" tells me that her and her performance partner, MC Nem "The Mistress," (Figure 2) started to enact wife versus mistress rhyming battles on stage called "duels" back in the mid-2000s. These battles revolve around MCs fighting over whose performance is going to persuade the audience. MC Kátia and MC Nem's "duels" depict an obvious contrast in performances of racialized femininities. This becomes clear in the presentation the pair recorded live for the aforementioned Furacão 2000 *Twister* DVD. MC Nem, who is a slim but curvy Black woman, wears tight pants with a shiny belt and a bra-like cropped top. Her moves imitate sexual activity, while she sings in a high pitch and uses an animated tone: "I'm fucking your husband!" Distinctively, MC Kátia maintains an aggressive posture typically associated with masculinity. She uses a lot of hand gestures, looking and sounding "tough" like a male rapper, though she dresses in somewhat feminine fashion: tight jeans, fit black top, a black beanie, and black pumps. At some point, she sings loudly and furiously, thumping her chest, "I'm not worried/Because the husband is *mine!*" Though the performance is generally belligerent, derision is also part of the dynamic of making the other woman look morally defeated. From the standpoint of the mistress, MC Nem mocks faithful wives for staying home and doing housework while mistresses are sleeping with

Figure 2: MC Kátia, posing. Credit: Brenda Barbosa

their men. MC Kátia, on the other hand, points out that the mistresses are the ones being fooled, since men are using them solely for sexual purposes. Though distinct, their performances of femininity reproduce common stereotypes: the wife, who is also a lighter-skinned Black woman, wears more modest clothes and performs in sexually contained ways. The mistress is played by a darker-skinned Black woman whose performance is more sexualized and who also happens to wear more sexually revealing clothes.

These stage "duels" featuring MC Kátia and MC Nem evolved into different versions until the two stopped performing together. On the second version of the battle, recorded live in 2006 for another Furacão 2000 DVD, *Tsunami I*, MC Kátia's performance of femininity looks different from the first version.[10] Her mockery and aggressiveness persist, but the MC invests in a more sensual performance. This time, MC Kátia wears a denim short skirt and a yellow top with generous cleavage. She replaces the rap-style hand gestures with sensual body movements to indicate that to perform from the standpoint of the wife, she does not need to embody femininity in more contained, discreet ways.

Lopes argues that the enactment of those two characters, the faithful or wife and the mistress, reinforces the virgin/whore binary—a duality that saturates ideas about women's identities in the West.[11] In the updated version of such an old dichotomy, Lopes emphasizes that the focus is on who is "sexually superior."[12] Furthermore, winning the battle depends on declaring who is inferior. Finally, she also states that these performances are necessarily non-feminist, since feminism emphasizes solidarity among women. Thus, feminine funk cannot be considered feminist.

Pinho calls the faithful/mistress duality a "controversial" topic noted in interviews he conducted in a community on the outskirts of Rio back in 2003 and 2004.[13] About the relationship between these two common characters, Pinho says:

> Several songs reference the "faithful," the "mistress," and the one called "late night snack," the woman a guy chooses at the end of the night to have sex with—or simply to make out, with no consequences. There is a high moral and evaluative investment in these figures. If the faithful[...]is a "family girl," who is not very "active," nor has "too many friendships with men," does not use swear words, does not wear short clothes and is likely a virgin, the mistress has no morals, nor does she deserve respect because she is easy and goes with any guy just to satisfy his needs and eventually her own.[14]

Unlike Lopes's interpretation of the relationship between the faithful and the mistress being about sexual performance, Pinho focuses more on the moral tensions the two positions instigate. Pinho is also careful in evaluating the characters in terms of feminism, but he does suggest that women have a "clear sense of the gender inequalities and oppression" that permeate their relationships as "they talk about it with passion and detail."[15] This perspective is somewhat present when Lopes indicates that funkeiras recognize that men can do whatever they want.[16] However, what these studies also indicate is that there is still little attention dedicated to the relationship among funkeiras themselves.

Even though this type of rivalry between funkeiras seems to revolve around men's needs, a closer look reveals other possibilities. First, in the process of challenging each other, funkeiras involved in this dispute end up de-centering men and refocusing their performances on demanding respect from each other. Second, although the performances suggest competition between wives and mistresses, each position also relies on the support of others in the audience. These alternative interpretations may weaken the idea of funkeiras simply reproducing the virgin/whore polarity. If the wife/mistress duels are indeed less about how funkeiras relate to cismen and more about how they compete for respect and audience solidarity, then the virgin/whore dichotomy does little to explain how funkeiras are positioned vis-à-vis one another.

In July 2013, I was present for a radio interview of the bonde As Abysolutas (The Absolute) that included a live performance of the song "É Melhor Tu Dividir" ("You Better Share"). Michelle, the lead singer, is sitting behind a round table while singing. Josy, the founder and oldest member of the group, a curvy and muscular Black woman, dances with her back facing the male DJ, who blushes when she shakes her hips and buttocks in the tight space of the studio. The song is a negotiation between two women in which Michelle suggests that they share what the man possesses so no one will leave the relationship empty-handed: "His money is mine/His car is mine/You can have the rest." This song contrasts with others of the same style in which women are more concerned with keeping the man and the relationship. Additionally, it is not really clear if Michelle is performing from the wife's or mistress's standpoint. Finally, this tune from As Abysolutas touches on the pragmatic issue of financial security. If women and feminine folks of color face poverty at higher rates,[17] it makes sense that money is another component of this struggle over relationships with cismen.

The binaries of competition/solidarity and virgin/whore do not solely define the supposedly non-feminist stance of the wife/mistress duality because they are not always opposite poles in the funkeiras' performances. From a transgressive standpoint, those opposed realms coexist in nuanced ways. It is even possible to say that, in this case, solidarity enables competition. When MC Kátia and MC Nem take turns on stage with the line "let's look at the faithful's/mistress's face and mock her,"[18] they are indeed asking for the support of others in the audience.

Another example of audience solidarity happened during Pocah's performance mentioned above. A group of women watching the show in front of the stage were vigorously singing along with the lyrics of "Oh, I'll Kill Her," with their hands in the shape of a gun to imitate Pocah. This type of interaction happens in songs about the *recalcada* (the envious woman) as well, which I explore later, and seems to facilitate funkeiras' bonding with women in the audience. Moreover, it is not that there is no solidarity among women in these traditionally feminine and supposedly dualistic contexts; on the contrary, solidarity is a key element in forming alliances among women in bailes. Thus, more than being "active" in one's own oppression, as implied in Lopes's position,[19] the funkeiras dynamically negotiate rivalry and alliances with other women on and off stage.

Several MCs and bondes do not stick to only one perspective of the wife/faithful woman or the mistress/single woman performance but switch. Pocah sings, "Everything I have/your husband gave me,"[20] and Gaiola das Popozudas taunts, "Wife my ass/you're his little maid."[21] This is noteworthy because the fact that funkeiras take turns in performing these roles makes them somewhat fluid and not necessarily opposite. More than singing from different perspectives, the manner in which they perform femininities in those roles vary significantly. MC Kátia's distinct performances of femininity in the first and second battle with MC Nem are a good example of this. She was essentially enacting the same role, that of the faithful wife, but she negotiates her racialized femininity in those two performances in different ways. In the first show, she looks more normatively feminine, but she sounds and acts more aggressively. In the second one, her performance is more sexualized, which conveys that the faithful wife does not have to perform the "virgin" or the morally pure woman. Even when funkeiras enact normatively feminine characters, their performances of them are still transgressive—MC Kátia, Pocah, and Deize Tigrona all promote physical violence toward mistresses, something that is not in the realm of passive normative white femininity. As Soihet reminds us, white feminine bourgeois morality in Brazil did not apply to poor women of color, who were thought to have loose morals for being out in public spaces—the sphere of men.[22]

Finally, while funkeiras enact these roles, they may not actually live or believe in them. MC Kátia told me that when she and MC Nem started to perform the wife/mistress duel, MC Kátia was actually single and MC Nem was married. I asked MC Carol if there is a right or a wrong way to perform about these relationships, and her answer resonates with the points I convey throughout this book. She says, "I can't say I think it's wrong for an MC to sing about wives and mistresses, because I also sing about things I haven't personally experienced ....We sing to survive." Singing to survive means that funkeiras enact multiple roles in their performances that are often as tortuous and conflicting as favela funk itself.

"You Want to Be Me!": The De-Centering of Cismen in the *Recalcadas* Trend

Another side of feminine competition in favela funk that was fairly popular in the mid-2010s is the recalcada (envious woman) trope.[23] In this case, funkeiras compete with each other over physical appearance, material possessions, and social status. Next, I investigate some of the general themes present in this facet of feminine rivalry, which, like the wife/mistress relationship, also reinforces contradictory ideas of competition and solidarity. Unlike in the wife/mistress topic, men are mostly excluded from recalcada-themed performances. The recalcada tendency is starting to fade, as funkeiras now claim to want to make music to support women and other feminine folks, which I show later.

Funkeiras mentioned the popularity of this trend in every single interview I conducted in 2013. This type of performative rivalry between women was not necessarily a new phenomenon in favela funk. Deize Tigrona says that back in the late 1990s, female stage battles were very popular in City of God. Teenage girls and their bondes would go on stage to talk about each other's clothes, hair, and appearance in general, always with a mix of aggression and scorn. Even though there are similarities between what Deize Tigrona experienced in City of God, the recalcada trope has specific contextual characteristics, such as the growth in consumption of goods by the working poor in Brazil during the Lula and Dilma presidencies.[24]

Songs about recalcadas are both similar to and different from the wife/mistress segment. They are similar because the tension between competition and solidarity persists—funkeiras still compete for respect and admiration from the audience. They are different because they are not grounded in sexual and moral choices women make in relationships with men. In recalcada-focused performances, artists do not argue over who is morally good; instead, they battle over who is *better*—prettier, richer, with the best gang, and so on. In the next few paragraphs, I rely on performances and interviews with the funkeiras to try to unpack the theme of the "jealous woman."

Ludmilla's "Fala Mal de Mim" ("Say Shit About Me") from 2012 was credited by several funkeiras for inaugurating this new version of feminine competitiveness in favela funk. In fact, her song generated responses from several other funkeiras. Tati Quebra Barraco, for instance, released the song "Tu Quer Ser Eu" ("You Wanna Be Me"), which references MC Ludmilla's song by repeating the expression "closeted fan":

You walk by my street
Don't even look at me
When you're with your gang
You want to make jokes

But this is because …
You're jealous
You're jealous
You want to be me
You're a closeted fan.[25]

Other women set out to provoke Ludmilla, such as MC Kátia, who told me she was involved in a controversy with the other MC's fans because of a response song to "Fala Mal de Mim." According to MC Kátia, it all started when she saw a news report about a student who had been physically assaulted right outside of school by another girl and two other women in the aggressor's family, in what she called "bullying." "That story marked me because I was bullied in school," she said. Soon after the news story broke, MC Kátia says Ludmilla's song started to play in the local baile, especially the chorus: "Don't look to the side/The gang is walking by/If you fuck it up/We'll beat you up."[26] Kátia felt that the tune set a bad example for girls in favelas who were, according to her, reacting to little misunderstandings with other girls by attacking in groups (or bondes). Her response music video, "Froxona" ("Big Coward"), challenges the idea of a group of women or young girls assaulting a woman or girl by herself. In the video, MC Kátia is shown surrounded by Black and brown women from her community as though they were ready to physically attack the MC. She is able to disperse the crowd of women by shouting, "a real woman deals with her shit on her own."[27] MC Kátia says that once the video began to circulate, Ludmilla's fans kept reporting her official pages on social media in order to have them taken down. The fans also accused MC Kátia of being jealous of their idol, who was becoming nationally recognized at the time.

Some funkeiras believe that women in general are jealous of one another. This is something that happens among women, but it does not mean women are all enemies of one another, according to MC Pink. On the contrary, funkeiras need other women to legitimate the feeling of being envied. This point is supported by an exchange I observed in Pocah's live performance, mentioned earlier in the chapter. Pocah asks a woman in the audience, "Are you hot?" She continues by addressing all spectators: "Wherever there are hot and powerful women, there are people bothered by it. Am I right?" It is possible to hear women in the audience screaming in agreement. "And here there's a lot of women who are impactful, who are beautiful." As the tamborzão starts beating in the background, Pocah sings, "She's jealous of me/My presence bothers you/Sorry/Sorry/Sorry I'm hot." While singing the lyrics, Pocah's embodied performance is a mix of somewhat assertive hand gestures, as if she were using them to send a message to the audience, and sensual hip moves while saying the line, "sorry I'm hot." The MC performs the second portion of the tune in the plural first person with the clear intention of including other audience members in the lyrics. This performance translates well the tensions that surround funkeiras' relationships in favela funk: they are moved both by alliances with and opposition to other women and feminine folks. In the recalcada trend, however, men are out of the equation.

The typical mockery present in several aspects of favela funk certainly persists in the recalcada trend. In fact, funkeiras like MC Pink and MC Dandara both believe that, like with the wife/mistress topic, there is indeed a lot of playfulness among women when the subject is jealously. MC Pink, who performs mostly *funk melody*, a romantic and melodic strand of funk, says *"recalque"* (jealously) is a humorous game: "I think it's cool because they are there, talking about each other's personalities, each other's clothes, and it becomes a joke between them." I ask MC Pink if she thinks this kind of topic in funk pushes women into disunion. She replies,

> Not at all! They are more than united! They enact this little war on stage, but after the show, they are hugging. It's between women. They understand each other and solve things between them. It's not like it's a man that comes to them and says things ... it's different [when men talk to women]. We, women, we know how to talk to each other.

The MCs bring up an important point about the relationship between funkeiras: how else can women and feminine folks relate to one another besides being competitive (or competing for men)? The recognition of favela funk's characteristic playfulness exists both in terms of funk as a popular/folk genre (which mostly focuses on men) and in the relationships between men and women.[28] However, I have not yet encountered studies recognizing that the genre's scorn includes the funkeiras' live and recorded performances. MC Pink's testimonial confirms that humor is an important element for feminine funk as well. Accordingly, humor serves both to shed light into the performative aspects of gender role-playing and expose its ridiculousness.

The recalcada motif has sedimented funkeiras' presence in the corporate media spotlight. In addition to Ludmilla, former funkeira turned international pop star Anitta also released a recalcada-themed song called "Show das Poderosas" ("Powerful Women's Show") in 2013. It was then that the subject of feminine jealously crossed the boundaries of bailes to reach nationwide success.[29] It was around the same time, in July 2013, that I first heard Valesca Popozuda perform live her debut single as a solo artist, "Beijinho no Ombro" ("Kiss on the Shoulder"). The song sends a message to recalcadas when it suggests: "pick up your jealously and go fuck yourself."[30] "Beijinho no Ombro" invokes the two most common elements in this type of funk, notably humor ("I can barely see you from the VIP area") and belligerence ("If we clash, there will be gunshots, fist fights, and bombs"). Valesca's tune reached even greater popularity once she released its ostentatious music video in December of the same year.[31] "Beijinho no Ombro" became a cultural reference,[32] and Valesca achieved a type of mainstream popularity that had been unusual for funkeiras up until then.[33]

With over 100 million views on YouTube, "Beijinho no Ombro's" music video features Valesca wearing different queen-like red and golden outfits. Her blonde hair is in an updo, adorned with a thin gold band that cascades into her forehead and showcases a ruby pendant. Valesca appears serious and confrontational throughout the video. She is surrounded by scantily clad dancers from diverse races who embody different gender expressions. "Beijinho no Ombro's" choreography features a mix of favela funk sensual moves with others that reproduce what the lyrics say—"Bark louder/Because I can't hear you from up here." The dark cinematography of the video, along with the abundance of the color red, seem appropriate for a song that aggressively ridicules rivals. Gomes asserts that the tone of Valesca's "Beijinho no Ombro" was severely criticized by Brazilian feminists for promoting competitiveness and aggression among women.[34] These analyses focused on the tune's lyrics, with very little concern for understanding "Beijinho no Ombro" as part of a recurring dialogue among funkeiras.

Acknowledging that competition and solidarity happen concurrently is in line with Jenks's perspective on transgression, in which contradictory elements can coexist and create, in turn, a type of hybrid performance.[35] Using this approach does not suggest, as posed by Aragão,[36] Lopes,[37] and Oliveira,[38] that funkeiras do not conform to systems of domination, such as patriarchy under capitalism, but rather questions the hasty conclusions based mostly on lyrical analyses. It is limiting to interpret the ways funkeiras play and dwell with their racialized femininities in dichotomous manners that disregard markers of race, class, and gender identity. Above all, what I also demonstrate here is that funkeiras negotiate relationships with other women in diverse ways, from opposition to solidarity, which ultimately emphasizes the heterogeneity of their performances of racialized femininities.

Favela funk is an evolving movement. Since 2013, both the wife/ mistress and the recalcada themes have faded and/or have changed significantly. In a 2018 interview, Valesca said that, at a point in her career, she made the conscious decision to alter the messages in her songs in order to reach more of a feminine audience.[39] Pocah, who once was thoroughly invested in performing about recalcadas, said in 2019, "funk has given me voice; I now use it to help out other women."[40] MC Xuxú's 150 BPM song "Senzala" (something like "Slave Quarters") modifies the recalcada motif to assert her Black and poor travesti identity while confronting others' prejudice:

Woman of war, of chest, of dick
Your concept doesn't faze me
I'm favela
I know the spark of the slave quarters
I'm almost never welcome
I cause crashes wherever I go
I know I'm beautiful
To hell with everything.[41]

In the next section, I shed light on another vital aspect of funkeiras' performances of racialized femininities: their relationships with cismen. Like the wife/mistress and recalcada trends, funkeiras' ambiguous and varied approaches to their interactions with cismen are complex and shifting.

"My Boyfriend Is the Biggest Sucker": Funkeiras' Clashes with Men

Funkeiras' clashes with men are another significant aspect of their transgressive performances of femininities. Many favela funk songs performed by men during the early 2000s included funkeira cameos that endorsed men's desires. Some artists and scholars considered those controversial songs degrading to women.[42] This development shifted in the mid-2000s with the popularity of Deize Tigrona and Tati Quebra Barraco,[43] when funkeiras started to respond to male MCs' sexual demands with scorn and aggressiveness. These responses, which at first were mostly connected to aggression or revenge via sex, are another essential aspect of funkeiras' transgression against normative white femininity. Funkeiras defy heteronormative demands that prescribe that feminine folks cater to men's desires.

"Eu Sento Rebolando" ("I Sit Shaking My Hips") by Pocah illustrates how funkeiras countered men's degrading songs about women. In this song, a woman just needs her sexual desires met for the night and has no intention to start a romantic relationship. Pocah, known as MC Pocahontas at the time, stands at the front edge of the stage at a live performance I attended in July 2013. She casually takes turn between talking to her audience and singing the lyrics:

> Look deeply into his eyes, and tell him, but let him know that it's just for tonight. There's no point in calling you tomorrow, because you won't answer him. "Ugh, what an annoying guy who keeps calling me!"... So tell him it's just for tonight. Tonight, I'll be your woman! And you'll be my man! I sit shaking my hips, calling your name!

As she moves from talking to the audience to singing the song, Pocah's voice changes significantly. She sounds smoother, sexier, her voice almost a moan. She moves up and down shaking her hips when the lyrics suggest. Pocah next takes turns singing lines with feminine voices in the audience. She starts with "I'll be your woman," and the crowd replies, "And you'll be my man." The audience sings in unison, and the exchange with Pocah happens in perfect synchrony.

By openly expressing her sexual needs while rejecting the imperative that ciswomen should seek committed relationships, Pocah subverts the gendered subordination of heterosexual desires. Normative femininity has been historically subordinated to masculinity by which cismen and patriarchal institutions regulate ciswomen's sexualities in a heteronormative context.[44] Ostensibly, ciswomen *should* desire cismen if heteronormativity is to be naturalized and reinforced. However, heteromasculine norms suggest that there are appropriate ways for women to display those desires, since they are seen as "the moral guardians of society whose behaviour must set the standard for men."[45] Pocah's performance violates the norm that control over sex should be a cisman's prerogative in a heteronormative relationship because she actively voices her sexual needs and endorses casual sex. Ultimately, the funkeira is not just performing about sex; she is also challenging normative white femininity by determining what kind of emotional arrangements ciswomen may present in their sexual encounters with cismen.

Pocah is not the only funkeira to transgress heteronormative values on stage. Many others, in fact, became famous for demanding sex at their own convenience. Another example is Tati Quebra Barraco's "Cachorra Solta" ("Loose Bitch"), which is a direct response to male MC Taizinho's "Cachorro Solto" ("Loose Dog"). In the song, she makes fun of a man who thinks that getting her pregnant would "trap" her into a monogamous relationship. Tati Quebra Barraco's song subverts the common assumption that women of color are the ones interested in using pregnancy to "trap" men: "I'm a loose bitch/You're not going to trap me/I'm going to the orgy and you'll be the one watching the baby!"[46] In this instance, Tati rejects motherhood, a potentially redeeming aspect of normative femininity per heteropatriarchal values,[47] in

order to have sex with other men. These funkeiras transgress normative white femininity not by inverting meanings of masculinity and
femininity but by questioning the strict boundaries of those categories
and producing versions of racialized femininities that clash with what
is hegemonically prescribed.

In June 2013, I make a last-minute decision to attend a live performance by Tati Quebra Barraco. The show takes place at a private
college party in a venue in downtown Rio. I am conflicted about going
to the performance. On one hand, the thought of going to a college
party filled with white, upper-class young adults makes the event
less appealing or exciting; on the other hand, I am curious to witness
how the audience will react to Tati and vice versa. I spend an hour
waiting and feeling out of place until the performance starts. Tati, a
Black woman in her late thirties at the time, wears a short black and
silver dress and black stilettos. Her curly, dark brown hair is in a bun,
and the braces on her teeth make her look much younger than she
is. Along with MC Deize Tigrona, also from City of God, Tati was
one of the first women to become popular for performing dirty funk,
and both women are known for navigating between elite and popular
stages.[48] Tati opens the show with her hits from the mid-2000s and
receives an animated response from the young, mostly white, female
audience members who dance and sing along to tunes like "Fama de
Putona" ("Bitch's Reputation") and "Boladona" ("Pissed Off"). I am on
the right front side of the stage when her performance of "Os Direitos
São Iguais" ("The Rights Are Equal") begins. This song was released
just months before this performance, and soon it is obvious the audience is not familiar with the lyrics:

> The rights are equal, the rights are equal!
> If men are cheating, women will cheat more!
> There's no being a little saint
> Stuck at home, washing and ironing
> While you fool around
> With Tati Quebra BarracoYou don't mess around
> If you make a fool out of meI'll make a sucker out of you

Tati's mocking tone and belligerent hand gestures contrast with the grin on her face; she challenges and ridicules men's "right" to cheat, as well as women's domestic obligations. She also plays with feminist language when stating "the rights are equal" to suggest that there's no equality in the "right" to cheat: women will in fact cheat *more*. Thus, Tati does not simply invert gendered language; instead, she transgresses gender norms by publicly refusing and taunting heterofeminine roles that limit women's activities exclusively to the domestic realm. Tati's transgressions entail hybridization and mixing of supposedly bounded categories, such as masculine and feminine, public and private. However, other elements of her performance suggest that she also attempts to conform to normative femininity. Tati's outfit is properly feminine, but not *too* feminine. Her dance moves are not hypersexual and are somewhat constricted in comparison to other funkeiras.

Perhaps these variations in performance illustrate the ways in which funkeiras handle public scrutiny, given the stigma they face for wearing skimpy clothes and employing excessively sexual dance moves—a sexist and classist backlash that certainly intersects with racism. Despite their different tones and postures, funkeiras disrupt heteronormative desires and practices. By performing that her "fucking pussy" is hers or that men will be the ones "watching the baby" while funkeiras "cheat more" or "go to the orgy," funkeiras confront white patriarchal (and heteronormative) values of ownership and control cismen claim to have over women's bodies and sexual autonomy.

Confronting and Scorning Male Privilege and Violence

Rhyme battles were relatively popular in favela funk in the late 2000s and early 2010s, especially as the movement spread throughout the rest of Brazil. Funkeiras participate in stage battles not only to confront other women, like in the previously mentioned "duel" between MC Kátia and MC Nem or in Deize Tigrona's narrative about female bondes. MC Marcelly and *funkeiro* MC Maiquinho perform a battle in 2012 especially for the funkeira's live DVD.[49] MC Marcelly, who is a light-skinned brown woman, wears black pants with a white strip on the sides, a yellow and red Wonder Woman top, and a light pink cardigan. Her curly mid-back length hair is loose, and she wears a headband. Her gestures are firm; her voice is strong and belligerent. Compared to the voice of MC Maiquinho, a young Black man, Marcelly's voice is deeper. The performance spotlights men's infidelity and physical abuse. While the MCs perform their first introducing rhymes, there are gunshot-like sound effects in between their spoken words. After a minute of playful introductions, MC Marcelly suggests:

> A real man doesn't go back and forth
> He knows how to appreciate
> The beautiful woman he has
> Don't complain later
> Saying things about me in the streets
> Wants to belong to several women
> Can't handle none of them
> The rights are equal
> Check this out, honey
> If men are gonna cheat
> Women will cheat too

MC Marcelly arouses voices from women in the audience, who in turn make noises with their hands up, in the shape of guns, while the gunshot-like sound effects continue. MC Maiquinho reacts by claiming that there's no such thing as equal rights, as women are not allowed to cheat: "Women here tonight/You're full of shit/Talk about cheating/Ask to be beaten/I'm Maiquinho from South Side/I'm the one with the mic/As of today/Cheating's just for men!"

Suggesting that men and women have equal rights when the topic is infidelity hints that being unfaithful is a *right* that men already have and that women are now trying to achieve. This idea is not exclusive to MC Marcelly's rapping, as Tati Quebra Barraco's aforementioned "The Rights Are Equal" implies. Cisheterosexual men emphasize that they will cheat, period. From women's perspectives, we see a type of "reactive cheating," in which they threaten to or actually find other men when their partners are being disloyal.

Another issue that comes up in this portion of the battle is how MC Maiquinho says that women who insist on cheating should be beaten. Herschmann and Freire Filho pose that in Brazilian folk/popular culture, women do not necessarily take songs that suggest violence against them in a serious manner.[50] Indeed, MC Marcelly ends the performance by reaffirming that what the audience had just seen was a staged battle. While this might be true, it would be problematic to disregard that the suggestion of violence against women is not grounded in any sort of cultural beliefs and life experiences. The suggestion is so problematic that funkeiras have started to react to men's intimidation, as references in Chapter Two to Valesca Popozuda's and Pocah's songs suggest. MC Marcelly, herself, recorded a song in 2015 to honor a fellow funkeira—a dancer—who was murdered by her fiancé.[51]

As the battle continues, MC Marcelly responds to MC Maiquinho:

There's no beating
What the hell are you talking about, Maiquinho?
Women like to be spanked
In bed, behind closed doors
Every cheated man
Has this "angry dude" pose
Always out in the streets
Picking up leftovers
Better be careful with feminine anger
Women don't cheat …

MC Marcelly raises the microphone to let women in the audience complete the verse: "Women take revenge!" She repeats the rhyme with the help of the spectators, and for a brief period, the gunshot-like sound effects turn into the tamborzão. The dynamics of the stage, a "war of the sexes" type rivalry, is extended to the audience: masculine voices support MC Maiquinho and feminine ones loudly back MC Marcelly.

MC Marcelly counterargues MC Maiquinho's threat to beat an unfaithful woman by saying that she only accepts being "spanked" in bed and then implying women do not cheat but rather "take revenge" on abusers and cheaters. This ambiguous move represents a transgression against normative white femininity. MC Marcelly conforms to heteronormative gender hierarchies when she asserts that women will only cheat in response to men's infidelity and not because they simply want to. Thus, the fate of the relationship depends upon men's choices. MC Marcelly dismisses MC Maiquinho's threats while blatantly reaffirming her sexuality and mocking his performance of masculinity by highlighting the ridicule of his "angry dude pose." Therefore, MC Marcelly affirms gender hierarchies by letting the men lead the relationship while challenging them by using her display of hyperheterosexuality—like when she publicly affirms that she enjoys being spanked in bed—to disregard threats of masculine violence.

Linn da Quebrada often contests and derides cismasculinity in her work. In the opening shots for "Talento" ("Talent"), the camera focuses on a close-up of Black travesti Linn da Quebrada with her mouth half-open as she gives the camera a mischievous, sensual look.[52] In the background, the lyrics begin: "There's no point in asking me/I won't blow you while hiding in a bathroom/You know I'm insatiable/I don't want just dick/I want the whole body." The following shot displays different shades of brown and Black bodies lined up close together, with only tights and hands visible, and then cuts to several shots of Black and brown travestis as the lyrics continue:

> So you don't fuck femmes?
> Who said that as fabulous as I am
> I'm gonna want to give ass to men
> Especially of your kind
> Of such specific race
> Who thinks you can do it all
> With the force of god
> And in the glory of the cock
> It was obvious
> You were about to be extinct
> That there was no point being a macho
> Using your dick

In "Talento," Linn transgresses normative white femininity first by acknowledging and then pushing against feminine folks' normative sexual desire for cismasculinity. More than just remarking on normative choices of partners in LGBTQIA+ interpersonal relationships that tend to value masculinity over femininity, Linn's references to "force of god" and "glory of the cock" point to the systemic dominance of cismasculinity through Christianity. What is remarkable about Linn's lyrics is that she seems to be simultaneously snubbing cismasculinity's virility and challenging the idea that transfeminine folks necessarily want to be with a cisgender man, no matter their sexuality. In fact, she suggests that cismasculinity will disappear—or become extinct—and perhaps so will the institutions it created that also maintain it. The music video is also a beautiful homage to travesti identity, a topic I further investigate in Chapter Six.

To illuminate how funkeiras openly talk about using their bodies to take sexual and material advantage of cismen's privileges, I now turn to Gaiola das Popozudas' performance of "Minha Buceta É o Poder" ("My Pussy Is the Power"). As I stand close to the 6-foot tall stage in the live show I attended in July 2013, Valesca is right in front of me when she starts singing the lyrics to the song. She squats and extends her hand to a male fan to my right while singing: "In bed I do everything." The music is so loud that the sound seems distorted, especially the bass. Valesca stands back up and continues: "I'm the one giving you pleasure/I'm a sex pro and I'll show you why." The tone in her voice sounds suave, considering her timbre is deep and husky. Those characteristics vanish as soon as she starts yelling the chorus: "My pussy is the power" (repeated three times). With one hand holding the microphone and the other arm raised, she sings loudly, with her eyes closed, almost as though she is preaching.

The lyrics expose how Valesca can have anything she wants from a man, supposedly based on the power of sex. She performs the song in first person, squats several times to talk to people in the audience, and teaches us how to use and take advantage of the power emanating from pussies: "Stupid women remain poor/but I'll tell you why/if they're smart, might even get rich/my pussy is the power/for 'her' men cry/for 'her' men spend/for 'her' men kill." The performance goes on as she enumerates the material advantages brought by her vagina and points out people in the audience, who sing along with the funkeira: "car, apartment, liposuction, 'an actress face,' silicone implants, and hair extensions."

Valesca scorns both men and women by suggesting that women should exploit men financially, while the ones who do not do that are considered stupid. Instead of relying on euphemisms to illuminate her success with men, she unashamedly exposes how she uses her hyper-sexuality to teach the "smart" funkeira formula: having sex for material gain. Valesca benefits from these arrangements by not only possibly enjoying the sex but also by achieving material stability. As a mixed race working-class woman, ideas of purity and chastity applied to bour-geois white women were never meant to include people like Valesca anyway.[53] The funkeira, thus, employs her racialized femininity to take material advantage of those who have financial power.

Valesca's performance is transgressive as she affirms and protests traditionally feminine roles. However, even though she upholds hetero-femininity via using her body to achieve a particular look, Valesca still does not fit within the boundaries of normative white femininity. First, she positions herself as the agent who is going to have sex; there is no passivity in her performance. Second, it is not clear whether the look she is trying to gain through sex—with silicone implants, hair exten-sions, and liposuctions—conforms to white feminine beauty standards. In sum, Valesca embodies a confluence of different types of feminini-ties. The multiplicity and tensions present in her performances cannot be explicated in simplistic binary terms. The racialized femininities Valesca and other funkeiras enact is specifically localized, while still in dialogic relationship with hegemonic notions of what it means to be a ciswoman. In fact, funkeiras construct their transgressive feminini-ties by picking up fragments from both their own marginalized context and from dominant discourses and placing them together to form their own culturally located versions.

MC Carol's 2012 hit "Meu Namorado é Mó Otário" ("My Boyfriend's the Biggest Sucker") is another song that encapsulates well the mockery and bellicosity with which funkeiras handle male privilege. This song, however, suggests a slight shift in funkeiras' relationships vis-à-vis men, as sexual activity is de-emphasized. In 2013s "Roda de Funk" ("Favela Funk Circle"), MC Carol performs in what looks like a bar.[54] Favela funk circles have been inspired by samba circles, in which artists sit around a bar table to perform live for a small audience while drinking beer and eating appetizers. In this particular setup, the tables are arranged rectangularly, with chairs positioned facing the camera. MC Carol, who identifies as a fat Black favela woman, sits in the middle of a long row of mostly men. Now-acclaimed MC Nego do Borel is sitting next to MC Carol, and the two interact when she starts performing "Meu Namorado é Mó Otário." As the DJ breaks from the previous song to introduce the new beat, MC Carol sensually stares into the camera, moves her head to the side and eyebrows up and down, and makes eye contact with Nego do Borel. When the intro breaks, she grabs the microphone and starts singing vigorously:

> My boyfriend's the biggest sucker
> He washes my panties [turning to Nego do Borel, waving her fingers and saying]
> ("Wash the whole fucking thing because I said so!")
> If he gets too cocky
> I'll send him to the kitchen ("go to the kitchen, do something!")
> If you don't like it
> Go sleep outside
> Because I'm going to the baile [singing smoothly, quieter]
>> I'm going to party.

While Nego do Borel uses the ice bucket to pretend he is washing clothes, MC Carol points her finger to it, and says "wash it all! Wash it because I said so!" The tamborzão pulsates in the background, rendering the atmosphere electrifying. Much of the appeal in this performance is grounded in MC Carol's intense energy. She concurrently embodies contempt and humor in her voice and changes her facial expressions from anger to smirks in the same verse.

MC Carol is often asked about these lyrics during interviews, usually in connection with questions about feminism. This is the case because MC Carol's song focuses on house chores, which are still mostly performed by women in heterosexual relationships.[55] When questioned about it by a reporter in 2015, she states that her boyfriend is not a loser for cooking and cleaning and that "men have to be less machistas and share house chores."[56] During our interview in 2019, MC Carol reflects on her journey of survival to arrive at her current understanding of feminism:

> I'm a really fucking complicated woman, you know? But I'm working really hard to be better ...Because I used to be really aggressive, you know? I was raised to be aggressive. I had to be aggressive at school; I had to be aggressive in the streets. If I got beaten up in the street and got home crying, I'd get beaten up even more .... I went to live with a person, so everything was fist fights and aggression. I was raised by men, hearing all this stuff. I had to become a man. I was forced to become a man, that's why the nickname [bandida, which can also be translated as thug]. What kind of woman am I? I don't even know! ["Are you under construction?" I ask, and we both laugh.] I'm under construction. It's really hard being a chill woman in such a machista world, in a country that is so machista like ours, you feel me?... It's too much trauma, you know? The traumas that machismo causes us ... when I realized, I had become a machista dude. You know those men who come home and want everything ready or otherwise they beat the shit out of their women? I was that man. But nowadays I have the conviction that I don't need to be this way anymore ....To me, feminism is about equality. I've always wanted equality ... but with machismo, there's no equality! With time I realized that you're either the person who beats up or the one who gets beaten.

MC Carol, who ran for office in 2018, claims that women began to call her a feminist in 2016. She tells me that she did not know what that meant at the time and credits the Black woman who works as her manager as the person who has been teaching her about racism and sexism. In 2016, she released the song "100% Feminista" with São Paulo-based Black female rapper Karol Conka, which I analyze in the next chapter.[57] In 2019, MC Carol and Tati Quebra Barraco collaborated with music producer Heavy Baile on the song "Mamãe da Putaria" ("Mother of Hoeness").[58] The music video for the single features the Black funkeiras as the owners/managers of a car wash business in which mostly Black men (and one white man) sensually clean up cars half-naked while women sit down fully clothed waiting for the service to be complete.

Right after the video's first minute, we see a closeup shot of a white woman holding Djamila Ribeiro's book, *Who's Afraid of Black Feminism*.[59] The lyrics are an homage to Tati Quebra Barraco's legacy of *funk putaria* (dirty funk), which she is passing down to MC Carol:

> I'm Tati Quebra Barraco and don't need introductions
> I'm the nightmare of dudes who think they're man hoes
> Tati from CDD has a story to tell
> The mother of hoeness is here to teach you
> If I tell you to lick, you're gonna lick
> If I tell you to put it on, you're gonna put on all of it ...
> Speaking of hoeness, I've arrived hot like the sun
> I have a lot of energy, me, MC Carol ...
> I'm a young hoe
> She's been a hoe for a long time
> Now go down on your knees and show me your talent.

Toward the end of the video, Tati and MC Carol come together to discuss how one of their "employees" was doing a poor job at the car wash, and MC Carol admonishes him. "Boy, this is your last chance! Stop by my office later," she says her with a smirk on her face, touching the man's hand. Tati, who up until then had been performing with rap-like hand gestures, joins the men on the floor of the car wash to dance alongside them. Meanwhile, MC Carol is shown blowing smoke from a cigar and watching the man from the previous interaction perform on a pole.

Hyper-femininity and hyper-heterosexuality have been historically linked with discourses about lower class and non-white women. As Soihet,[60] Batista,[61] and Freire Filho and Herschmann[62] hint, Brazilian elite and middle-class have a historical fear of uncontrollable sexualities that emerged in colonial times and persists in contemporary Brazil, especially when it comes to the sexuality of poor Black women. Correspondingly, Brazilian culture and institutions have long deemed poor women of color's performances of gender and sexuality simultaneously repulsive and desired.[63] The category "women," hence, was both inclusive and exclusive of certain performances of femininity, with white bourgeois femininity at the top of the normative gender hierarchy. Butler reminds us that identities are simultaneously inclusive and exclusive, affirming and pathologizing.[64] That is precisely why investigating how embodied performances break with restrictive identities has such a promising possibility for funkeiras whose classed, racialized femininities have been historically marginalized.

Feminist Funkeiras

MC Carol's 2016 feminist awakening happened at a time when many funkeiras started to openly discuss machismo. In 2014, Valesca Popozuda became the face of São Paulo's SlutWalk (Marcha das Vadias, in Portuguese) when she used feminist lingo during an interview to assert that "to be slut is to be free."[65] Gomes notes that Valesca Popozuda, indeed, was the only funkeira in 2014–2015 who openly called herself a feminist.[66] In a 2018 tweet, veteran MC Tati Quebra Barraco posted the following: "Don't visit my tweets from 2012/2013/2014. I was shitty and my mentality was extremely machista. I won't delete them though. I don't see a reason to hide that I was shitty one day. Who hasn't, right? Good afternoon."[67] Despite not being "perfectly" feminist and not knowing about it early in her career, Tati claims that she always wanted to be able to do what men do—"and even more."[68] Now in her openly Black feminist phase, Tati still maintains the playfulness for which she is known. One of her more recent mottos encapsulates these ideas well. Tati tweeted the following for the first time on June 18, 2017, and then several times after that: "Be a hoe, but don't forget to study. Be an educated hoe."[69] Here, the MC cleverly blends feminism and favela funk. Funkeiras Deize Tigrona and Linn da Quebrada are also open about their anti-machistas commitment, though both of them are more focused on LGBTQIA+ issues, as I explore in Chapter Six. Pocah stated in 2019 that she became a feminist in 2016:

> I really like being able to use my voice to bring awareness to women, and it makes me extremely happy when they say that I inspire them and use my songs as an incentive to leave toxic relationships ....I support the feminist

movement, and I'm really happy I was able to understand a little more about this fight.[70]

When right-wing conservative politician Jair Bolsonaro was running for president in 2018, feminist groups in Brazil responded by creating a counter-movement called "Ele Não/#elenão" ("Not Him"). The feminist response to Bolsonaro highlighted the rape threats he made to another congresswoman and his espousing of violently homophobic ideas.[71] Some funkeiras joined in the movement. Tati Quebra Barraco tweeted on September 20, 2018: "First of all: HAPPY BIRTHDAY TO ME. Second of all: NOT HIM."[72] MC Carol posted several Instagram and Twitter messages supporting the Ele Não movement, including pictures from protests that happened a few days before the election on October 7, 2018, and the #womenagainstbolsonaro.[73] Valesca Popozuda responded to insults on Twitter in support of #elenão with the following message:

> Just a warning for those who've been offending me because of the #NOTHIM: saying "Your butt is made out of silicone" doesn't offend me, ok! I paid a lot of money for her … and to say, "Valesca is old and dates a young man," damn right I do, and whenever I can I fuck every day because it's great [wink face emoji].[74]

Funkeiras have now achieved more space in favela funk than in the last 15 years. More than visibility within the movement and in mainstream media, over time they have established more assertive ways to relate to men—the ones still in charge of the movement for most part. Challenging men on stage and being successful doing so seems to be having a continued impact on funkeiras' part in favela funk. Scholars should follow these political trends in favela funk in order to trace long-term consequences for funkeiras. Questions about impact on audiences, for instance, could generate more concrete answers in terms of the effects identifying as feminists has on funkeiras, their fans, and favela funk. Viana gives us a hint: while studying groups of feminine favela funk fans from Minas Gerais, she claims that these bondes produce a type of transgressive feminine sociability:

The girls/women in the studied bondes utilize images traditionally associated with femininity to construct their own ways of understanding and experiencing relationships of gender and power; therefore, they appropriate attributes such as malice and sensuality to compose their own gender identities.[75]

Rather than deductively trying to apply the feminist label on funkeiras, inductively investigating their performances is likely to generate better, deeper considerations of feminine folks involved with favela funk in any shape or form.

In their artistic performances, funkeiras use embodied politics to publicly affirm and embrace their marginalized bodies in movement. They use unconventional methods to impose their sexual desires on men and define the types of affective arrangements they want to engage in while also mocking those who try to dominate them via money and/or sex. All of these defying acts in funkeiras' performances not only contest normative white femininity but also provide diverse, contradictory practices for doing so. Similarly, the relationships with other funkeiras are full of paradoxes, including belligerence, mockery, competition, and solidarity. Gender-first and lyric-based analyses cannot capture the intricacy of these relationships.

Funkeiras went from challenging other women because of men to confronting other funkeiras over status, money, and looks to finally de-emphasizing these kinds of performances altogether. Accordingly, they moved on from punishing men via sex to affirming their sexual, financial, and romantic autonomy. Survival led funkeiras to feminism—their version of feminism, which is oftentimes not understood or respected by other (white) feminists.[76] Perhaps the version of feminism that best fits funkeiras' ambiguous, transgressive performances of racialized femininities is U.S.-based hip-hop feminism. Instead of relying on binaries that reinforce and elevate white middle-class femininity and its morality, hip-hop feminism trailblazer Joan Morgan argues for a "feminism brave enough to fuck with the grays."[77] Funkeiras performances of and negotiations with transgressive racialized femininities can broaden feminist understandings of embodied politics that do not clearly fit in dichotomous understandings of gender oppression and that are not simple matters of choice. An integral part of funkeiras' intricate performances of embodied politics is their relationships with race, racism, and whiteness. In the next chapter, I assess the way these issues further complicate funkeiras' embodied performances and negotiations with the movement and mainstream media, as well as how a renewed commitment to Black identity has impacted feminine favela funk.

Notes

1 Pocah, "Pocah—Pode Chorar (Clipe Oficial)," August 23, 2019, YouTube video, 2:45, https://www.youtube.com/watch?v=6XRJXGes0Bc.

2 Gabriel Adams Castelo Branco de Aragão, "O Discurso e a Construção da Imagem Feminina No Funk," *Cadernos de Pesquisa na Graduação em Letras* 1, no. 1 (2011): 80; Adriana Lopes, *Funk-se Quem Quiser: No Batidão Negro da Cidade Carioca* (Rio de Janeiro: Bom Texto, 2011).

3 D. Soyini Madison, *Critical Ethnography: Method, Ethics, and Performance* (Thousand Oaks: Sage, 2005).

4 Jim Thomas, *Doing Critical Ethnography* (Newbury Park: Sage, 1993).

5 Lopes, *Funk-se*.

6 Man Recordings, "Deize Tigrona Bandida Live," October 2, 2008, YouTube video, 3:29, https://www.youtube.com/watch?v=aLCt_Mby324.

7 Furacão 2000, "Twister Mc Kátia Marido e meu," January 17, 2011, YouTube video, 1:57, https://www.youtube.com/watch?v=gVKj-EVIhYA.

8 Mr Bongo, "Tati Quebra Barraco—Se Marcar," June 6, 2013, YouTube video, 2:33, https://www.youtube.com/watch?v=55BN3EH2mfU.

9 Lopes, *Funk-se*.

10 Furacão 2000, "DVD Furacão 2000 Tsunami I," January 11, 2011, YouTube video, 2:39, https://www.youtube.com/watch?v=gcOkX_CW1aQ.

11 Lopes, *Funk-se*.

12 Lopes, *Funk-se*, 176.

13 Osmundo Pinho, "The 'Faithful', the 'Lover' and the 'Charming Young Male': Gender Subjects in a Racialized Periphery," *Saúde e Sociedade* 16, no. 2 (May/August 2007): 138.

14 Pinho, "The 'Faithful,'" 138.

15 Pinho, "The 'Faithful,'" 135.

16 Lopes, *Funk-se*.

17 Fabio Queiroz Pereira and Jordhana M. C. Gomes, "Poverty and Gender: The Marginalization of Travestis and Transsexuals by the Law," *Revista Direitos Fundamentais e Democracia* 22, no. 2 (2017): 210–224; Sumaia Villela, "Na

Luta contra a Pobreza, Mulheres Buscam Autnomia por Conta Propria," *Agência Brasil*, March 8, 2016, https://agenciabrasil.ebc.com.br/direitos-humanos/noticia/2016-03/na-luta-contra-pobreza-mulheres-buscam-autonomia-por-meio-do.

18 Furacão 2000, "Tsunami."

19 Lopes, *Funk-se*, 175.

20 EliveltonMello FUNK, "Mc Pocahontas—Seu marido tá bancando," February 5, 2012, YouTube video, 2:14, https://www.youtube.com/watch?v=PrgXdNXg-CY.

21 Pheeno TV, "Valesca Popozuda—Fiél é o caralho / caçadoras de piru @ The Week Rio—Pheeno TV," July 3, 2012, YouTube video, 2:25, https://www.youtube.com/watch?v=Jlitw9rlqg4.

22 Rachel Soihet, "A Sensualidade em Festa: Representações do Corpo Feminino nas Festas Populares no Rio de Janeiro na Virada do Século XIX para o XX," in *O Corpo Feminino em Debate*, eds. M. I. Matos and Rachel Soihet (São Paulo: Unesp, 2003): 177–97.

23 Mariana Gomes, "My Pussy é o Poder. Representação Feminina Através do Funk: Identidade, Feminismo e Indústria Cultural" (Unpublished thesis, Federal Fluminense University, 2015); Raquel Moreira, "Bitches Unleashed: Women in Rio's Funk Movement, Performances of Heterosexual Femininity, and Possibilities of Resistance" (PhD diss., University of Denver, 2014).

24 Mariana Ceratti, "In Brazil, an Emergent Middle Class Takes Off," *The World Bank*, November 13, 2012, https://www.worldbank.org/en/news/feature/2012/11/13/middle-class-in-Brazil-Latin-America-report.

25 Inovashow, "Tati Quebra Barraco—Tu quer ser eu (CD se liberta)," December 11, 2014, YouTube video, 2:15, https://www.youtube.com/watch?v=I_cMb4LA3-k.

26 Ludmilla, "Ludmilla—Fala mal de mim," August 25, 2014, YouTube video, 3:30, https://www.youtube.com/watch?v=UKhdAumYKCc.

27 ArrebentaFunk, "MC Kátia—Froxona resposta Beyonce [clipe official]," October 9, 2012, 5:24, YouTube video, https://www.youtube.com/watch?v=3WM6k1lzzpI.

28 Denise Garcia, *Sou Feia, Mas Tô na Moda* (São Paulo: Imovision, 2005), Film; João Freire Filho and Micael Herschmann, "Funk Carioca," *Eco-Pós* 6, no. 2 (2003): 60–72.

29 Anderson Antunes, "Could Brazil's Latest Music Sensation Anitta Be a Global Superstar in the Making?" *Forbes*, August 30, 2013, https://www.forbes.com/sites/andersonantunes/2013/08/30/could-brazils-latest-music-sensation-anitta-be-a-global-superstar-in-the-making/#3b316dc0432a.

30 Valesca Popozuda, "Valesca Popozuda—Beijinho no Ombro (official music video)," December 27, 2013, YouTube video, 7:34, https://www.youtube.com/watch?v=73sbW7gjBeo.

31 Gomes, "Pussy é o Poder"; Valesca Popozuda, "Beijinho no Ombro."

32 Gomes, "Pussy é o Poder."

33 Fabrício Falcheti, "Com 'Beijinho no Ombro', Cachê de Valesca Popozuda Passa para R$ 60 mil" *UOL*, February 24, 2014, https://natelinha.uol.com.br/celebridades/2014/02/24/com-beijinho-no-ombro-cache-de-valesca-popozuda-passa-para-r-60-mil-71861.php.

34 Gomes, "Pussy é o Poder."

35 Chris Jenks, *Transgression* (London: Routledge, 2003).

36 Gabriel Aragão, "O Discurso e a Construção da Imagem Feminina No Funk," *Cadernos de Pesquisana Graduação em Letras* 1, no. 1 (2011): 73–85.

37 Lopes, *Funk-se.*

38 Edinéia de Oliveira, "A Expressão da Identidade Feminina No Gênero Musical Funk," *VI Semana Integrada das Licenciaturas*, Tubarão, October 22–26, 2007.

39 Universa, "Valesca Popozuda: 'Fico no baile até às 9h da manhã,'" October 5, 2018, YouTube video, 10:06, https://www.youtube.com/watch?v=BeuKVWsZulI.

40 Thiago Baltazar, "'O Funk Me Deu Voz e Eu a Uso para Ajudar Mulheres', Diz Pocah," *Vogue*, November 10, 2019, https://vogue.globo.com/celebridade/noticia/2019/11/o-funk-me-deu-voz-e-eu-uso-para-ajudar-mulheres-diz-pocah.html.

41 MC Xuxú, "MC Xuxú—Senzala (feat. Ingoma) áudio official," January 28, 2018, YouTube video, 2:24, https://www.youtube.com/watch?v=NrvNrJ1ijvo.

42 Aragão, "Discurso"; Freire Filho and Herschmann, "Funk Carioca"; de Oliveira, "Expressão."

43 Garcia, *Sou Feia.*

44 Gust Yep, "The Violence of Heteronormativity in Communication Studies: Notes on Injury, Healing, and Queer World-Making," *Journal of Homosexuality* 45, no. 2/3/4 (2003): 11–59.

45 Jane Arthurs and Jean Grimshaw, *Women's Bodies: Discipline and Transgression* (London: Casell, 1999), 141.

46 Diogo Santos Maxi, "Cachorra Solta—Tati Quebra Barraco," April 15, 2012, YouTube video, 2:22, https://www.youtube.com/watch?v=B1rL8OOSv4c&list=RDLj6Mk_1KHFQ&index=19.

47 Yep, "The Violence."

48 Garcia, *Sou Feia.*

49 FM Music BR, "MC Marcelly & Maikinho DVD—Duela rimeas na hora," January 30, 2012, YouTube video, 7:36, https://www.youtube.com/watch?v=A0NBwZmcxIo.

50 Freire Filho and Herschmann, "Funk Carioca."

51 Tabata Uchoa, "MC Marcelly Interpreta Vítima de Violência Doméstica em Clipe," *O Dia*, November 2, 2015, https://odia.ig.com.br/_conteudo/diversao/celebridades/2015-11-03/mc-marcelly-interpreta-vitima-de-violencia-domestica-em-clipe.html.

52 Linn da Quebrada, "Mc Linn da Quebrada—Talento—Clipe official," August 23, 2016, YouTube video, 5:59, https://www.youtube.com/watch?v=hkAHuRPGgNk.

53 Gomes, "Pussy é o Poder."

54 Funk Carioca, "MC Carol de Niterói:: Ao vivo em um video polêmico na roda de funk:: Especial," March 11, 2013, 6:39, YouTube video, https://www.youtube.com/watch?v=Eu-dsrtbuHE.

55 Karina Trevizan, "36% das Mulheres Dizem Dividir com Marido as Tarefas de Casa Igualmente," *G1*, June 15, 2016, http://g1.globo.com/economia/concursos-e-emprego/noticia/2016/06/so-36-das-mulheres-dividem-tarefas-domesticas-com-marido-diz-pesquisa.html.

56 Marina Novaes, "MC Carol: 'Meu Namorado Não é Otário. Homem Hem que Dividir Tarefa,'" *El País*, August 9, 2015, http://brasil.elpais.com/brasil/2015/07/27/cultura/1438026091_663516.html.

57 MC Carol Oficial, "MC Carol & Karol Conka—100% feminista (prod. Leo Justi & Tropkillaz)," October 7, 2016, YouTube video, 3:19, https://www.youtube.com/watch?v=W05v0B59K5s.

58 Heavy Baile, "Heavy Baile, Tati Quebra Barraco & MC Carol—Mamãe da putaria (clipe oficial)," March 8, 2019, YouTube video, 3:35, https://www.youtube.com/watch?v=vw09YpI_QMQ.

59 Djamila Ribeiro, *Quem Tem Medo do Feminismo Negro* (São Paulo: Companhia das Letras, 2008).

60 Soihet, "Sensualidade em Festa."

61 Vera Batista, "Na Periferia do Medo," in *Estudos Gerais da Psicanálise: Segundo Encontro Mundial* (Rio de Janeiro: Estudos Gerais da Psicanálise, October 30, 2003).

62 Freire Filho and Herschmann, "Funk Carioca."

63 Mariza Côrrea, "Sobre a Invenção da Mulata," *Cadernos Pagu* 6/7 (1996): 35–50.

64 Judith Butler, *Gender Trouble: Feminism and the Subversion of Identity* (New York: Routledge, 2006).

65 Graziele Oliveira, "Valesca Popozuda: 'Ser Vadia é Ser Livre,'" *Época*, April 11, 2014, http://epoca.globo.com/ideias/noticia/2014/04/bvalesca-popozudab-ser-vadia-e-ser-livre.html.

66 Gomes, "Pussy é o Poder."

67 Tati Quebra Barraco (@TatiQBOficial), "Não visitem os meus tts de 2012/2013/2014. Eu era uma merda e meu pensamento era extremamente machista. Mas não irei apagar. Não vejo motivo de esconder que já fui uma merda um dia. Quem nunca né? Boa tarde," Twitter, November 12, 2018, 9:18 a.m., https://twitter.com/TatiQBOficial/status/1062001722955055104.

68 Tati Quebra Barraco (@TatiQBOficial), "Não sabia de feminismo. A questão era, se os homens podem. Eu posso também e até mais," Twitter, June 24, 2020, 9:05 a.m., https://twitter.com/TatiQBOficial/status/1275792219136557057.

69 Tati Quebra Barraco (@TatiQBOficial), "Seja piranha mas não se esqueça dos estudos. Seja uma piranha formada," Twitter, June 18, 2017, 11:28 a.m., https://twitter.com/TatiQBOficial/status/876476726792134656.

70 Lucas Rocha, "Entrevista: Pocah explica novo nome e fase da carreira, se abre sobre feminism e bissexualidade, e dá detalhes de namoro: 'Não esperava que as coisas ficariam sérias,' " *Hugo Gloss*, September 10, 2019, https://hugogloss.uol.com. br/entrevistas/entrevista-pocah-explica-novo-nome-e-fase-da-carreira-se-abre-sobre-feminismo-e-bissexualidade-e-da-detalhes-de-namoro-nao-esperava-que-as-coisas-ficariam-serias/.

71 Pablo Uchoa, "Jair Bolsonaro: Why Brazilian Women Are Saying #NotHim," *BBC*, September 21, 2018, https://www.bbc.com/news/world-latin-america-45579635.

72 Tati Quebra Barraco (@TatiQBOficial), "Primeiramente: PARABENS PRA MIM Segundamente: ELENAO Terceiramente: SEGUNDAMENTE," Twitter, September 20, 2018, 11:07 p.m., https://twitter.com/TatiQBOficial/status/1042988667935936512.

73 MC Carol (@mc_caroloficial), "Ahhhh gente eu to tão feliz. Foram tantas palavras de carinhos, tantas pessoas pedindo adesivo e panfletos, eu não tinha noção dessa aceitação. Essa experiência está sendo tão importante em minha vida #ELENAO #mulheresunidascontrabolsonaro #mccarol 65100," Twitter, October 1, 2018, 12:53 a.m., https://twitter.com/mc_caroloficial/status/1046639339101466624.

74 Valesca Popozuda (@ValescaOficial), "Só um aviso pra quem tem me ofendido por conta do #ELENao falar 'sua bunda é de silicone' não me ofende tá! Pq eu paguei caríssimo por ela … E falar 'Valesca tá velha e namora um homem novo' namoro mesmo, e sempre que posso eu dou todo dia pq isso é ótimo," Twitter, October 11, 2018, 11:19 a.m., https://twitter.com/ValescaOficial/status/1050420525200277504.

75 Iara Pires Viana, "Funk Territory and Femininities: Subjectivities Built Between Power Relations, the Street and Violence," *Revista Brasileira de Estudos do Lazer* 3, no. 3 (2016): 123.

76 Gomes, "Pussy é o Poder."

77 Joan Morgan, *When Chickenheads Come Home to Roost* (New York: Simon & Schuster, 1999), 59.

Chapter Five

Anti-Blackness and Racial Consciousness among Funkeiras

Even though this book privileges a *transfeminista* approach to performance and embodied politics in which issues of race, class, and gender are weaved through the analysis, I feel that it is necessary to explicitly address the particular challenges Black funkeiras face in favela funk. This chapter has a twofold purpose: to address how the anti-Blackness present in Brazilian culture is expressed within favela funk and to highlight funkeiras' fight against it. First, I focus on a previous analysis of Tati Quebra Barraco along with two personal interviews of Black funkeiras, Deize Tigrona and MC Dandara, and their perspectives on how racism limits their career. These reflections on race are significant because they were generally unusual in Brazilian culture. Given that foundational myths of racial democracy have previously pushed racial discourses aside in favor of discourses about class and social mobility, making direct references to Blackness has been uncommon among funkeiras and in favela funk until very recently.[1] The chapter also examines the recent wave of public, Black-affirming positions held by several Black funkeiras. These come at a time in which there have been growing conversations about race in Brazil facilitated by Black folks, especially Black women and travestis.

This chapter relies on a variety of qualitative methods and a diversity of texts in order to capture how funkeiras handle issues of race in favela funk. I use personal and media interviews, news reports, analysis of music videos, and funkeiras' social media posts to provide a comprehensive picture of the transformations favela funk has been experiencing in terms of intersecting issues of race and gender. Perhaps more than the previous chapters, this section engages with funkeiras' social media presence, as they use it to communicate their affirmations of Black identity. For Piñero-Otero and Martínez-Rolán, the relative low cost associated with social media, along with the possibility of reach and rapidity of creation and diffusion of messages, make platforms like Twitter and Instagram "valuable for online political action."[2] Accordingly, political activity in digital platforms serves "as alternative tactics and expressions to traditional political structures."[3] More than expressing their opinions online, funkeiras use digital platforms to build personal and communal narratives about favela funk and Blackness without depending on hegemonic media.

Race, Racism, and Whiteness in Brazil

The debate about race in Brazil has been marked by two opposing ideas. The first notion, very popular during the nineteenth century, posed that the intense miscegenation that is part of Brazil's history is also what placed the country "behind" in terms of "progress"—Brazil had become "too dark" in this process, according to white elites.[4] The other idea, which is the one that prevailed in Brazilian culture, is the myth of different races (Black, white, and Indigenous, especially) coming together in a harmonious way that was popularized by Brazilian anthropologist Gilberto Freyre.[5] Brazil has been referred to by the UN as a unique and successful racial and ethnic experience in terms of accommodation of differences.[6] The ideological construction of the country's "miscegenated Brazilianness," thus, is grounded on concepts of "non-race,"[7] which then leads to beliefs that Brazil deals very well with racial differences.[8]

Recent literature on racial constructions in Brazil indicate a "structural blindness in Brazilian society" when it comes to racism.[9] Côrrea argues that, like other nations that enslaved people, these issues stem from the country's history of colonialism.[10] This foundational characteristic of Brazilian racism can be exemplified by the fact that the country "has officially incorporated whiteness into its nation-building project."[11] This policy, called *branqueamento* (whitening), facilitated the migration of white Europeans to Brazil in the first decades of the twentieth century with the purpose of lightening the population by encouraging miscegenation between Black and Indigenous Brazilians with white Europeans.[12]

Although under the veil of racial democracy, "the legacy of white superiority still holds much sway, to the effect that many Brazilians either identify or desire to identify as 'whiter' than their phenotype might suggest."[13] After all, there are material and social implications for claiming whiteness. Unlike in the U.S. context, in which race developed into a "strict and polarized white-black binary," with whiteness possessing very exclusive boundaries, in Brazil race is structured as a continuum: if one has any European ancestry, they have the chance to be considered potentially white, or at least *not* Black.[14] Colorism is also a result of this practice. To S. Ribeiro, colorism in Brazil is "about a society that, based on skin tone, defines which spaces people can and cannot occupy. That way, the darker a person's skin is in Brazil, the more she will suffer processes of exclusion."[15] From this, it is possible to grasp two closely related aspects of racial categories in Brazil. First, whiteness is somewhat fluid and inclusive, since one can claim it loosely based on phenotype; second, relatedly, miscegenation is simultaneously a weapon of whiteness and an expression of anti-Blackness. No wonder Brazilians are known for using countless racial identifiers based on color, usually to avoid identifying as Black.[16] For instance, since the 1960s, the Brazilian national census (measured by the governmental institute IBGE) has been using the same five categories of race/color (instead of origin or ethnicity): white, black, brown (*moreno* or *pardo*, the most popular category among Brazilians, which varies from "light brown" to "dark brown"), "yellow," and "indigenous" (the only category related to origin/ethnicity). Yet, there is also a more recent open-ended self-declaration question in which people do not have to choose their color/race from options presented in the form. The usual result for this question is approximately 200 different types of self-declared colors/races.[17]

Black activists and scholars have been working hard to undo the damage of Freyre's racial democracy façade for white supremacy. Since the 1970s, Black feminist intellectuals like Lélia Gonzalez have been organizing around intersecting issues of race, gender, and class.[18] Still, Silva argues that Brazilian political movements, even those on the left, still continue to relegate race to the margins of conversations about restructuring the country's systems.[19] Recently, however, a new generation of Black activists and scholars is emerging and garnering the power of social media to call out the left and organize politically.[20] These young Black folks from different parts of the country have been openly defying anti-Blackness in Brazilian culture. According to S. Ribeiro, these young people are "tired of the imposed aesthetic invisibility and of the denial of their physical characteristics, seen as negative by a racist society."[21] Perhaps related to this rise in Black activism is the fact that in seven years, from 2012 to 2018, the number of people who self-identified as Black in the Brazilian census increased by 32%.[22] In 2015, the Black Women's March gathered 50,000 women in Brazil's capital, Brasília, to protest against racism and violence and for their community's right to life.[23] Black feminists in Brazil consider this event an important turning point in contemporary Black activism in the country.[24] According to one of the march's organizers, Black journalist Juliana Gonçalves, "many [Black] girls who were not familiarized with issues of racism became involved with the fight [against anti-Blackness and sexism] through the events and meetings leading up to the march."[25] Weschenfelder and Fabris argue that the current visibility Black feminism has in Brazil is due to Black women's tireless efforts to organize, in academia or otherwise. Proof of this is the growing number of spaces, be them in universities or in social networking sites, that have emerged to promote discussions around Black identity and social justice issues. Accordingly, "this visibility has not only guaranteed new members for the [Black feminist] movement, but it has also catched [Brazilian] society's attention to the inequities Black women face in the country."[26]

S. Ribeiro's mention of aesthetics in this new Black movement in Brazil is especially important to understanding funkeiras' recent engagement with issues connected to race.[27] This generation is comprised of "a large amount of Black folks, mostly poor, that through aesthetic and culture transform their bodies, up until then marginalized and criminalized by an exclusionary system."[28] These young people utilize "activism and politics to affirm their Blackness."[29] Like favela funk, which is a product of the African diaspora[30] and is thus simultaneously indigenous to Rio and an expression of a Black struggle globally, S. Ribeiro calls attention to the fact that this new tendency to value Black beauty and bodies goes beyond national borders; it is a worldwide movement. The analyses below spotlight the different stages and aspects of questions of race among funkeiras. After investigating backstage racism and the invisibility of race in favela funk, I delve into funkeiras' recent public performances of Blackness and Black femininity.

"Nobody Wants to See the Black Doll's Mouth": Favela Funk and Sexist Racism

While favela funk's roots are clearly Black and *favelada*, explicit mentions of race were fairly uncommon among funkeiras between the early 2000s and the mid-2010s.[31] As mentioned above, because race relations in Brazil are saturated with ideas about racial democracy and peaceful miscegenation, overt references to race in general and anti-Black racism in particular were unlikely;[32] instead, coded racist language was/ is frequently associated with geographic location and physical attributes.[33] In favela funk, Lopes notes that up until the publication of her book in 2011, there were only two songs containing obvious mentions of race: Amilcka and Chocolate's "Som de Preto" ("Black Sound") and MC Dandara's "Agora Tô Piranha" ("Now That I'm a Whore"), which has the line "I go to the baile looking for my big Black man."[34] Moreover, "although bodies are spoken about all the time and the majority of the women who perform dirty funk can be considered Black or brown, it is only implicitly that they articulate racial signifiers in the constitution of their gender identities."[35] This subsection exposes these paradoxical propensities in favela funk, especially up until 2014.

Tati Quebra Barraco has used coded language to talk about race via physical attributes in her performances. She released the album *Boladona* (Pissed Off) in 2004, which contains the hit song "I'm Ugly but Trendy." In it, Tati says, "I'm ugly, but trendy/I can pay for the motel room/And that's what matters." The lyrics to this tune assume ugliness without much detail. In fact, it is unclear what makes Tati physically unattractive. However, in other moments, the MC has hinted at what she meant. One of Tati's early career sayings was something along the lines of "My hair isn't straight, I'm not hot, but I fucked your husband."[36] Lopes contends that the MC's reference to ugliness is traversed by otherwise silent allusions to race—in this case, straight hair: "Tati is 'ugly' and her 'hair isn't straight' in relationship to a white standard of womanhood."[37] It is not unusual for Black and brown funkeiras to go through a process of "whitening" or masking phenotypically Black characteristics in order to succeed in public. According to Pinho, in a white supremacist society, it becomes necessary for Black folks "to manipulate appearance as a way to 'control' threat and fear associated with the Black body."[38] For women and transfeminine people, this process may include plastic surgery, blue or green contact lenses, blonde extensions, and straightened hair.[39] This might work for brown or light-skinned funkeiras, like Valesca Popozuda. For undoubtedly Black artists like Tati, working to conceal Blackness in their physical attributes while avoiding explicit mentions to race does not mean that their bodies and performances were not still perceived as classed and racialized. Thus, Tati was already facing significant financial, emotional, and perhaps even physical risks for choosing to perform about sex and poor Black women's sexuality as a poor Black woman. It is understandable that Tati Quebra Barraco worked to evade her Blackness early in her career; it was a matter of survival.

Black funkeiras who spoke with me in 2013 understood that racial prejudice plays a role in their ability to go mainstream. "Dirtiness is all over media, and it's not because of funk," says Deize Tigrona. The MC from City of God protests the fact that favela funk's sexually explicit lyrics are singled out in corporate media. While commenting on her racy song "Prostituto" ("Male Prostitute") from 2008, Deize says:

> If I release two or three more like that one, it will be played. I know it. So, I don't want the media coming to me and saying that the lyrics are "too heavy," that it won't be on TV "cause it's 'too heavy.'" Ok, so what?

After protesting the lack of space for funkeiras like her in the media, Deize Tigrona looks at me with an inquisitive expression and wonders, "You know, sometimes I ask myself, 'Is this because I'm Black?' This is with funk in general, not just with me."

Deize is not the only one to question racial discrimination. MC Dandara also points out during our interview that race affects her ability to succeed as a Black woman. I spoke with Dandara at her manager's office in a slum in the west side of Rio. She had her one-year-old daughter on her lap while she explained to me, between laughter, how racially ambiguous funkeira Valesca Popozuda achieved success performing Dandara's song, "Now That I'm a Whore." According to the MC, Valesca made the equivalent of "240 minimum wages" off of the track's popularity, which included an invitation to pose for Brazilian *Playboy*. Referring to her vagina, MC Dandara stated: "If I had [performed it] myself, I wouldn't have shown my doll's mouth, because nobody wants to see a Black doll's mouth." Dandara believes that the mainstream success certain light brown funkeiras achieve, which often comes with lucrative invitations to pose nude, would unlikely be there for her because she is a Black woman. This reflection is significant because Dandara is able to point to *material* benefits of being light-skinned. Consequently, opportunities that involve significant financial gains for women in general are not available for dark-skinned Black women. These reflections on race are significant because they were unusual in Brazil at the time. Perhaps funkeiras avoided public references to race and racism, as pointed out by Lopes,[40] but in my fieldwork, during informal conversations with funkeiras, those who are Black always found a way to mention favela funk's lack of commitment to Black issues and Black beauty.[41]

Performances of Black Femininity among Funkeiras

Funkeiras' public embracing of their Black identities came at a time when there was a movement of young people using social media to construct and assert their Blackness.[42] I started noticing this trend among funkeiras in 2015 while following MC Carol on Facebook. She tells me during our August 2019 phone interview that she has been using social media, including Instagram and Twitter, to express opinions related to gender and race. However, this is not to say that is exactly when it started; rather, I would like to draw parallels between the political and cultural moment Brazil was experiencing in the second half of the 2010s and the rise in funkeiras' engagement with intersecting issues of race and gender. In this section, I utilize diverse types of texts, including personal and news media interviews, music videos, song lyrics, and social media posts in order to thoroughly grasp funkeiras' performances of Blackness. I trace these performances in their music-related favela funk work as well as in their public personas.

MC Carol performs Blackness both in her favela funk work and in her public persona. In March 2016, for instance, she was a guest artist in São Paulo's music festival Lollapalooza, where she performed with Karol Conka, a rising Black female rapper. After the event, MC Carol commented, "Brazil is a very prejudiced country, not only with racial issues but with everything. Here, everything has established standards. To see two Black women singing together opens people's minds, and that's great!"[43] In it, the two artists performed their song, "100% Feminista,"[44] which mixes the beats of hip-hop and favela funk. The lyrics to the tune provide a Black feminist standpoint on gendered violence, as they also honor a series of famous Black and brown women:

> I witnessed all of this in my own family
> Woman with a black eye, beaten up every day
> I was 5 years old but I already understood
> That women will get mauled if there's no food
> Oppressed woman, no voice, obedient
> When I grow up, I'll be different
> I've grown

Pleased to meet you, Carol Bandida
I represent women
100% feminista

The song continues as MC Carol pays homage to Black ancestry by citing a series of important Black women in Brazilian history: Congolese princess and maternal grandmother of Zumbi dos Palmares, Aqualtune; Black novelist Carolina Maria de Jesus; colonial Black queen and warrior, Dandara; and Black free woman born into slavery, Chica da Silva. She then proceeds to affirm her Black femininity using a hostile rapping tone that ends with her shouting: "I'm a woman, I'm Black/My hair is kinky/Strong, demanding/Sometimes fragile, I confess/My fragility doesn't diminish my strength/I'm the boss of this shit, I won't wash the dishes." MC Carol offers a perspective of her identity as a Black woman that involves a series of assertive and vulnerable moments. Black women in Brazil are recognized for their strength and sense of survival,[45] which at times can hinder the perception that they are vulnerable as well. MC Carol concomitantly embraces these apparently disparate characteristics. The tune is also a cry against gendered violence, to which Black women are more susceptible than white women in Brazil.[46] Using the same commanding tone from the previous verse, MC Carol says "I'm an independent woman/I don't accept oppression/ Lower your voice/Lower your hand!" Favela funk songs are rarely as explicit as "100% Feminista" in their political commentary, especially when the topics involves intersections of race, class, and gender.

Other songs from MC carol also offer some kind of social commentary about race, even when they are not necessarily focused on gendered issues. In the 2015 tune "Não Foi Cabral" ("It Wasn't Cabral"), for instance, the MC narrates an interaction with a teacher in history class in which she challenges the colonial narrative that Portuguese explorer Pedro Alvarez Cabral "discovered" Brazil, like it is usually taught in grade schools in the country.[47] The song opens with the Brazilian national anthem and a few seconds later favela funk's tamborzão mixes with it. The lyrics reference the genocide of indigenous people by Portuguese colonizers ("Thirteen caravels/Brought a lot of death/ One million Indians/Died of tuberculosis"), as well as the struggles and resistance of enslaved Africans, especially women ("If it wasn't for Dandara [female Black warrior]/I'd still be getting flogged"). MC Carol also challenges the double standard poor people of color face in the Brazilian justice system in "Delação Premiada" ("Plea Deal"), which protects political and police corruption while incarcerating and killing Black favela folks. Her overt references to racism, colonialism, sexism, and state violence attest to favela funk's shifting context and artistic possibilities.

MC Xuxú tells me during our June 2020 interview that it is difficult trying to survive as a Black and travesti artist. She says that often "brands want people who are skinny, with straight hair," which is one way to ensure that they will only sponsor white and/or light-skinned people. Still, MC Xuxú asserts that her audience, mostly comprised of Black and LGBTQIA+ folks "from the hood," provides a good support for her work. Like MC Carol, whom she mentions in one of her tunes ("... pray to Jah about how much all of this hurts me/Praise while listening to the anthems of Carol de Niterói"), MC Xuxú also uses references to other Black women in her work. In the music video for "Meus Desapegos" ("My Detachments"), a song about ditching guys on social media, several shots of framed photos of diverse Black women adorn a bedroom where MC Xuxú performs.[48] Among them are Brazilian soul singer Elza Soares, slayed Rio councilwoman Marielle Franco, U.S. transwoman Laverne Cox, and international superstar Beyoncé. I asked MC Xuxú why she chose these particular people, to which she replied, "I wanted to have examples of strength, you know, of struggle." She comments that her and her team collectively selected these folks. Often during our conversation, MC Xuxú made references to the importance of communal work and support for her success, which is something that I further explore in Chapter Six.

Linn da Quebrada is another artist whose performances of Blackness are apparent in her artistic work. The opening shots of her 2016 music video for "Bixa Preta" ("Black Fag") show flickering lights, while feminine-presenting bodies of color move sensually.[49] The background audio sounds like an evangelical preacher delivering a sermon: "There's a whole generation promoting homosexualism [sic]! And God is telling you, 'Be a man! Dress like a man! Behave like a man!

Talk like a man!' " The subsequent frame quickly focuses on Brazilian Black travesti artist Linn da Quebrada, who runs her fingers through her long, pink braids. Next, the video cuts to another close shot of a Black, feminine-presenting person who stares at the camera while the preacher's frantic voice echoes in the background: "Be a man!" The artist from São Paulo overtly engages with her Black and favela identities in this music video, such as the lyric, "Because I'm a crazy Black fag from the favela." In a white supremacist context that pushes false ideas around "racial democracy," Linn da Quebrada's blunt enunciation of her positionality matters. More than noting her other identities, Linn da Quebrada first insinuates that to be Black in Brazil requires courage, and second, that Blackness enhances queerness: "My black skin is my cloak of courage/it boosts the movement/it flatters the *viadagem*."* Linn's music videos and live performances often feature Black and brown gender nonconforming folks dancing and sharing affection. In the next chapter, I turn my attention to the connections between race, gender identity, and sexuality in favela funk.

Since roughly around 2017, previously mentioned MC Tati Quebra Barraco began releasing songs in which she directly affirms her Blackness. In "Berro" ("Scream"), for example, there is a verse that says, "Our time is now, damn it/Understand if you can/I'm Black, I don't get intimidated/Respect me, I'm a woman."[50] The music video for the song, which is a collaboration with Heavy Baile, features Tati and singer and drag queen Lia Clark at a favela rooftop party. Tati wears a hot-pink bodysuit with one of her popular sayings on it—something along the lines of "who is fucking me isn't complaining" ("quem tá comendo não tá reclamando"). It is significant to point out that, in this music video, Tati's embodied performances are not that different from those of the mid-2000s. In fact, funkeiras' ways of singing, dancing, and dressing did not change dramatically from what I discussed in chapters three and four, which mostly focused on performances from the mid-2000s

---

* *Viadagem* is a term stemming from the word *viado* and could refer to a group of *viados* or to folks engaging in *viado*-like activities. The term *viado* is considered the antithesis of masculinity in Brazilian sexual culture—the opposite of macho. See chapter six for further contextualization of the moniker.

until the mid-2010s; they have, nonetheless, reframed some of favela funk's popular roles by, for instance, adding more overt symbolic references to race.

Lopes compares the ways in which Black female rappers in the U.S. and Black funkeiras perform their femininities, specifically noting how the former elevate Black femininity in comparison to the latter.[51] She notes that the Brazilian historical context helps explain these differences. However, I would like to call attention to the fact that it is precisely because of the contextual differences that we should be able to evaluate these performances using different, more culturally located lenses. While I agree that the more evident symbolic expressions of Blackness among funkeiras is a positive change in the movement, I want to reaffirm one more time that their performances were still racialized and classed, often deemed uncontrollable and inappropriate, and at times criminalized by both the state and mainstream media. The particular ways they have been performing their racialized femininities, though not always unproblematic, have allowed them to survive. On that note, Linn da Quebrada interviewed Brazilian Black feminist Djamila Ribeiro in one of the many Instagram live events she facilitated during the Covid-19 pandemic quarantine.[52] When discussing the different ways Black Brazilians have been organizing and fighting against racism in comparison to U.S. Americans in light of Black Lives Matter protests, D. Ribeiro contends that Brazil is an extremely dangerous place for activists in comparison to the United States. Resistance to racism, thus, takes many forms because the Brazilian context makes Black lives very precarious. Linn da Quebrada's interview of D. Ribeiro illustrates the ways in which funkeiras perform their Black feminine identities on social media, as I analyze next.

Black Femininity on Social Media

Using connective ethnography as a stance that understands what happens in online spaces as extensions of everyday life,[53] I examine funkeiras' performances of Blackness and Black femininity on social media. Specifically, I have been following Black funkeiras MC Carol, Tati Quebra Barraco, Deize Tigrona, Linn da Quebrada, MC Rebecca, and MC Xuxú on Twitter and/or Instagram since at least 2018—except Deize Tigrona, who was not on social media until she joined Instagram in May 2019. Three main themes have emerged from my observations: funkeiras engage in political commentary related to Blackness; funkeiras use social media to affirm their Blackness and Black femininity; and funkeiras challenge whiteness, especially white women, on social media. The messages I depict below are a representative sample of the ways in which funkeiras perform Blackness online. In no way do I intend these posts to be interpreted as all-encompassing of their social media presence.

On the night of March 14, 2018, Rio's city councilwoman Marielle Franco was murdered by militia men one day after publicly denouncing police brutality in a Rio favela.[54] Marielle, who was a member of the Socialism and Liberty Party, identified as a Black feminist, favelada, and bisexual.[55] Her murder evidenced Rio's dangerous connections between the state's politicians, the military police, and paramilitary members who control several of its areas.[56] Amid public protests,[57] many funkeiras, especially Black artists, made public statements mourning Marielle and asking for justice. On March 15, 2018, MC Carol shared a black and white photo of Marielle's smiling face on Instagram. The post accompanying the picture reads as follow:

> I'm searching for words, but all I fell is anger and a lot of fear … now more than ever, I'm feeling oppressed and weak …. Marielle and Talíria [another Black woman politician] encouraged me to fight, to be strong. They had been at my house where we talked for hours about my fears …. I was feeling so confident, so hopeful after talking to them. Today, all I feel is fear. Actually, I've always been afraid because I'm Black, because I live in the favela, because I'm a woman, because I sing funk …. Today, I'm sure that nothing protects you, no matter who you are. If you're Black and fight for Black people, you always end up EXECUTED!!![58]

On the same day, MC Carol posted a photo of a graffiti on a wall that says, "There's no justice if the murderer is in uniform,"[59] in reference to the now-confirmed speculation that former cops were involved in Marielle's murder.[60] Linn da Quebrada also shared the black and white image of Marielle's face on the 15th, with the caption below:

It is the blood of my own that runs through the margins. Marielle Franco, present. Let us transform the grief into struggle. Black, lesbian, favelada, activist, who used her body to move the structures. And we know that when a Black woman moves, the whole societal structure moves with her. #itwasntburglary #shewasexecuted.[61]

Like in MC Carol's message, Linn's response has the dual function of shedding light on misogynoir by crafting a message that addresses both race and gender while also denouncing the act itself. When news about Marielle's murder came out, the military police said that it looked like Marielle, her communications staff, and her driver had been targeted by robbers. However, those familiar with Marielle's fight to expose police brutality knew that she was likely executed for that reason. MC Xuxú also posted something that referenced gender and race, a quote that reads: "Look at her, the glow of the slave quarters," followed by a message asking international organizations to demand justice for Marielle.[62] Tati Quebra Barraco tweeted a few months later on June 8, 2018, "Marielle, present!"[63] in reference to the popular protest chant supporters of the councilwoman have coined. Unlike Black funkeiras, Valesca Popozuda mourned Marielle Franco by emphasizing her connection with feminism and fight against machismo. The funkeira's Instagram post on March 15, 2018, shows a black and white photo of Marielle at the beach, in which she is holding several fans with the motto "no means no" and pointing to a temporary tattoo on her arm with the same words. Valesca's caption makes no explicit mentions of race, and the hashtags use feminist jargon: "We're not going to be quiet, they're not going to silence us. Marielle fought for human rights, for our rights! And they took away her right to live. #justice #sorority #nomeansno."[64]

Rio-based funkeiras MC Carol, Tati Quebra Barraco, and Deize Tigrona often use social media to speak out against racist police violence targeting Black folks. MC Carol tweeted on February 16, 2019,

Dead with a bullet to the head, his name was Zé and he was 13 years old. He … was going down the favela and they killed him. Zé's color was Black ….This is not a coincidence, this is racism, and RACISM KILLS![65]

Tati Quebra Barraco, whose son was killed by the military police (PM), tweeted about it on December 10, 2016: "the PM took away a piece of me that will never be refilled. The PM killed my son. This pain will never heal."[66] On October 31, 2017, she posted, "Arguing with the PM really is the greatest cause of death in Rio."[67] City of God-based Deize Tigrona used her Instagram to promote Vidas Negras Importam (Black Lives Matter) protests in Rio on May 31, 2020. The first image in Deize's message is a poster of the protest containing pictures of young Black people, mostly children, who were murdered by Rio's police. The caption reads, "THOSE WHO DON'T FIGHT ARE DEAD. TODAY EVEN WITH THE QUARANTINE, THERE WILL BE A PROTEST FOR LIFE. #stopkillingus #blacklivesmatter EVERYONE OUT IN THE STREETS WEARING MASKS [TO PROTEST] AGAINST THE MURDER OF OUR BROTHERS AND SISTERS."[68] Messages against police brutality are not uncommon among funkeiros in general, especially those who are not mainstream artists.[69] Nevertheless, the overt mention of Black lives, especially by popular funkeiras, is indeed relevant and more common after 2017.

Funkeiras also use social media to affirm their Blackness in general and their Black femininity in particular. Accordingly, many of these social media manifestations from Black funkeiras are gendered; their sense of Blackness seems to be inevitably attached to their gender identities. Beginner MC Rebecca posted a photo of herself wearing braids. In the picture, the MC poses like she is taking a selfie, but we only see the profile of her head and shoulders, with the blurred background image of a mirror reflecting the scene. The description of the photo is an homage to Black hairstyles:

> BRAIDS [black heart emoji]. Afro hairstyles are part of the history of Black people, especially Yoruba people ... braids saved a lot of Black women who were sold as slaves and would hide seeds in their hair to have something to eat. This and other stories are part of the rich culture we created and respecting it is fundamental! Hair is resistance, ancestry; it's culturally important and part of an identity that is embedded in our roots! [black fist and black heart emojis][70]

Linn da Quebrada shared a photo framing the upper part of her chest, her chin, and the tip of her fingers, which hold a thin black rope.[71] A smaller image of Linn in a fetal position works as a pendant for the black rope. The words "és cura" (you're a cure) are written in cursive on her chest. "És cura" is a play with words, as it is also the Portuguese feminine term for dark, "escura." Linn complements the image with a poem:

> Your skin is cure.
> Make your body your lucky charm. Sharp knife on a satin table.
> Deep cup. Lucky charm and not a cane.
> Kill and get killed.
> Kill the white macho colonizer master patroller.
> Kill and die in you,
> And feel it too
> The strength of my ancestors.

MC Xuxú (Figure 3) shared a photo of herself on July 25, 2019, to celebrate the Day of the Afro-Latina and Caribbean Woman.[72] In the picture, MC Xuxú poses with her hands on her face, fingers slightly spread out, curly loose hair covering part of her eyes, with a longer strand touching her nose. MC Xuxú wears a light-brown, long sleeve shirt that blends in with the background, as her facial expression is serious but tender. Although the caption mostly describes the important date, she ends the message with "Long live Tereza de Benguela [quilombola leader]," along with hashtags that pay homage to Black women, such as "#dayoftheblacklatinacaribbeanwoman #blackwomanday #blackwomensjuly." Similarly, MC Carol habitually posts about the struggles and particularities of being Black. She shared a video excerpt from an interview with Linn da Quebrada and her performance partner Jup do Bairro with the following tweet: "Before I knew my gender I was already getting beaten up EVERY DAY at school for being Black."[73] In the video, we see MC Carol saying that the most painful time in her life was in grade school, when she used to be bullied for being Black.

Figure 3: MC Xuxú.
Credit: Marina Costa

Not all funkeiras maintain this level of seriousness in their self-affirming of Blackness. Tati Quebra Barraco often uses humor to underscore her difficult trajectory as an artist. On January 21, 2019, she tweeted, "Being a Black favelada woman who has made it with controversial songs isn't easy, y'all. But I'll keep resisting [black fist emoji]. The hoeness cannot end, I'm made of it [emoji covering mouth]."[74] The funkeira, mentioned early in this chapter to exemplify Lopes' argument that in the 2000s female MCs lacked racial consciousness,[75] now frequently uses Twitter to make all sorts of political statements, including about her Blackness, as far back as 2016. The funkeira seems to know that now there is space to affirm her Blackness instead of trying to dissimulate it. Still, Tati maintains the authentic and humorous style that has made her a successful MC.

Lastly, Black funkeiras perform Blackness by calling out and/or mocking whiteness and white people. This development is especially noteworthy if we consider the revered yet invisible place whiteness has occupied in Brazilian culture. Linn da Quebrada retweeted with comment an image with the caption in English, "Whites forming a barrier between Black protestors and police." In her commentary, Linn expresses how important it is for Black folks that white people become antiracist by coming out of their "supposed universal neutrality."[76] Linn does not usually call out white people in general for their racism. Conversely, she possesses a particularly scornful way to address cismen, especially those who are white, as I show in Chapter Six.

Tati Quebra Barraco and MC Carol perform Blackness in ways that seem more adversarial vis-à-vis whiteness, usually in response to attacks from white folks. In these public interactions, Tati and MC Carol shed light on the racial and gendered dynamics in place by calling out different levels of violence against Black women. On August 28, 2018, Tati tweeted a message challenging the possibility of widespread gun ownership in Brazil that suggested Brazilians would not know how to use a gun. Twitter user Malvino replied, "if we shoot as much as your plastic surgeon works, then I'll be worried."[77] Tati, in turn, responded to this user by copying his profile picture, which clearly shows his face, and commenting the following: "white privilege is having this monkey face and Dumbo ears and being called handsome."[78]

MC Carol also uses a more belligerent and humorous tone in her dealings with white folks. In a tweet in which her feminist identity was once again questioned by a white woman, a constant occurrence in Carol's public life,[79] she says: "Here's what I feel like doing when privileged rich white women say 'I'm a feminist activist but this MC Carol doesn't represent me.'"[80] The tweet is illustrated with a popular cartoon that shows a Black woman covering the mouth of a blonde white woman. Additionally, MC Carol often responds to fatphobic comments by exposing the commenters and mocking their whiteness. On September 17, 2018, Carol published the screenshot of an interaction she had with Instagram user mauro_o_98, who tagged her in a political post with the following message: "Haddad [presidential candidate who ran against Bolsonaro] has more voter rejection than fat women, like @ mccaroldeniteroi in the club." MC Carol's reply was: "Being rejected by a white man with a skinny dick is called luck [wink emoji]."[81]

Funkeira and pop star Ludmilla relies on a much subtler approach, as evidenced by a controversy with former funkeira and international celebrity Anitta. Ludmilla accused Anitta of several misdeeds in a now-deleted emotional video posted to Instagram, including that Anitta did nothing to stop racist attacks made by her fans against Ludmilla.[82] Shortly after this controversy, Ludmilla released the music video for the 150 BPM song "Cobra Venenosa" ("Poisonous Snake").[83] The video showcases a post-apocalyptic world inhabited by mostly Black women. The lyrics to the song spotlight the conflict between two women in which one of them is slippery and untrustworthy. Coincidently or not, the white woman representing this behavior in the video looks very similar to Anitta[84] and, thus, creates a scenario in which Black women are up against the poisonous snake. In a July 3, 2020 tweet, Ludmilla says that she was criticized by feminists for pitting women against each other in "Cobra Venenosa's" lyrics and music video.[85] She provided a lengthy response defying both the interpretation of the music video as well as established concepts around feminine rivalry. Ludmilla says,

The lyrics to the song are, actually, much more about the unity of women. So much so that the character who plays the "poisonous snake" is invited to join the squad. When a woman does something that hurts you, that belittles you or does something you think is wrong, it has to be possible for us to talk about it, to get things sorted out …. it's not because it's another woman that we can't point out their contradictions and mistakes. When men call out other men, we never talk about masculine rivalry. But since as women we're only taught to be rivals, we can only occupy that space. It's important to break with this idea that criticism between women is always the result of feminine rivalry so we can have healthier and more authentic relationships between us …[86]

Based on this statement, the racial and gendered dynamics in the music video have concurrent explanations. First, they indeed seem to point to Ludmilla's personal issues with Anitta, and second, the problematic relationship between the two also suggests that there are larger issues among women, especially related to race. Ludmilla's message clarifying her intentions with the music video subtly addresses white feminist assumptions about "sorority" that disregard differences among women—women must remain united under any circumstances. Funkeiras' diverse modes of shedding light on the pervasive and subtle ways whiteness functions, especially in feminine and feminist contexts, point to a changing racial context that is inevitably impacting the way feminism is publicly discussed.[87] Black funkeiras now openly hold white people accountable, including white feminists.

Funkeiras and the Politicization of Black Femininity

Funkeiras' public relationship to Blackness in general and Black femininity in particular surely is a developing one. I want to be careful here not to provide hasty conclusions about the visible shift in funkeiras' racial performances. Nonetheless, it is possible to highlight a few key takeaways. Black funkeiras from the mid-2000s were doing their best to survive in a context in which their bodies and performances were openly pathologized, as favela funk was under intense government and media scrutiny. It is unsurprising that they did not engage in public performances about race. However, that does not mean funkeiras were not racially conscious. My interviews with MC Dandara and Deize Tigrona suggest that, at least in 2013, they were aware of Brazil's mainstream media's anti-Blackness. Second, questions surrounding funkeiras' status as feminists emerged long before public conversations about race, as chapters two through four suggest.[88] Perhaps this is yet another indication that feminism in Brazil tends to favor gender-first analyses, which function in ways that concurrently erase references to Blackness while normalizing white middle-class femininity. Third and lastly, funkeiras' public performances of Blackness and femininity point to Brazilian Black feminists' assessment of their movement's recent expansion, especially via social media. S. Ribeiro contends that Black youth uses social media to engage in activism and self-expression via aesthetic, as well as to strengthen their collective and individual identities as a diverse, heterogenous group.[89] Weschenfelder and Fabris argue that Black feminists continue to carve out public spaces of discussion and political organization, be them online or in the physical world.[90] This chapter hopefully illustrated the myriad ways in which Black funkeiras affirm their Blackness and perform Black femininity. Accordingly, it would be important for scholars to trace funkeiras' more explicit connections and contributions to this new wave of Brazilian Black feminism.

More than creating a particular favela funk aesthetic, Black funkeiras are helping construct a narrative around race, gender, and class that is both personal and collective. Black feminist Stephanie Ribeiro uses the Black-owned, queer friendly party collective *Batekoo* as an example of a group of young folks whose work goes beyond aesthetic and parties.[91] Similarly, Black funkeiras' embodied politics are a combination of their public visibility and survival, their artistic performances, and the political work with which they engage. As pointed out by S. Ribeiro, more than just surviving and defending their Black femininity, Black women and transfeminine people are able to create public spaces of self-affirmation.[92] These practices happen in tandem with their Black-centered activism. Tati Quebra Barraco became outspoken against Rio's military police violence after her son was murdered by them in 2016. MC Carol ran for office in 2018 with a platform against the criminalization of favela funk and police brutality. As of September 2020, Linn da Quebrada hosts interviews with Black activists and intellectuals on her Instagram and YouTube channel. Deize Tigrona is part of a community initiative in City of God that has been providing food, hygiene products, medicine, and masks to struggling families in the favela during the 2020 coronavirus pandemic. These developments indicate that Black funkeiras' embodied politics are no longer limited to favela funk; instead, these artists engage in Blackness as envisioned by Weschenfelder and Fabris, as "a set of discourses that operate in different frontlines, and that produces regimes of truth and subjectivizing processes."[93] These funkeiras, thus, are helping develop and solidify affirming messages about Blackness in their own process of "becoming Black" women and transfeminine people.[94] In the final chapter of this book, I delve into another relatively recent development in favela funk, namely the emergence of transfeminine artists of color whose powerful performances showcase and strengthen travesti politics.

Notes

1 Adriana Lopes, *Funk-se Quem Quiser: No Batidão Negro da Cidade Carioca* (Rio de Janeiro: Bom Texto, 2011); Raquel Moreira, "'Now that I'm a Whore, Nobody is Holding Me Back!': Women in Favela Funk and Embodied Politics," *Women's Studies in Communication* 40, no. 2 (April 2017): 172–89.

2 Teresa Piñero-Otero and Xabier Martínez-Rolán, "Memes in the Internet Feminist Activism. #ViajoSola as an Example of Transnational Mobilization," *Cuadernos.Info* 39 (2016): 18.

3 Piñero-Otero and Martínez-Rolán, "Memes," 18.

4 Mariza Corrêa, "Do Feminismo aos Estudos de Gênero no Brasil: Um Exemplo Pessoal," *Cadernos Pagu*, 16 (2001): 13–30.

5 Liliane Cambraia Windsor, "Deconstructing Racial Democracy: A Personal Quest to Understand Social Conditioning about Race Relations in Brazil," *Social Identities* 13, no. 4 (July 2007): 495–520.

6 Sérgio Costa, "A Construção Sociológica da Raça no Brasil," *Estudos Afro-Asiáticos* 24, no. 1 (2002): 35–61.

7 Costa, "Construção Sociológica," 43.

8 Márcio M. Aguiar, "A Construção das Hierarquias Sociais: Classe, Raça, Gênero e Etnicidade," *Cadernos de Pesquisa do CDHIS* 36–37, no. 20 (2007): 83–8.

9 Corrêa, "Do Feminismo," 25.

10 Corrêa, "Do Feminismo."

11 Helen Marrow, "To Be or Not To Be (Hispanic or Latino): Brazilian Racial and Ethnic Identity in the United States," *Ethnicities* 3, no. 4 (2003): 441.

12 Costa, "Construção Sociológica"; Marrow, "To Be."

13 Marrow, "To Be," 441.

14 Marrow, "To Be," 428.

15 Stephanie Ribeiro, "Quem Somos: Mulheres Negras no Plural, Nossa Existência é Pedagógica," in *Explosão Feminista: Arte, Cultura, Política e Universidade*, ed. Heloísa Buarque de Hollanda (São Paulo: Companhia das Letras, 2018), 275.

16 Stephanie Nolen, "Brazil Colour Bind," *The Globe and Mail*, July 31, 2015, https://www.theglobeandmail.com/news/world/brazils-colour-bind/article25779474/.

17 Simon Schwartzman, "Fora de Foco: Diversidade e Identidades Étnicas no Brasil," *Novos Estudos CEBRAP* 55, (November 1999): 83–96.

18 Cidinha da Silva, "De Onde Viemos: Aproximações de uma Memória," in *Explosão Feminista: Arte, Cultura, Política e Universidade*, ed. Helosia Buarque de Hollanda (São Paulo: Companhia das Letras, 2018), 252–60.

19 da Silva, "De Onde Viemos."

20 S. Ribeiro, "Quem Somos."

21 S. Ribeiro, "Quem Somos," 273.

22 Daniel Silveira, "Em Sete Anos, Aumenta em 32% a População que se Declara Preta no Brasil," *G1*, May 22, 2019, https://g1.globo.com/economia/noticia/2019/05/22/em-sete-anos-aumenta-em-32percent-a-populacao-que-se-declara-preta-no-brasil.ghtml.

23 Helena Martins, "Após dois anos da marcha, mulheres negras continuam mobilizadas contra racism," *Agência Brasil*, November 18, 2017, https://agenciabrasil.ebc.com.br/direitos-humanos/noticia/2017-11/apos-dois-anos-da-marcha-mulheres-negras-continuam-mobilizadas-contra-racismo.

24 S. Ribeiro, "Quem Somos."

25 S. Ribeiro, "Quem Somos," 265.

26 Viviane Inês Weschenfelder and Elí Terezinha H. Fabris, "Becoming Black Woman: Self-Writing in an Intersectional Place," *Revista Estudos Feministas* 27, no. 3 (2019): 4.

27 S. Ribeiro, "Quem Somos."

28 S. Ribeiro, "Quem Somos," 273.

29 S. Ribeiro, "Quem Somos," 273.

30 Lopes, *Funk-se*.

31 Lopes, *Funk-se*.

32 Liliane C. Windsor, "Deconstructing Racial Democracy: A Personal Quest to Understand Social Conditioning About Race Relations in Brazil," *Social Identities* 13, no. 4 (2007): 495–520.

33 Lopes, *Funk-se*.

34 Lopes, *Funk-se*.

35 Lopes, *Funk-se*, 186.

36 Tatiana Amin, "Tati Quebra Barraco Agita Festival na Argentina," *O Fuxico*, November 21, 2006, https://www.ofuxico.com.br/noticias-sobre-famosos/tati-quebra-barraco-agita-festival-na-argentina/2006/11/21-53983.html.

37 Lopes, *Funk-se*, 189.

38 Patrícia de Santana Pinho, *Reinvenções da África na Bahia* (São Paulo: Annablume, 2004), 117.

39 Lopes, *Funk-se*; Moreira, "Women in Favela Funk."

40 Lopes, *Funk-se*.

41 Raquel Moreira, "Bitches Unleashed: Women in Rio's Funk Movement, Performances of Heterosexual Femininity, and Possibilities of Resistance" (PhD diss., University of Denver, 2014).

42 S. Ribeiro, "Quem Somos."

43 Lucas Pasin, "MC Carol Relembra Participação no Lollapalooza: 'Choro ao Ver Vídeos,'" *Ego*, March 16, 2016, http://ego.globo.com/lollapalooza/2016/noticia/2016/03/mc-carol-relembra-participacao-no-lollapalooza-choro-ao-ver-videos.html.

44 MC Carol Oficial, "MC Carol & Karol Conka—100% Feminista (prod. Leo Justi & Tropkillaz)," October 7, 2016, YouTube video, 3:19, https://www.youtube.com/watch?v=W05v0B59K5s.

45 Djamilla Ribeiro, *Quem Tem Medo do Feminism Negro?* (São Paulo: Companhia das Letras, 2018); S. Ribeiro, "Quem Somos."

46 Paula A. Idoeta, "Atlas da Violência: Brasil Tem 13 Homicídios de Mulheres por Dia, e Maioria das Vítimas é Negra," *BBC Brazil*, June 5, 2019, https://www.bbc.com/portuguese/brasil-48521901.

47 Funk Mídia, "MC Carol—Não foi Cabral," July 3, 2015, YouTube video, 3:17, https://www.youtube.com/watch?v=XchG_QRQ6Rc.

48 MC Xuxú, "Mc Xuxú—Meus Desapegos (Clipe Oficial)," May 14, 2019, YouTube video, 3:36, https://www.youtube.com/watch?v=Z2hQJ9QM08A.

49 Linn da Quebrada, "Mc Linn da Quebrada—Bixa Preta," September 30, 2016, YouTube video, 4:28, https://www.youtube.com/watch?v=ZeMa942nYe4.

50 Heavy Baile, "Heavy Baile—BERRO (feat. Tati Quebra Barraco e Lia Clark)," December 1, 2017, YouTube video, 3:30, https://www.youtube.com/watch?v=NzILPU8PG2s.

51 Lopes, *Funk-se.*

52 Linn da Quebrada, "[LIVE] Linn da Quebrada e Djamila Ribeiro: O que Vem Depois da Ocupação?" June 30, 2020, YouTube video, 1:19:39, https://www.youtube.com/watch?v=tYI4ZxZRGYc.

53 Kevin M. Leander, "Toward a Connective Ethnography of Online/Offline Literacy Networks," in *Handbook of Research on New Literacies*, eds. Julie Coiro et al. (New York: Routledge, 2010).

54 Ernesto Londoño, "A Year After Her Killing, Marielle Franco Has Become a Rallying Cry in a Polarized Brazil," *The New York Times*, March 14, 2019, https://www.nytimes.com/2019/03/14/world/americas/marielle-year-death.html.

55 Anna Virgínia Balloussier, "Família de Marielle Reivindica Legado e Bissexualidade da Vereadora," *Folha de Pernambuco*, July 1, 2019, https://www.folhape.com.br/noticias/familia-de-marielle-reivindica-legado-e-bissexualidade-da-vereadora/109281/.

56 Londoño, "A Year After."

57 Dom Philips, "Protests Held Across Brazil After Rio Councillor Shot Dead," *The Guardian*, March 15, 2018, https://www.theguardian.com/world/2018/mar/15/marielle-franco-shot-dead-targeted-killing-rio.

58 MC Carol (@mccaroldeniteroioficial), "Estou buscando palavras, pq eu só sinto ódio, só sinto raiva e mt medo, realmente, eu nao sei o que falar, mas do que nunca ...," Instagram photo, March 15, 2018, https://www.instagram.com/p/BgVR76Hgy1A/.

59 MC Carol (@mccaroldeniteroioficial), "Photo of graffiti on a wall," Instagram photo, March 15, 2018, https://www.instagram.com/p/BgW6FSKAgk8/?igshid=3hmxwcdb391y.

60 Londoño, "A Year After."

61 Linn da Quebrada (@linndaquebrada), "Baseado em carne viva e fatos reais, é o sangue dos meus que escorre pelas marginais ...," Instagram photo, March 15, 2018, https://www.instagram.com/p/BgV1izBHArm/?igshid=pebho31qs3l1.

62 MC Xuxú (@mcxuxu), "Olha pra ela, o brilho da senzala," Instagram photo, March 15, 2018, https://www.instagram.com/p/BgWU5WSHh6S/?igshid=1sh87v6ahekgk.

63 Tati Quebra Barraco (@TatiQBOficial), "Marielle Presente!!!!" Twitter, June 8, 2018, 8:46 a.m., https://twitter.com/TatiQBOficial/status/1005083604630810624.

64 Valesca Popozuda (@valescapopozuda), "Hoje o meu bom dia, não vem nada bom, #QuemMatouMarielleFranco Não vamos nos calar, não vão nos calar," Instagram photo, March 15, 2018, https://www.instagram.com/p/BgWFTx4nUcs/?igshid=r7qp6t270h2n.

65 MC Carol (@mc_caroloficial), "morto com um tiro na cabeça, o nome dele era Zé ele tinha 13 anos, ele era empacotador de mercado, estava descendo o morro e mataram ele, a cor do Zé era negra ...," Twitter, February 16, 2019, 9:21 p.m., https://twitter.com/mc_caroloficial/status/1096972904481411075.

66 Tati Quebra Barraco (@TatiQBOficial), "A pm tirou um pedaço de mim que jamais será preenchido A pm matou o meu filho Essa dor nunca irá se cicatrizar," Twitter, December 10, 2016, 10:40 p.m., https://twitter.com/TatiQBOficial/status/807807225012121600.

67 Tati Quebra Barraco (@TatiQBOficial), "Discutir com pm é a maior causa de morte natural no RJ mesmo," Twitter, October 31, 2017, 7:21 p.m., https://twitter.com/TatiQBOficial/status/925518000459059200.

68 Deize Tigrona (@deizetigrona), "Quem não luta está morto. Hoje mesmo com essa quarentena vai ter um ato pela vida. #paremdenosmatar #vidasnegrasimportam," Instagram photo, May 31, 2020, https://www.instagram.com/p/CA24E9Rn1L6/.

69 Adriana Facina, "'Não Me Bate Doutor': Funk e Criminalização da Pobreza," *Encontro de Estudos Multidisciplinares em Cultura*, Salvador, May 27–29, 2009; Lopes, *Funk-se*.

70 MC Rebecca (@mcrebecca), "TRANÇAS♥ Penteados afros fazem parte da história do povo negro, e o nagô é um deles," Instagram photo, July 3, 2020, https://www.instagram.com/p/CCMmW8bp6UR/.

71 Linn da Quebrada (@linndaquebrada), "tua pele és cura. faça de seu corpo seu patu á. faca amolada em mesa de cetim. corte profundo. amuleto & n ão muleta. mate & morra," Instagram photo, July 2, 2020, https://www.instagram.com/p/CCKE39MlaPz/.

72 MC Xuxú (@mcxuxu), "25 de julho, dia da Mulher Afro-Latina-Americana e Caribenha, uma data extremamente significativa para nós. Salve Tereza de Benguela!" Instagram photo, July 25, 2019, https://www.instagram.com/p/B0WuOFJllwR/?igshid=3di9zkbcikzt.

73 MC Carol (@mc_carolofficial), "Antes de eu saber meu gênero eu já apanhava DIARIAMENTE na escola por ser preta," Twitter, April 26, 2020, 12:10 a.m., https://twitter.com/mc_caroloficial/status/1254276615120605184.

74 Tati Quebra Barraco (@TatiQBOficial), "Ser mulher preta e favelada que venceu na vida através de músicas polêmicas não é fácil gente. Mas sigo resistindo. A putaria não pode acabar, fui feita dela," Twitter, January 21, 2019, 8:18 p.m., https://twitter.com/TatiQBOficial/status/1087535005797101568.

75 Lopes, *Funk-se.*

76 Linn da Quebrada (@linndaquebrada), "uma das coisas q mais tem me chamado atenção nesses protestos sobre o caso d Georg Floyd é o posicionamento da popu-lação branca, saindo da suposta neutralidade universal. isso eh mto importante e fundamental. principalmente pra nós. e pra aquelas aqui q se dizem anti-racistas," Twitter, May 29, 2020, 9:04 a.m., https://twitter.com/linndaquebrada/status/1266369778031013890.

77 Malvino (@MalvinoIgor), "Se a gente atirar igual teu cirurgião plástico trabalha aí eu fico preocupado," Twitter, August 28, 2018, 11:06 a.m., https://twitter.com/MalvinoIgor/status/1034472222373629953.

78 Tati Quebra Barraco (@TatiQBOficial), "Privilégio branco é ter essa cara de mico e orelha de dumbo e ser chamado de lindo," Twitter, August 28, 2018, 2:32 p.m., https://twitter.com/TatiQBOficial/status/1034524050993938433.

79 Rodrigo Soares, "Com Visões Políticas Distintas, MC Carol e Antonia Fontenelle Trocam Farpa," *UOL Famosos*, October 1, 2018, https://tvefamosos.uol.com.br/noticias/redacao/2018/10/01/com-visoes-politicas-distintas-mc-carol-e-antonia-fontenelle-trocam-farpas.htm?cmpid=copiaecola.

80 MC Carol (@mc_caroloficial), "O que da vontade de fazer quando uma mulher branca rica privilegiada diz: 'Sou feminista MILITANTE mais essa Mc Carol não me representa,'" Twitter, April 23, 2019, 5:57 p.m., https://twitter.com/mc_caroloficial/status/1120823980875833345.

81 MC Carol (@mccaroldeniteroioficial), "Alo mulheres gorda de pernão bundao … APRENDAM, não é você! É ELE! A maioria que rejeita é porque não tem pau.

É mta areia pro caminhãozinho deles, é sério ... Deus me livre de pau branco pequeno e fino," Instagram photo, September 17, 2018, https://www.instagram. com/p/Bn0OdtAnqfI/?igshid=d4ltolns6q5g.

82 "Anitta Se Pronuncia Sobre Racismo Após Ataques Contra Ludmilla: 'A Justiça Vai atrás de Você,'" *Extoína*, June 17, 2020, https://exitoina.uol.com.br/noticias/famo-sos/anitta-se-pronuncia-sobre-racismo-apos-ataques-contra-ludmilla-justica-vai-atras-de-voce.phtml.

83 Ludmilla, "Ludmilla—Cobra Venenosa feat. DJ Will 22 (Official Music Video)," July 3, 2020, YouTube video, 2:44, https://www.youtube.com/watch?v=H9OCyYPQ7J8.

84 Leonardo Ribeiro and Ricardo Rigel, "Atriz em Clipe 'Cobra venenosa' de Ludmilla Já foi Apontada Como Sósia de Anitta," *Extra*, July 3, 2020, https://extra.globo.com/ tv-e-lazer/atriz-em-clipe-cobra-venenosa-de-ludmilla-ja-foi-apontada-como-sosia-de-anitta-24513824.html.

85 Ludmilla (@Ludmilla), "É sobre isso," Twitter, July 3, 2020, 8:24 p.m., https://twit-ter.com/Ludmilla/status/1279224569098878976.

86 Ludmilla, "É sobre isso."

87 D. Ribeiro, *Quem Tem*.

88 Nelito Fernandes and Alice Granato, "Mulherada de Respeito," *Revista Época*, January 16, 2006, http://revistaepoca.globo.com/Revista/Epoca/0,,EDR72874-6011,00.html; Kate Lyra, "Eu Não Sou Cachorra Não. Não? Voz e Silêncio na Construção da Identidade Feminina no *Rap* e no *Funk* no Rio de Janeiro," in *Comunicação, Consumo e Espaço Urbano: Novas Sensibilidades nas Culturas Jovens*, eds. Everardo Rocha et al. (Rio de Janeiro: Mauad, 2006), 175–95.

89 S. Ribeiro, "Quem Somos."

90 Weschenfelder and Fabris, "Becoming Black Woman."

91 S. Ribeiro, "Quem Somos."

92 S. Ribeiro, "Quem Somos."

93 Weschenfelder and Fabris, "Becoming Black Woman," 3.

94 Weschenfelder and Fabris, "Becoming Black Woman."

Chapter Six

"Sit Down and Observe Your Own Destruction, Macho!": Travesti Performances in Favela Funk

Is Travesti Queer?

Perhaps, at this point, it has become apparent that I avoid using the term "queer" in my description of gender nonconforming performances in favela funk. There are a few important reasons for doing so. First and foremost, as Ochoa notes, queer is a category local to the U.S. that has traveled a great deal because of the "theoretical hegemony that allows for the publication and circulation of American texts around the world."[1] Scholars writing in different settings must be careful, as queer "does not have the same resonance" everywhere it goes.[2] Additionally, as Eng, Halberstam, and Muñoz contend, the supremacy of U.S.-based scholarship reproduces dynamics that go beyond academia, in which meanings of queerness, and gender and sexuality categories more broadly, are subsumed by "U.S. nationalist identity and political agenda globally."[3] My work is committed precisely to undoing Western-centric readings of transgressive performances from women and transfeminine people of color, and a careless use of "queer" could inadvertently reinforce these tendencies.

Queer theory has been accused of failing "to address culturally specific texts of knowledge(s) embedded in the material realities of non-White American middle-class LGBTQ people."[4] Moreover, queer theory's focus on "selfhood, individual agency, and experience"[5] comes at the expense of recognizing the impact class, race, citizenship, and more has on individual identity while simultaneously failing to acknowledge the importance of culture, community, relationships, and collective resistance so vital for the survival of LGBTQIA+ people of color.[6] Relatedly, Cohen warns scholars of the problematic propensity to use queer in opposition to heterosexuality, which mistakenly reproduces the binaries it is intended to combat—that of queerness *versus* everything else.[7] This view disregards the intricacies and distinctions of people of color's personal and communal experiences with gender and sexuality.

Scholars of color have made important efforts to remedy the shortcomings of a white-washed version of queer theory. They have proposed "quare"[8] and "kauer"[9] analyses, both of which challenge prevalent Western, white, middle-class takes on queerness. These rearticulations of queerness more accurately encompass the ways in which gender identity and sexuality intersect with race, class, citizenship status, and ability. According to Yep, queerness, when functioning intersectionally, uncovers contingent "systems of body normativity."[10] Disidentificatory practices by queer people of color in transnational contexts, in many ways, led to critiques and challenges to queer theory. The ways in which queerness has been reimagined are in line with, and expand upon, Muñoz's disidentifications project, in that they attend to classed, raced, ableist, and other systems of oppression queer folks of color navigate in transnational contexts.[11] Although I avoid labeling the artists "queer" in this chapter, I nonetheless rely on some versions of queerness and queer theory that consider issues of race and class.

While scholarship focusing on queerness, especially Muñoz's disidentifications, is fundamental for elucidating the culturally located and possibly powerful ways in which funkeiras' performances operate, labeling the artists "queer" seems counterproductive for a couple of reasons. First, the funkeiras in this chapter either directly or indirectly embrace the travesti label. Second, travesti is a historically situated, contingent term that evades Western categorizations of gender and sexuality, with strong racialized and classed connotations. Hence, there is no reason to refer to funkeiras as queer when they do not identify as such. The same is true for other terms these funkeiras use, such as *viado* and *bicha*, which can be loosely translated as "queer" and "fag," respectively. *Viado* seems to be more connected to sexuality while *bicha* relates to effeminate gender performances.[12] Translating them all as "queer" would erase the cultural nuances attached to these words. Third, previous research on trans and travesti identities was largely conducted by cisgender people, many of whom were Western scholars and most of whom imposed their Western lenses on their subjects' experiences. As a result, many of these studies were committed to "uncovering" how certain practices and bodies fit binary categories of gender and/or sexuality familiar to Western academia.[13]

In this chapter, I turn my attention to the performances of three Black funkeiras who embody different iterations of travesti identity. Each artist performs according to and/or beyond the limitations and possibilities favela funk and Brazil at large allows. Through a critical cultural analysis of mediated performances, along with funkeiras' personal and media interviews, I start with dancer Lacraia, who rose to fame in 2002 and who never explicitly identified as travesti—though her practices and media interviews suggest a subjugated, de-historicized travesti identity. Next, I move on to MC Xuxú, a funkeira whose performances combine personal and collective narratives of current travesti struggles. Finally, I end with Linn da Quebrada, an artist who materializes her visions of travesti futurity in her performances. Using favela funk's aggressive performative style, these funkeiras destabilize cisnormative white femininity while re-centering performances of racialized travesti femininity. This chapter utilizes theories of queerness, but it mostly spotlights the peculiarities of travesti subjectivities in an effort to decolonize Western cisnormative, and perhaps even queer, conceptualizations of sex, gender, race, and class.[14] Although I hope to demonstrate that the multiple iterations of travesti identity function as means of survival and beyond, the analysis of each performer's idiosyncrasies paints a more complete picture of the challenges and possibilities of travesti identity within and outside favela funk.

Stuck in the Present: Lacraia's Fabulousness and the Burden of Liveness

"I think [she] would've been happier today," said Lacraia's mother on the fourth anniversary of the dancer's death.[15] In 2002 and 2003, Black dancer Lacraia (Centipede) and her performance partner, MC Serginho, were among the most popular favela funk acts in Brazil.[16] MC Serginho sang hits like "Eguinha Pocotó" ("Pocotó Little Mare") and "Vai, Lacraia!" ("Go, Lacraia!") to the beats of the Miami bass, while Lacraia energetically danced to the tunes. As a favela funk act, having a Black transfeminine artist on stage was indeed a novelty. Lacraia recognized the importance of her presence on national TV in an interview with Lopes:

> Lacraia is a figure that inspires respect, that Serginho and I created together. Before her, the guys in the bondes would say, "go, fucking fag, go." Now, they respect my art and say, "go, Lacraia, go." I was a hair stylist, make-up artist, drag queen, but now I'm Lacraia. I know there's still a lot of discrimination, but I consider Lacraia a milestone in Brazilian TV: a gay, Black, poor [person] that … has better moves than a lot of [cis]women out there.[17]

Based on her interviews and on reporting at the time of her death on May 5, 2011, Lacraia's identification seems ambiguous. To Lopes, she defined herself as an "almost woman" while also self-describing as "gay."[18] While Serginho only referred to Lacraia in the feminine,[19] he also said that having her on stage was a shock at first "because nobody had the courage to put an openly homosexual person on stage."[20] Now, however, Lacraia seems to be more accurately remembered as a Black travesti.[21] The diverse and contradictory ways Lacraia identified are more of a testament to the limitations of language and colonial heteronormative categories of gender and sexuality than a result of any kind of gender and sexuality "confusion" on her part.

Lacraia's ambiguity appears to reflect the scholarly path to try to understand travesti identity. Some scholars link this identification more to sexuality than to gender. Garcia,[22] for instance, partially agrees with Kulick's assessment that travestis "desire to embody homosexuality."[23] Garcia, however, understands travesti identity as patchwork or as a series of complex, at times contradictory, performances of traditional and peripheral femininities and masculinities, which include sexual practices.[24] Studies focusing on "homosexuality" in Brazil also suggest that the travesti identification should not be used cross-culturally in uncritical manners—as a Western classification of sexual deviance—since Brazil has a culturally specific system of sexual practices and relationships.[25] Because these categories are contingent upon cultural meanings that Western scholars at times miss, it is not uncommon for travestis to be perceived as "gays who cross-dress" with the understanding that it is their sexuality that determines their gender expression.[26] These assessments, as Vartabedian argues and with which I agree, remove the idiosyncrasies of travesti identity[27] while also reinforcing colonial, heteronormative understandings of gender and sexuality.[28] There is great social stigma associated with travesti existence,[29] which may have discouraged someone like Lacraia to openly identify with the term at the time. My intention, however, is not to impose an identity on this artist. Rather, the analysis below assumes Lacraia's complexity through her stage performances, her own words, and the comments of others who were close to her. Additionally, I refer to Lacraia in the feminine because that was the artist's and her partner's choice of pronouns when referring to the stage persona.

There was certainly something distinct about MC Serginho and Lacraia's act. Unlike other favela funk dancers (usually brown and Black ciswomen) who tend to stay in the corners or the back of the stage during performances, MC Serginho and Lacraia truly shared the spotlight. In a 2004 performance at the musical festival Nokia Trends, the pair performed with famous favela funk DJ Marlboro.[30] MC Serginho performs a medley of his own songs along with other popular favela funk tunes from the early 2000s. Lacraia is seen moving around the stage, mixing choreographed arm and hip moves with favela funk's signature twerking. She wears a tight, zip-up, black top with neon yellow edges and collar and black tights with a short neon yellow skirt over it that accentuates her slender but muscular dark brown body. Hoops adorn her ears, and a newsboy-style black cap covers her head. At multiple points in the performance, it is as though Lacraia is the star of the show. She maintains a steady smile throughout the performance, and when she is in the center of the stage, MC Serginho moves to the side and sings to her.

Lacraia's display of femininity is often over-the-top and vibrant. This is not unusual among travestis who perform. Indeed, Brazil has a history of travesti shows.[31] Based on Ochoa's argument of travestis' agentic move to "become fabulous" in order to negotiate their transgressive existence,[32] Soliva poses that Brazilian travesti performers engage in "glamorous practices"[33] in order to survive. These practices are associated with a particular type of femininity that tends to make travestis more legible to cisheteronormative culture. However, Lacraia does not fully align with these historical roles of "professional travesti" performers.[34] That is because professional travestis usually possess other physical markers of traditional femininity, such as long hair, breast implants, and light skin, that Lacraia did not have.

Normative race and gender are parodied in MC Serginho and Lacraia's song "Caetano Disse Não" ("Caetano Said No"). The lyrics are a version of another popular favela funk tune, MC Sapão's "Eu Tô Tranquilão" ("I'm Chill"). In MC Serginho's song, he tells the story of a hot girl—represented by popular white, blonde, blue-eyed Brazilian actress and model Luana Piovani—who is asking for a song. As MC Serginho reveals that the woman in the song is Luana Piovani, the audience instead sees Lacraia presenting herself on stage and claiming to be the famous white actress.[35] To Lopes, Lacraia "seems to obscure race and gender signifiers, causing a mix of discomfort, curiosity, and fascination in the audience. Lacraia cites these race and gender standards in order to subvert them, in that she claims them to herself."[36]

The atmosphere of playfulness around Lacraia's performances can take vicious turns. MC Serginho shares in an interview that the pair used to enact a game on stage in which he would offer 50 reais to an audience member who volunteered to French kiss Lacraia.[37] The dancer seemed to be fine with the arrangement. So much so that she mentions in the interview with Lopes that she is "a gay who is popular on TV, before any other homosexual showed up in a soap opera. By the way, what can't be done in the soap opera can be done on stage: the French kiss."[38] Lacraia is referencing the fact that at the time, soap operas would usually cut same-gender kissing scenes. MC Serginho reports pushing cismen off the stage for refusing to smooch the dancer.[39] In his interpretation of it, he was caring and protective of Lacraia.

The "kissing Lacraia" game became a consistent expectation of her live TV appearances. However, unlike stage performances in which Lacraia and Serginho had ownership over the script and some control over the situation, on live TV, Lacraia was often presented as the laughingstock of the audience and other guests. Coelho recalls a time in which Lacraia played the bride in a mock wedding at *Programa da Eliana* (Eliana's Show): "The groom refused to repeat the words of the 'priest' ('faithful wife') and did not kiss her at the end of the ceremony. This was supposedly the 'funny' part about the sketch."[40] Later in 2009, Lacraia was once again a guest in *Programa da Eliana*, and this time, she participated in a segment called "Opposites Attract."[41] Lacraia is paired with her assumed "opposite," a hypermasculine, muscular white man, with whom the dancer became friends as a result of her participation in the show. The whole segment boils down to the host, other guests, and the audience mocking Lacraia's "opposite" for claiming he gets along with her. The host asks if they should kiss, to which the man refuses. At some point, one of the male guests stands next to Lacraia and, putting his hands on her stomach, tells the man's father who was sitting in the audience: "sir, you don't know: you're going to become a grandfather." The whole room bursts into laughter while Lacraia stands there with an uncomfortable smile on her face. In another instance, Lacraia is invited to Rodrigo Faro's TV show, *Hora do Faro* (Faro's Time).[42] The host, who is a white man, is known for dressing up as his guests. Faro wore blackface in his impersonation of Lacraia for this episode. More than ridiculing Lacraia's performance of femininity by tripping over high heels and stating "don't laugh at me, I'm a family man," Faro is also deriding her Blackness by making it part of his costume. Lacraia seemed fine with the "joke."

Becoming the first Black travesti performer to achieve national popularity as a favela funk dancer came at a high price for Lacraia. Favela funk can be both inviting and exclusionary to LGBTQIA+ folks, especially travestis.[43] MC Serginho claims that they were taken in by DJs and other artists in the movement,[44] but Lacraia was very aware of the prejudice against her, especially pre-fame.[45] The country at large, however, was/is generally hostile to travestis, though they also elide fascination. To Ochoa, "society violently imposes itself" on the bodies and existences of travestis in order to "demarcate gender territory."[46] This establishment of boundaries results in their "social, economic, legal, political, and interpersonal exclusion."[47] Since travestis evade clear, heteronormative categories of gender and sexuality, their presence is met with disparate reactions:

> One of the most striking dimensions of the Brazilian preoccupation with travestis is that despite the habitual presence of travestis in both what we might see as the "high" contexts of popular culture and the "low" contexts of seeing them on city streets and in the crime pages of the local newspaper (frequently in lurid close-ups as murdered corpses), there appears to be no clear consensus about what exactly travestis are.[48]

Lacraia's performative fabulousness as a strategy of survival has possibly led to what Muñoz terms "burden of liveness."[49] In this work, I have been highlighting the political power of performances, but performances alone, in their pure corporeality, cannot undo subjugation. Muñoz clarifies that performances' liveness can become an affliction for marginalized folks.[50] The "burden of liveness" comes from the fact that "the minoritarian subject is always encouraged to perform, *especially* when human and civil rights disintegrate."[51] Muñoz relates the "burden of liveness" to late capitalism's limited possibilities for the racialized working-class, especially women and transfeminine folks, who are in turn pushed into performing for the amusement of majoritarian groups.[52] Travestis are excluded from the labor market in Brazil, with around 90% of them depending on sex work to survive.[53] This, in turn, makes them more susceptible to poverty, discrimination, and violence.[54] There are urgent and material reasons for someone like Lacraia—a Black travesti from one of Rio's favelas—to perform: survival.

The live TV examples from the previous paragraphs support Muñoz's point that "not all performances are liberatory or transformative."[55] Lacraia's existence was reduced to those moments of entertainment— very little was known about her other than what live shows and live TV presented.[56] This role of the Other as entertainer of dominant groups "affords the minoritarian subject an extremely circumscribed temporality,"[57] that of the "the live" only, which ultimately denies the marginalized performer a history or a sense of futurity: "If the subject can only exist in *the moment*, she or he does not have the privilege or the pleasure of being a historical subject."[58] That way, Lacraia's temporality was limited to an ahistorical, depoliticized present. As a result, she was exploited and dehumanized.

In 2015, Lacraia's mother gave *Ego* an interview in which she states that the dancer "wasn't happy," despite being regularly represented as a joyful person.[59] At home, Lacraia was quiet and introspective, which her mom attributed to the dancer's need to find peace in a frantic routine. The constant prejudice to which Lacraia was subjected contributed to her sadness.[60] In 2011, Lacraia died of some kind of chronic illness that was not revealed by her family—some reports speculated that she died of pneumonia while others suggested she had tuberculosis.[61] To Vieira, trans people face a double bind by being both invisible and hypervisible. This paradox is expressed through a "lack of imagination" or an "excess of imagination in the form of stigmas."[62] Either way, the result is erasure and depreciation of "the concrete existence of trans people in society."[63] Lacraia's subjectivity was confined to a perpetual present in which she was constantly under the spotlight, while the depth and complexity of her existence and struggles were erased. The fact that Lacraia's mother believes she would be happier today connects to the next theme of this chapter: travestis' ability to disidentify from the toxic ways the label functions in normative discourses.

Performance, Disidentification, and New Travesti Subjectivities

Disidentification is a practice in which subjects "tactically and simultaneously work on, with, and against a cultural form."[64] In their revisiting of Muñoz's work, Eguchi and Asante pose that "a theory of disidentifications is a process of highlighting the *material* realities produced by the hegemonic ideology that work for and/or against minoritarian subjects" (emphasis in original).[65] The process of disidentification is not one of selecting what to keep or take out of normative identification.

Instead, disidentification is a third option to the binary identification/ counteridentification that allows marginalized folks to rearrange their selves within and against oppressive systems. It postulates "ways to look at, critique, and shift embodied performances of minoritarian identities and subjectivities that reveal nuanced forms of neither assim- ilation nor resistance."[66] Subjects who disidentify, thus, labor to admin- ister an identity that has been degraded in dominant discourses. To Muñoz, "This management is a critical negotiation in which a subject who has been hailed by injurious speech, a name, or a label, reterrito- rializes that speech act and the marking that such speech produces to a self."[67] Disidentification works similarly to transgression in that both propose that identities be enacted not as pure subscription to or denial of normativity but as a way to work against *and* within the status quo.

Disidentification defies traditional notions of identification that prioritize metaphorical processes, which in turn translates embodied events into tidy systems of symbols and identities—translations that are detrimental to marginalized people. The artists whose perfor- mances Muñoz investigates experience identity in rather ambiguous, fractured ways. Hence, conventional forms of dealing with identity, identification, and representation would likely undermine the politi- cal potential their performances might have. In disidentificatory per- formances, Muñoz sees possibilities for cultural transformation from within, "always laboring to enact permanent structural change while at the same time valuing the importance of local or everyday struggles of resistance."[68] Disidentification allows subjects to dispute the interpella- tion process put forth by hegemonic ideologies.

Although Muñoz's work[69] is valuable for the analysis of travesti per- formers in favela funk, it evokes a particular meaning of queer that is culturally specific to the U.S. context. Accordingly, I want to be mind- ful not to replicate Global North/Global South dynamics that assume that marginalized folks in the South exist solely as case studies (and not as producers of knowledge) for theories formulated in the North. Brazilian trans scholar Vergueiro effectively argues that "scientific colo- nialities negatively impact gender perspectives that are different, more complex, than the Eurocentric models that guide the construction of knowledge about gender identities [...] It is necessary to decolonize, intersectionally, the diversity of bodies and of gender identities."[70] What remains of this chapter is the result of the thoughtful reverberation of these funkeiras' voices. Indeed, both MC Xuxú and Linn da Quebrada are producers of knowledge. Their experiences, performances, and perspectives contest controlling iterations of travesti identity as they simultaneously re-envision the meanings of travesti.

MC Xuxú and Linn da Quebrada use favela funk to engage in disidentification by embodying established categories in Brazilian sexual culture (such as femininity, masculinity, *travesti, viado,* and *bicha*) in order to reframe the meanings they exude and the material consequences these terms have on the lives of travestis of color. Muñoz asserts that "to perform queerness is to disidentify, to constantly find oneself thriving on sites where meaning does not properly 'line up.' "[71] These funkeiras' performances function as a way to make discursive sense of their own bodies and of those in their community by way of simultaneously challenging discourses about the duality and stability of hetero- and cisnormativity,[72] as well as racism, sexism, and classism. Even though MC Xuxú and Linn da Quebrada both engage in disidentificatory practices, they do so in idiosyncratic, particular ways that reveal distinct outcomes. MC Xuxú fashions travesti identity by relying on personal and collective subjectivities. Her performances highlight current travesti relationships, practices, and struggles. Differently, Linn da Quebrada's performances suggest a utopian vision of travesti, a worldmaking that uses present-time performances to foresee a travesti-centric future.

MC Xuxú and the Politicized Travesti Identity

"Auntie, do you prefer the one who commits to you or the one who pays for you?/Both! One to pay me and another one to make me happy!"[73] In "Kit Assume" ("Commit Kit"), transfeminine funkeiras MC Xuxú and featured guest Mulher Pepita narrate the types of romantic and sexual relationships in the lives of travestis over tamborzão beats. MC Xuxú often performs about the pains, joys, and current reality of travestis in Brazil. Unlike Lacraia, who was stuck in the present in a manner that stripped her existence and performances off the historical and political struggles her presence represented, MC Xuxú embodies a disidentificatory travesti subjectivity that grants her more agentic power. She disidentifies from mainstream discourses about travestis, be them about the "professional" travesti who is usually white and depoliticized or the dehumanized, othered travesti often present in crime news pages. Rather, MC Xuxú's embodiment of travesti subjectivity is multidimensional. It is evident in both speaking with her and through listening to her songs and watching her music videos that her subjectivity is proudly traversed and shaped by her Black, travesti, and *favelada* identities.

MC Xuxú often take turns speaking in both singular and plural forms of the first person during our June 2020 interview. These changes in position move seamlessly as she tells me her life story over WhatsApp video chat, which indicates an existence that is both idiosyncratic and collective. Contrary to Lacraia's experiences with male funk bondes who would deride her before she became famous, MC Xuxú tells me that it was precisely at a male bonde baile that she was invited to dance on stage:

> Have you heard of a bonde called Ousados (Bold Boys)? I went to one of their performances in the very beginning of my transition; then their lead MC invited me to dance on stage. I was treated so well, and I was so confused! Because I was obviously a trans person in the very beginning of her transition .... I now have passability [the ability to appear cisgender], but I was definitely not passible then. So I got super excited, you know?!

She tells me, as she fixes her curly brown hair, that that was enough to lure her into favela funk, along with another pragmatic reason: favela funk is popular, especially in comparison to her other preferred genre— rap. When I ask her why so many travestis have chosen favela funk, she says with a penetrating conviction, "because funk has a force from the hood, like, the message will be delivered. Because funk is straightforward and it takes no turns. That way, it's easier to penetrate ears, hearts, and diverse spaces." The warm welcome MC Xuxú received from Ousados was a reality in her everyday life while residing in Rio das Pedras, a militia-controlled favela on the west side of Rio that hosted one of the most popular bailes in the city in the 2000s: "When I went to Rio, I saw how the *bichas* [fags, transfeminine people] were treated in the bailes. I felt respected there more so than here, though I wasn't very involved with funk in Juiz de Fora [her hometown and place she currently resides in the state of Minas Gerais]." The reputation that Rio das Pedras is a safe haven for travestis and other transfeminine people exists beyond MC Xuxú's testimonial. In the documentary *Favela Gay*, LGBTQIA+ folks report that Rio das Pedras is indeed a welcoming place.[74] In addition to feeling welcomed, MC Xuxú tells me that Lacraia and Garota X—both travestis she mentioned a few times during our interview—were artists who served as favela funk examples that she could emulate.

MC Xuxú's music videos function as extensions of these particular and communal existences I hear in her interviewing voice. The video for "Eu Fiz a Chuca"* ("I Douched")[75] is an interesting mixture of a risqué and candid representation of a travesti practice and wholesome content. As it opens, a naked MC Xuxú sits on a toilet with arms covering her breasts and hands holding the sides of her face. Her bright-blue yarn dreadlocks are in a side ponytail held by a yellow hair tie that matches her large, drop-shaped earrings. The bathroom in which MC Xuxú sits has bare brick walls, the kind that you would see in a Brazilian favela shack. The screen is covered with small poop emojis, and at some point, MC Xuxú waves around a douche hose and looks at the camera with a mischievous expression. The scene then cuts to the artist strolling around a favela, dressed, while greeting residents and holding hands with a small child. Then, the scene cuts to other feminine-presenting people, mostly Black, dancing to the beats together, out in the community. This group unites with MC Xuxú, and all start dancing choreographed moves on a favela rooftop.

The lyrics to "Eu Fiz a Chuca" are playful and sexually suggestive but certainly not explicit—like many favela funk songs: "To not be embarrassed/so things go right/I've douched really good to get rid of all the/I … I … I … smell good/I'm hot for you …/show me what you can do." Together, the music video and the lines for "Eu Fiz a Chuca" make public this travesti practice that is a part of her quotidian life. This

---

* Chuca is a queer slang for rectal douching done in preparation for anal sex.

may seem trivial, but travesti identity is often confined to strict corners of normative discourses, such as crime, sex work, and live entertainment. MC Xuxú's performance moves away from these restrictive representations while also managing to avoid assimilationist narratives. She affirms the everydayness of travesti identity by strolling around a neighborhood in broad daylight. Additionally, while the lyrics suggest sexual activity will happen, the fact that she appears naked in a bathroom, sitting on a toilet further humanizes her, as does greeting members of her community. The video's spirited opening sequence juxtaposes with the fact that she is nude and singing sexually suggestive lyrics. The playfulness with which MC Xuxú narrates this practice did not matter in terms of the tune's marketability. In reflecting on the obstacles of being a travesti funkeira and releasing this song, she sighs and tells me the following: "It's really hard. Brazil has censored me a lot because of my performances. When I sang 'I did the chuca,' it wasn't allowed, but É o Tchan could sing "she made the snake rise" [popular *axé* song in the 1990s]… being travesti is really hard."

In "Eu Fiz a Chuca" and other music videos, MC Xuxú is seen in community with other transfeminine and queer people, a strategy that fellow funkeira and travesti Linn da Quebrada also utilizes. "Meus Desapegos" ("My Detachments")[76] narrates MC Xuxú's romantic/sexual relationship adventures as she "detaches" from (or breaks up with) different men. The 150 BPM favela funk beat sounds like a human voice performing beatbox, and the tone in the MC's voice is disdainful. I previously mentioned this music video in Chapter Five, when analyzing funkeiras' racial politics. As stated, one of the three scenarios in the music video includes MC Xuxú sitting on a bed in front of a wall with several framed pictures of trans and cis Black women. On her left, one can also spot a white, blue, and pink flag, which represents trans people in Brazil. Curiously, this is the only setup in which MC Xuxú is alone. The idea behind the pictures might be to suggest that she is not really isolated but has the company of those women who look over her. Early in the video for "Meus Desapegos," MC Xuxú is seen placing her hand on the photograph of Black soul singer and activist Elza Soares, as if asking for her blessing. In another scene, MC Xuxú is surrounded by mostly Black feminine-presenting people who are gathered around a pool table and wear revealing, colorful clothing. Occasionally, the video cuts to close-ups of the faces, breasts, and buttocks of these folks. A feeling of a welcoming queer-like community is created and is not surprising, given that during our interview, I could notice subtle movements between MC Xuxú's individual and collective identities. As MC Xuxú continues to consider the personal and communal barriers she faces as a travesti funk artist, she says,

> We've been achieving things, each one of us opening one door .... We haven't had a travesti reach the popularity level of [drag queen pop star] Pabllo Vittar, but Linn [da Quebrada] is the one who got the closest. Little by little, we discover our strengths, and lately, well, I've always focused on collective work, but lately I've been learning and studying the collective, how we can support each other ..."My god, I may not have been able to get what they got, but I'll promote their work because it'll be for all of us."

Because she moves through life as a Black travesti artist from the favela, her way of doing favela funk reflects those experiences. I ask her if there is a right or a wrong way to perform dirty funk, to which MC Xuxú replies, "I think so. You can sing about dirty things without being sexist ... without being prejudiced, you know? There's a lot of dirtiness that degrades *bichas*, women ... and then there's dirtiness that everyone has fun." Her dirty songs, thus, are intended to allow all to have fun—"I Douched" is an example of that. This does not mean that her songs do not make explicit political statements. Her lyrics often oscillate between the type of relational ridicule funkeiras perform and travesti-affirming/transphobic-shaming positions. "Cuida do Seu" ("Take Care of Yours"),[77] for instance, at first sounds like a typical song about relational misunderstandings ("Stalk me day and night/Fine, do you/Loves to put me down/But when you zoom in on my pic/Can't find any flaws"). However, in the second half of the song, MC Xuxú makes its theme more explicit:

> Take care of your own excretory system
> Because with mine, I like to make love
> Don't come at me, prejudice is so tacky
> Say shit about me but loves a finger in the ass

But I don't care, here's my middle finger
And I wanna see who's got a problem with it
Because this drive it was God who gave me
So I can take care of mine and tell you to take care of yours

A scantily clad, bare chested MC Xuxú, who stars in the music video, is surrounded by Black and brown feminine folks dancing through the busy downtown of Juiz de Fora. Every single scene of this video features the whole crew, with Black dancers always in the front row. About halfway through the music video, the provocative bodysuit that MC Xuxú is wearing is covered with a boyfriend-cut white blazer and a Brazilian presidential sash. This sequence of frames starts with the MC standing in front of a rainbow flag, making animated hand gestures, and giving the camera direct eye contact as she sings the stanza mentioned above. In the scenes that follow, MC Xuxú leads a procession through the busy city downtown. She, indeed, looks like a politician and her followers. Together, the lyrics and music video make a powerful statement about homophobia/transphobia and body autonomy—her own and others'.

Even though MC Xuxú often refers to herself as travesti, she also used the label "transwoman" during our interview. I asked her about these categories, to which she replied,

> I've read several explanations that I even agree with, but I don't think there's any difference between the transwoman and the travesti. We all have dicks, and no dick is different when there's prejudice involved …. The thing is having passability, knowing it's a privilege to have it, and making it a space of struggle.

MC Xuxú's reasoning seems to contest the distinction between these categories that Bento puts forth on her foundational work about Brazilian travestis and transsexual folks.[78] Specifically, Bento reports that those who identify as transwomen want to distance themselves from the travesti label, which often carries raced, classed, and nonbinary undertones. Instead, MC Xuxú shifts the conversation from the labels to what she perceives to be most important, namely the lived realities of those with and without passability. This is a disidentificatory move: MC Xuxú does not repudiate these categories or even the need to pass; rather, she blurs these labels' dissimilarities to fit an understanding of her own identity. It is important to investigate these variations in identification, especially as travestis and other transfeminine people gain public space. As I show later in this chapter, Linn da Quebrada interprets the travesti identity differently from MC Xuxú.

MC Xuxú's appearance frequently presents feminine. Towards the end of our interview, I ask her how she conceives her femininity, to which she replies, "I really like what people deem 'feminine,' but I also like what people deem 'masculine.' " These negotiations support Garcia's research with travestis who report that they adopt an assortment of peripheral femininities and masculinities in their performances of gender.[79] MC Xuxú understands the significance of binary gender passing; yet, her actual gender performance is more dense than simple compliance with what is considered feminine. Our conversation ends up taking a different turn when MC Xuxú starts to talk about her body, her recent weight gain, and how that process is shifting her identity: "I now consider myself a fat Black travesti from the favela." She continues,

> I'm getting used to being fat. We hear all the time that we have to love ourselves, love our bodies. But lately I've been criticized for promoting some weight loss products in exchange for samples. People are like "you have to love yourself," and I'm like, "hold up, y'all. I'm still becoming familiar with my fat identity. We deconstruct ourselves, so calm down. I'll love myself, but it doesn't happen overnight."

I ask her to unpack this sentiment by suggesting that it seems like there are two related issues in her answer: first, the pressure from what she pointed out early in our interview of being a celebrity and subscribing to white, normative looks, and second, the pressure that comes from being an activist. I tell her, "you have to be this perfect person, always empowered …" MC Xuxú interjects to continue my reasoning with an animated tone: "You have to speak very well. You have to understand all topics really well. You can never make mistakes; you have to be perfect. Can't do it like this. Nobody learns anything that way." MC Xuxú understands that the demand for her to be perfect is unrealistic, especially as someone whose identities make her especially vulnerable to scrutiny.

The material and symbolic elements in MC Xuxú's subjectivity indicate that the artist disidentifies from restrictive travesti discourses. The performances that compose this "empowered travesti"
subjectivity suggest that MC Xuxú labors from within and against a
white supremacist cisnormative system. She alludes to the "empowered travesti" in her song, "Vingancinha" ("Little Revenge").[80] After
singing about travesti struggles in the lines, "Resistance is to survive …. They're putting travestis down, humiliating travestis/If I'm
here today, it's because travestis get killed," the following verse says
"Why should I give up, be quiet?/Nice to meet you, empowered travesti." Hours after our conversation ended, I sent MC Xuxú a voice
message asking her to explain the meaning of "empowered travesti."
Her response came shortly after: "she has autonomy; she's her own
person." MC Xuxú often situates her concerns in present struggles by
denouncing violence against travestis and lack of professional opportunities. She molds and performs her subjectivity with the intention to
both survive and thrive in a context in which travestis are murdered
at alarming rates. Unlike MC Xuxú, Linn da Quebrada's performances
propose a transformed world for travestis and other gender nonconforming folks. As I show next, Linn works to materialize a utopian
future in the present.

Linn da Quebrada's Travesti Worldmaking

Funkeira and multimedia artist Linn da Quebrada is a self-identified
Black *bicha travesti* from the favela. Unlike other travesti and LGBTQIA+
artists in favela funk, Linn's self-affirming, in-your-face rhetorical and
bodily moves that especially target cisgender men clash with the ideologies of normalization and acceptance in Brazilian LGBTQIA+ culture—
Linn does not wave rainbow flags. She enacts gender in ambiguous ways,
but she centers her performances around femininity and transfeminine
people; she is open about her energetic, non-heterosexual sexuality. For
example, she frequently performs about seducing, having sex with, and
rejecting cisgender masculine men. Finally, her Blackness and favela
origins are woven through her travesti identity and worldmaking.

In contrast to MC Xuxú, Linn da Quebrada does not understand travesti as a synonym for transwoman—and passability is not even mentioned during our interview. After almost a year of back and forth between Linn's agent and me, she finally set a date for us to talk via WhatsApp video chat. Linn cancelled several live, public performances because of the 2020 Coronavirus global pandemic. Consequently, it became easier to schedule an interview around her busy schedule. On an April 2020 afternoon, Linn answers my call with a clean face. Her barbed wire forehead tattoo is visible, although looking a little faded. She asks me if it is ok for her to wash dishes while we talk. I say, "of course!" When I ask Linn about her identification, she tells me that, even though she believes "all these [identity] categories are doomed to fail" and that "our identities cannot handle how complex we are," she believes that travesti encapsulates her the most: "Travesti is where I see the most power to act over my own body .... And I see myself as (re)inventing a new possibility of travesti. Travesti is an identity in transformation, always."

Linn da Quebrada's disidentificatory performances from normative discourses around gender, sex, sexuality, race, and class are also slightly distinct from MC Xuxú's. As the analysis of three of her favela funk music videos—"Talento," "Enviadescer," and "Bixa Preta"—and our personal interview show, the self and the world Linn constructs are not ones of simple acceptance of already-established categories; rather, Linn envisions a world in which marginalized, racialized femininities are leading a path of transformation. In her conceptualization of queer temporality, Calafell poses that queer folks are included in dominant discourses in ways that de-emphasize and marginalize their lived experiences in favor of confining narratives.[81] Accordingly, Calafell argues, these folks "employ disidentificatory strategies such as memory and queer temporality to challenge these constructions and power interests, offer counter narratives, and create communities based upon these feelings of difference and excess."[82] Similarly, Muñoz understands queerness as "a structuring and educated mode of desiring that allows us to see and feel beyond the quagmire of the present."[83] Later on, he adds, "Often we can glimpse the worlds proposed and promised by queerness in the realm of the aesthetics."[84] Linn's performances foresee a world beyond tolerance in which travestis of color and other queer feminine folks shape social relations and networks. This world is not "an escape from the social realm";[85] on the contrary, it is the materialization of Linn's individual and communal longings. Linn da Quebrada consciously constructs her performances with these radical, transformative intentions. I have organized the main themes that emerged out of our interview and performances in three topics: de-centering cismasculinity, communal performances of racialized femininities, and travesti worldmaking.

De-Centering Cismasculinity

Linn da Quebrada tells me that she uses "music as a weapon." In a calm, reflective manner, she talks about the underlying belligerent purpose music has for her:

> Music occupies this warlike space for me, because it's where I point the gun to my own head. People think I'm pointing it [the gun] to the macho—which is also true—but indeed, it's an attitude to help me understand that I needed to kill the white colonizer macho that lived inside of me, that colonized my emotions, my affects, my relationships, and my body.

Western colonial norms of gender and sexuality still prevail in Brazil.[86] In the country's cisheteronormative culture, control over feminine individuals, aggressiveness, and virility are desirable qualities in cismasculinity, which is constructed in opposition to, and it is considered superior to, femininity and passivity.[87] Moreover, sexual virility and hypermasculinity are desirable in both travesti and gay culture.[88] Linn da Quebrada's work suggests two disidentificatory moves from these norms: first, she seemingly uses binary discourses of masculinity/sexual activity and femininity/sexual passivity to, second, engage in the de-centering of cismasculinity while privileging a travesti femininity. This section explores the former.

Masculine-presenting cisgender men are virtually nonexistent from Linn da Quebrada's performances. While she references them verbally, they are not physically represented in her work. Linn notes that her intention is to kill the "macho" in herself and not to destroy masculinity per se, as "masculinity is not essentially toxic because multiple masculinities exist." In my conversation with her, she explains why she chose music and favela funk to re-envision interpersonal, social, and communal relationships that do not depend on cismasculinity to exist: "I thought funk would be a great tool because it produces desires, and I wanted to produce *my* desires. I didn't want to talk about already-existing desires. I wasn't interested in producing something phallocentric, because that already exists."

Although Linn understands the ubiquity of white cisheteropatriarchy, the tactic to use her performances to clash with the narratives that support it is motivated by the fact that "these discourses are also fragile." In the opening shots for "Talento" ("Talent"),[89] the camera focuses on a close-up of Linn da Quebrada with her mouth half-open as she gives the camera a mischievous, sensual look. In the background, the lyrics begin: "There's no point in asking me/I won't blow you while hiding in a bathroom/You know I'm insatiable/I don't want just dick/ I want the whole body." The following shot displays different shades of brown bodies lined up close together, with only tights and hands visible, and then cuts to several shots of Black and brown travestis while the lyrics continue:

So you don't fuck femmes?
Who said that as fabulous as I am
I'm gonna want to give ass to men
Especially of your kind
Of such specific race
Who thinks you can do it all
With the force of god
And in the glory of the cock
It was obvious
You were about to be extinct
That there was no point being a macho
Using your dick

In "Talento," Linn's disidentificatory move first acknowledges and then pushes against the normative desire for cismasculinity. More than just remarking on normative choices of partners in LGBTQIA+ inter-personal relationships that tend to value masculinity over femininity, references to "force of god" and "glory of the cock" point to the systemic dominance of cismasculinity through Christianity. Linn tells me that she became a Jehovah's Witness at a young age, and the experiences in the church—"good and bad, traumatic and otherwise"—really shaped her subjectivity and her relationship with her body. Between fear of sin and guilt, Linn thought that once she started to explore her body, she would be "destroyed" by God. That, in turn, pushed her to live life as she wanted. Unsurprisingly, her songs are traversed by challenges to Christianity.

What is also remarkable about "Talento" is that Linn seems to be simultaneously snubbing cismasculinity's virility while also defying the idea that feminine-presenting folks necessarily want to be with a cisgender man, no matter their sexuality. In fact, she suggests that cis-masculinity will disappear—or become extinct—and perhaps so will the institutions it created that also maintain it. Per the quote in the open-ing of this subsection, Linn metaphorically kills the white macho colo-nizer in her art. The intention is indeed to make that particular mode of existence—which dictates everybody else's way of life—disappear.

Similarly, in "Enviadescer,"[90] Linn throws a favela block party filled with Black and brown feminine-presenting, nonbinary folks to scorn masculine cisgender men, who are again virtually absent from the video. "Enviadescer" derives from the term *viado*, and it means to be become *viado*. These terms are considered the antithesis of masculin-ity in Brazilian sexual culture—the opposite of macho "and a threat to an ideal of masculinity centered upon ideas of force, power, violence, aggression, virility and sexual potency."[91] Accordingly, *viado* suggests the feminization of cisgender men and is often used in degrading manner. In Linn da Quebrada's music video, she disidentifies from the normative understanding of the term; "enviadescer," instead, becomes desired—"If you want to be with me, boy/You'll have to enviadescer." Both "Talento" and "Enviadescer" dislocate cismasculinity by disiden-tifying from the dominant yearning for cisgender masculine men that is aligned with sexual vigor. Linn pokes fun at the "discreet macho," the man who performs gender and sexuality in normative ways.

Furthermore, Linn disavowals cis- and heteronormativity by proposing that transfeminine folks in fact desire other transfeminine folks.

Scorn is not the only emotion Linn da Quebrada's music videos express in relationship to cismasculinity. The idea that she uses her music as her "weapon" becomes evident in "Bixa Preta."[92] In it, Linn embodies a more confrontational tone. As mentioned in Chapter Five, this live performance-turned-music video starts with a series of dark, out of focus images of Black and brown transfeminine folks with what sounds like the sermon of an evangelical preacher demanding listeners to "be a man!" in the background. The preacher's aggressive voice sets the tone for the rest of the performance and also potentially represents that which Linn might be ideologically up against—gender and sexuality norms enforced in spaces now dominated by evangelicalism, such as favelas.[93] Using the sound of the last syllable in "Bixa Preta," the chorus has Linn prolonging that note and rolling the "r," imitating the sound of gunshot sounds—"Bixa pretrrrrrraaaaaaáahh!!! Tá tá tá!" while holding her left hand up in the shape of gun. The lyrics demand that "machos" "sit down and observe" their own "destruction" over the hypnotic beats of the tamborzão. Here, more than making fun of the "discreet macho" or the one who requests fellatio while hiding in a bathroom, Linn wants the destruction of the hierarchy that privileges machos, as it dehumanizes her existence as a Black travesti. Narratives from travestis of color work to understand who they are in relationship to their marginalization—in this case, the systems that create and privilege cismasculinity—but also seek to construct and express who they are because of, and in spite of, these oppressive systems. As Linn da Quebrada works to de-center—and destroy—cismasculinity, Black travesti femininity is the political weapon of choice in her performative arsenal.

Communal Performances of Racialized Femininities

When marginalized folks engage in disidentificatory practices, they rework their existence within systems that deem them as "others." In order to survive in "a phobic majoritarian public sphere,"[94] Linn da Quebrada's embodied performances restructure normative categories of gender, sex, and sexuality in ways that dislocate cismasculinity to the margins and privilege working-class, Black and brown transfeminine practices. In addition, her music videos suggest that these disidentificatory moves happen in community, which challenges Western understandings of queerness that focus on "selfhood, individual agency, and experience."[95] This communal performance of racialized femininities that Linn da Quebrada fosters could possibly function as a coalitional model for engaging in truly intersectional decolonial politics.[96]

While the contemptuous references to "machos" in Linn da Quebrada's work indicate an understanding of masculinity in hegemonic terms, her idea of femininity is clearly non-normative for a few reasons. First, as a Black, working-class travesti, Linn da Quebrada's femininity will inevitably be marked as "othered." Second, and in tandem with the previous point, all three music videos I analyze are in favela funk style and incorporate, specifically, the bass line and beats, the singing, the scorn and belligerence in the tone and in the lyrics, the dance moves that include a lot of twerking, the provocative clothes folks wear, and the mostly working-class settings of the videos. As I have argued throughout this work, the femininities associated with favela funk are perceived as exaggerated, inappropriate, and most importantly, in tension with the normative white femininine version that is so dominant in Brazilian culture. Taking these points into consideration, I examine disidentificatory ways in which Linn da Quebrada constructs and enables diverse peripheral, racialized femininities. It is via these performances that, as suggested by Muñoz,[97] cultural transformation from within might emerge.

A meticulous look at Linn da Quebrada's three music videos indicates that her work is an homage to Black and brown feminine-presenting persons, travestis and otherwise. The most obvious indication of this is how prevalent those folks are in her videos. If cismasculinity is alluded to in somewhat one-dimensional ways in Linn's videos, femininity is shown as thickly multilayered; people in Linn da Quebrada's videos present diverse types of bodies, skin colors—with a noticeable presence of Black and brown folks—style of clothes, makeup, and hairstyles. And although all three videos share this common aspect, each advances unique aspects of these rebellious femininities. In our interview, when

I interject to ask Linn about the obvious presences and absences in her videos, she provides a detailed explanation for these conscious choices. While sitting in her living room after washing dishes, she explains the following:

> I realized love is beneficial almost exclusively to men. Men are made and raised to be loved by women and by the feminine, and women are always raised to love men. Women exist to serve and protect [men]. Love is very useful to men. At the same time, [cis]masculinity is so problematic that they [men] convince us that that's what forms us, what forms the feminine: it's love. Love is part of the essence of what is masculine and what is feminine …. As I realize these things, I begin to want to deviate from this narrative to focus on us, on our bodies.

"Talento" enforces the absence of masculine cisgender men by focusing solely on travestis, who perform for the camera by dancing, lip-synching to the lyrics, and tenderly exchanging affection with one another. The video looks like it was shot outside of an abandoned warehouse during a sunny day. A blue wall in this isolated space frames many of the frenetic twerking images of Linn and other Black and brown travestis, who put their hands on the wall with their backs to the camera and sensually slant their upper body while keeping their hips up. These images that happen outside are alternated with shots from inside of what looks like a house, with sunlight coming through the windows. Later, we learn that this enclosed space is a shelter for travestis who are in a situation of homelessness. Toward the end of the video, each travesti introduces themselves; each person talks about their concerns and aspirations, as images of the interviews take turns with shots of them putting on feminine outfits:

> Hello, my name is Gi … Carla, and someday, I want people to see me as Gilson during the day and, well, when I'm dressed as a woman, [I'd like to be seen] as Carla. Recognized, seen, transformed … You see? I wish I could be all that. Actually, I *want* to be all that.

As the introductions continue, it becomes clear that travestis are not homogenous in the way they fashion their identities. Aside from Carla/ Gilson, one by one travestis introduce themselves in diverse ways: as women ("I was born a woman"), as "the one who's a woman in the body of a macho," as the one with "velvet hands and a porcelain mouth," and as not always travesti ("I consider myself gay; sometimes I'm travesti").

Dressed in hyper-feminine, provocative ways while dancing around and showing affection, travestis in "Talento" seem to reclaim a public space at daytime. Conversely, the isolated video location reminds us of the great physical risk travestis face in Brazil. As Brazilian trans activist and scholar Viviane Vergueiro points out, Brazilian institutions concurrently ignore and inflict a great deal of physical violence and psychological pain in the lives of trans people.[98] In this sense, the shelter plays an important role in "Talento" because they are able to escape the threats of public spaces, albeit temporarily. As Linn mocks and attacks cismasculinity, she likewise recognizes the struggles travestis face (in a lot of ways, *because* of cismasculinity) by, first, promoting the shelter at the end of the video and, second, by illuminating how complex their identities are.

Filmed partly in a favela and partly in a busy street, "Enviadescer" combines close-ups of cleavage, buttocks in short skirts and shorts, bare legs, and feet in high heels with dancing—mostly twerking—and lip-synching. Close to the second minute of the video, there is a sequence of images displaying feminine-presenting folks hugging, touching tongues, and kissing each other on the lips. At one point, the camera shifts to the back of Linn's head and shoulder while her arms are tangled around another Black, feminine-presenting person's neck, whose face reveals a wide-open smile, dark lipstick on the lips, and hoop earrings in their ears. Their bodies are in proximity and demonstrate intimacy and affection. After rebuffing "discreet machos," the lyrics continue, "I really like the bichas!/The effeminate ones who show lots of skin/Go out with makeup on." "Enviasdescer" is suggested as an antidote to cismasculinity—the embracing of a working-class racialized femininity that has nothing to do with assigned Western binaries, biological sex, or sexual orientation. "Enviadescer" is, in fact, a performance:

> Oh, my god
> What are these bichas doing?
> Everywhere I look

They're all [gender neutral "todes"] enviadescendo
But this has nothing to do with liking cock or not
Come on closer, dykes and transviadas!†
Let's enviadescer until we hit our butts on the floor!

It is not incidental that Linn da Quebrada is never alone in the three analyzed music videos. Several other travestis and feminine-presenting folks often surround the performer while singing and/or dancing, which gives the impression that she exists in community with these other marginalized folks. In "Enviadescer," Linn twerks right outside of a Military Police battalion surrounded by others of different shapes and sizes who are also sensually moving their bodies. Moreover, as the lyrics above point out, Linn invites other queer folks to twerk in community. Having strength in numbers might defy the rules of when and how they can occupy public spaces where their bodies and performances are coded as "deviant" while challenging institutions that perpetuate their oppression, such as the Military Police.[99]

"Bixa Preta" is the only video in which Linn is in the more formal role of the performer—on a stage during a live show, holding a microphone, and with an audience around her. But even then, images of Linn's audience, or co-performers, abound. Like in the other two videos, "Bixa Preta" offers a collection of images of travestis and other feminine-presenting folks of different shades and shapes dancing, as well as close-up shots of body parts like legs, crotches, chests, breasts, and buttocks. On stage, Linn da Quebrada wears a black dress with a generous neckline that exposes her chest, a white beaded short necklace, and high-heeled lace-up boots. She wears hot-pink yarn braids in a half-up half-down style. Her bodily movements combine firm hand and head gestures with sensual hip movement. The lyrics follow the melody's aggressive tone:

What a weird bixa, mad
Loose, perverted [...]

---

† *Transviadas* is the feminine of transviado, which means corrupted or immoral, commonly used to designate non-normative genders and sexualities.

I go out in high heels
Wearing makeup in the favela
But too bad, you just now noticed this beautiful aberration?
It's too late, alpha male
I'M NOT FOR YOUR ENJOYMENT

Like *viado*, the word *bixa*—a modified spelling of the original *bicha* (loosely translated as "fag")—is connected to persons who are perceived as sexually passive and "exaggeratedly" feminine in comparison to cisheteronormative standards.[100] Klein argues that travestis often incorporate the word *bicha* into their lexicon to refer to themselves[101]—Linn da Quebrada frequently identifies as a *bicha* travesti. This, in turn, complicates normative associations of sexual activity with masculinity and passivity with femininity because some travestis, indeed, have control over active, masculine men.[102] Linn's use of *bixa* is disidentificatory: she concurrently acknowledges its pejorative, cisnormative meaning—"mad," "loose," "perverted"—and embraces its abjectness by referring to herself as a "beautiful aberration" whose existence is not meant for cismasculinity's gratification.

Linn da Quebrada's framing of herself as an "aberration" resonates with a point she made during our interview. At 23 years old, Linn was diagnosed with testicular cancer. (She mentions that she found it ironic, given the body part's association with masculinity.) Cancer forced her to reevaluate her relationship with her body, a body that no longer felt invincible and immortal:

> My body was fragile; I was sick. That was the moment I got the closest to myself, because that's when I understood that I could turn my fragilities into potency. The fact that I was Black, the fact that I was a bicha, the fact of the feminine in my body, the fact of the disease itself—these were all "fragilities" that the world would frame as weaknesses. But I looked at these fragilities and wanted to turn them into potentials.

Linn's Blackness, her nonconforming femininity and sexuality, and her working classness all become potencies in "Bixa Preta." The verse "My Black skin is my cloak of courage/It boosts the movement/

It flatters the *viadagem*"‡ not only indicates that Blackness is an essential aspect of her femininity and sexuality, but the reference to a "movement" also points to Linn da Quebrada's political purpose. When taken together, along with the images of Black and brown folks performing in community, these moves signal a powerful coalitional opportunity. Linn's coalition is anchored in the opposition to cismasculinity and its oppressive institutions, as she invites other marginalized folks to mock it and eventually destroy it. Moreover, in Linn's world, working-class Black travesti femininity does not exist in relationship to cismasculinity. On the contrary, it exists to defy it, destroy it, or to ultimately survive and thrive irrespective of it.

Travesti Worldmaking

Linn da Quebrada's (Figure 4) music videos suggest a few disidentificatory moves. She relies on hegemonic terms and their meanings to make her work intelligible while concomitantly disrupting the hierarchy that organizes them—travesti and bicha are examples of this. Like the dominant understandings of travesti and bicha, in Linn da Quebrada's world, these too exist in opposition to cismasculinity. Unlike the dominant use of the terms, such opposition is not grounded in cismasculinity's superiority to, and dominance over, travesti femininity but in the lack of relationality between the two—the independence of travesti femininity. These contradictions are also present in tone and physical behaviors and expressions in Linn da Quebrada's music video performances. At times, anger seems to be the dominant affect, such as in "Bixa Preta;" at other times, scorn sets the tone, like in "Talento." As an "ambivalent structure of feeling,"[103] Linn's disidentificatory performances are affectively wavering, with scorn and anger existing concurrently with communal love.

---

‡ *Viadagem* is another term stemming from the word *viado*, and it could mean a group of *viados* or engaging in *viado*-like activities.

Figure 4: Linn da Quebrada. Credit: Gabriel Renne

The communal love Linn da Quebrada's performances envision is radically different from the cisheteronormative love that dictates and shapes social relations, which she calls "a fantasy, a parable, a tale." Additionally, Linn postulates that cisheteronormative "love is one of the tools that help maintain this system," precisely because it "organizes us socially, forms families, distributes inheritance, [and] promotes economic circulation." This cisheteronormative "love" is what Linn aims to "kill" and replace it through her music:

I needed to destroy love and its collateral affects. Because if we're able to build other affective networks, we'll then be able to reorganize socially. Foucault says this ... the problem with homosexuality is not to give ass. The problem is that if we use that as motivation, our social relations will transform. If this is taken radically, if this becomes a radical experiment, our whole social structure could change, because then other things [and not romantic, heteronormative love] would lead us to create connections.

In many ways, Linn da Quebrada's disidentificatory practices engage in "a remaking and rewriting of a dominant script."[104] Linn da Quebrada's performances are unquestionably political, and her end goal is a travesti worldmaking—a present vision of a possible future. Grounded in the power of performances, be they theatrical or quotidian, Muñoz understands "worldmaking" as "the ability to establish alternate views of the world. These alternative vistas are more than simply views or perspectives; they are oppositional ideologies that function as critiques of oppressive regimes of 'truth' that subjugate minoritarian people."[105] In Linn da Quebrada's travesti worldmaking, cismasculinity is a joke; it is going extinct. Transfeminine folks, especially those who are from working-class backgrounds, Black and brown, dance freely and show affection in public spaces during the day. They are free from racist, transphobic violence and dehumanization, and they are the ones who perform gender and sexuality in the most desirable ways.

The centering of these bodies in affection and communion, according to Linn, could lead to "new networks of survival," such as "a psychological support network [and] a material support network." It is only by imagining new social relations that they can be materialized. Linn utilizes her body in performance and her provisional iteration of travesti subjectivity to envisage a transformed social, cultural, and economic landscape. Travesti enables her to "create diverse femininities, virile femininities, courageous femininities, furious femininities" as part of the process to decolonize identities and relationships.

Embodied Politics and Survival

All three performers examined in this chapter contribute to the shifting knowledge about travesti identity and performance within and beyond favela funk. As travestis gain more prominence in public spaces, the least that scholars can do is work to echo their voices, their subjectivities, and their political projects—including their use of embodied politics—as a way to help combat the systemic violence to which they are subjected. I feel fortunate that I was able to interview MC Xuxú and Linn da Quebrada. Our exchanges felt true to Conquergood's call for ethnography to move "from Other-as-theme to Other-as-interlocutor."[106] In addition, critical ethnography's interviewing methods, which aim to illuminate subjects' memories, desires, contradictions, and more, allowed me to bring to the surface the political possibilities in both MC Xuxú's and Linn da Quebrada's voices.[107]

Intercultural communication, feminist, and queer scholars should pay close attention to the knowledge production of travestis. Their experience-based insights provide powerful ways to dismantle and reconceptualize Western systems of gender and sexuality, especially as they relate to coloniality and whiteness. The political strategies these groups generate under precarious structural conditions both seek to alleviate their existence under the current system while reimagining a political project in which they are fully entitled to human and civil rights. Because their lived experiences are so immersed in racist, transphobic, sexist, and classist struggles, their bodies indeed play a fundamental role in the process of reconceptualizing our social relations. In this context, embodied politics is fully entangled with structural changes as it is a matter of survival.

Notes

1 Marcia Ochoa, "Ciudadanía perversa: divas, marginación y participación en la 'loca- lización,'" in *Políticas de ciudadanía y sociedad civil en tiempos de globalización*, ed. Daniel Mato (Caracas: FACES, Universidad Central de Venezuela), 254.
2 Ochoa, "Ciudadanía," 254.

3 David Eng, Judith Halberstam, and José Muñoz, "Introduction: What's Queer About Queer Studies Now?", *Social Text* 23, no. 3–4 (2005): 15.

4 Shinsuke Eguchi and Godfried Asante, "Disidentifications Revisited: Queer(y)ing Intercultural Communication Theory," *Communication Theory* 26 (2016): 173–74.

5 Eguchi and Asante, "Disidentifications Revisited," 174.

6 Cathy Cohen, "Punks, Bulldaggers, and Welfare Queens: The Radical Potential of Queer Politics?" *GLQ: A Journal of Lesbian and Gay Studies* 3, no. 4 (1997): 437–65.

7 Cohen, "Punks."

8 E. Patrick Johnson, " 'Quare' Studies, or (Almost) Everything I Know About Queer Studies I Learned from My Grandmother," *Text and Performance Quarterly* 21, no. 1 (2001): 1–25.

9 Wenshu Lee, "Kauering Queer Theory: My Autocritography and a Race-Conscious, Womanist, Transnational Turn," *Journal of Homosexuality* 45, no. 2/3/4 (2003): 147–70.

10 Gust Yep, "Queering/Quaring/Kauering/Crippin'/Transing 'Other Bodies' in Intercultural Communication," *Journal of International and Intercultural Communication* 6, no. 2 (2013): 120.

11 Eguchi and Asante, "Disidentifications Revisited"; Yep, "Queering/Quaring."

12 Marcos Roberto Garcia, "Identity as a 'Patchwork': Aspects of Identity Among Low-Income Brazilian Travestis," *Culture, Health & Sexuality* 11, no. 6 (July 2009): 611–23.

13 Fernanda Belizario, "Gênero: Feminilidade Travesty," *Medium*, March 7, 2019, https://medium.com/@febelizario/g%C3%AAnero-feminilidade-travesti-aaffaf7fb386; Yep, "Queering/Quaring."

14 Viviane Vergueiro, "Por Inflexões Decoloniais de Corpos e Identidades de Gênero Inconformes: Uma Análise Autoetnográfica da Cisgeneridade como Normatividade," *Repositório UFBA*, 2015, https://repositorio.ufba.br/ri/handle/ri/19685.

15 Luciana Tecidio, "Mãe de Lacraia conta que o filho não era feliz: 'Sofreu muito preconceito,' " *Ego*, May 10, 2015, http://ego.globo.com/famosos/noticia/2015/05/mae-de-lacraia-conta-que-o-filho-nao-era-feliz-sofreu-muito-preconceito.html.

16 Matias Maxx, "A funkeira Lacraia é um ícone dos LGBTs no Brasil," *Kondzilla*, June 28, 2019, https://kondzilla.com/m/a-funkeira-lacraia-e-um-icone-dos-lgbts-no-brasil.

17 Adriana Lopes, *Funk-se Quem Quiser: No Batidão Negro da Cidade Carioca* (Rio de Janeiro: Bom Texto, 2011), 192.

18 Lopes, *Funk-se.*

19 Juliana Maselli, "Morre dançarina de funk Lacraia," *Ego*, May 10, 2011, http://ego.globo.com/Gente/Noticias/0,,MUL1661583-9798,00-MORRE+DANCARINA+DE+FUNK+LACRAIA.html; Maxx, "A funkeira Lacraia."

20 Maxx, "A funkeira Lacraia."

21 Caia Coelho (@travestiviva), "THREAD, Lacraia era uma travesti e ficou conhecida nacionalmente em 2003 através do funk, eu tinha 11 anos ...," Twitter, June 3, 2020, 5:20 p.m., https://twitter.com/travestiviva/status/1268306593441091590.

22 Garcia, "Identity."

23 Don Kulick, *Travesti: Sex, Gender, and Culture Among Brazilian Transgendered Prostitutes* (Chicago: The University of Chicago Press, 1998).

24 Garcia, "Identity."

25 Richard Parker, "Masculinity, Femininity, and Homosexuality: On the Anthropological Interpretation of Sexual Meanings in Brazil," *Journal of Homosexuality* 11, no. 3–4 (1986): 155–63.

26 Julieta Vartabedian, *Brazilian Travesti Migrations* (Cham: Palgrave Macmillan, 2018), 2.

27 Vartabedian, *Travesti Migrations.*

28 Viviane Vergueiro, "Despatologizar é descolonizar," *Global Action for Trans Equality,* October 26, 2015, https://transactivists.org/viviane-vergueiro-despatologizar-es-descolonizar/.

29 Don Kulick and Charles Klein, "Scandalous Acts: The Politics of Shame Among Brazilian Travesti Prostitutes," in *Recognition Struggles and Social Movements: Contested Identities, Agency, and Power,* ed. Barbara Hobson (New York, NY: Cambridge University Press, 2003), 215–38.

30 Showlivre, "DJ Marlboro, MC Serginho e Lacraia no Nokia Trends—arquivo radar Showlivre 2004," June 12, 2009, YouTube video, 2:37, https://www.youtube.com/watch?v=BIvHaD9YuoU.

31 Thiago Barcelos Soliva, "About the Talent of Being Fabulous: The 'Transvestite Shows' and the Invention of the 'Professional Transvestite,'" *Cadernos Pagu* 53 (2018): 1–40.

32 Ochoa, "Ciudadanía."

33 Soliva, "Being Fabulous," 3.

34 Soliva, "Being Fabulous."

35 Lopes, *Funk-se.*

36 Lopes, *Funk-se,* 194.

37 Maxx, "A funkeira Lacraia."

38 Lopes, *Funk-se,* 192.

39 Maxx, "A funkeira Lacraia."

40 Coelho, "THREAD."

41 SBT do Brasil, "4/6—Os Opostos Se Atraem—Eliana—22/11/09," November 24, 2019, YouTube video, 7:21, https://www.youtube.com/watch?v=qkHj1Tk_htI.

42 "Rodrigo Faro se transforma em Lacraia," *R7,* March 20, 2010, http://tv.r7.com/record-play/melhor-do-brasil/videos/rodrigo-faro-se-transforma-em-lacraia-21102015.

43 Silvio Essinger, *Batidão: Uma história do funk* (Rio de Janeiro, Editora Record, 2005); TV Onix, "Documentário Favela Gay completo," November 16, 2017, YouTube video, 1:11:45, https://www.youtube.com/watch?v=4gjjXLvhOXo.

44 Maxx, "A funkeira Lacraia."

45 Lopes, *Funk-se.*

46 Ochoa, "Ciudadanía," 242.

47 Ochoa, "Ciudadanía," 242–43.

48 Kulick and Klein, "Scandalous Acts," 221.

49 José Esteban Muñoz, *Disidentifications: Queers of Color and the Performance of Politics* (Minneapolis: University of Minnesota Press, 1999).

50 Muñoz, *Disidentifications.*

51 Muñoz, *Disidentifications,* 187.

52 Muñoz, *Disidentifications,* 187.

53 MG2, "Cerca de 90% das travestis e transexuais do país sobrevivem da prostituição," *G1,* May 18, 2018, https://g1.globo.com/mg/minas-gerais/noticia/cerca-de-90-das-travestis-e-transexuais-do-pais-sobrevivem-da-prostituicao.ghtml.

54 Lucas Paoli Itaborahy, "Pessoas LGBT vivendo em probreza no Rio de Janeiro," *Micro* Rainbow *International,* December 2014, https://mrifoundation.global/wp-content/uploads/2014/12/20141204-report-port.pdf.

55 Muñoz, *Disidentifications.*

56 Tecidio, "Mãe de Lacraia."

57 Muñoz, *Disidentifications,* 189.

58 Muñoz, *Disidentifications,* 189.

59 Tecidio, "Mãe de Lacraia."

60 Tecidio, "Mãe de Lacraia."

61 Maselli, "Morre Dançarina;" Tecidio, "Mãe de Lacraia."

62 Helena Vieira, "Transfeminismo," in *Explosão feminista,* ed. H. Buarque de Hollanda (Rio de Janeiro: Companhia das Letras, 2018), 345.

63 Vieira, "Transfeminismo," 345.

64 Muñoz, *Disidentifications,* 12.

65 Eguchi and Asante, "Disidentifications Revisited," 175.

66 Eguchi and Asante, "Disidentifications Revisited," 183.

67 Muñoz, *Disidentifications,* 185.

68 Muñoz, *Disidentifications,* 11–12.

69 Muñoz, *Disidentifications.*

70 Vergueiro, "Despatologizar."

71 Muñoz, *Disidentifications,* 78.

72 Julia Johnson, "Cisgender Privilege, Intersectionality, and the Criminalization of CeCe McDonald: Why Intercultural Communication Needs Transgender Studies," *Journal of International and Intercultural Communication* 6, no. 2 (2013): 135–44.

73 MC Xuxú, "Mc Xuxú—Kit Assume (feat. Mulher Pepita) ÁUDIO OFICIAL," January 28, 2018, YouTube video, 2:44, https://www.youtube.com/watch?v=EbJ4A9-R_z4.

74 TV Onix, "Documentário Favela Gay."

75 MC Xuxú, "Mc Xuxú—Eu fiz a Chuca," March 27, 2016, YouTube video, 3:10, https://www.youtube.com/watch?v=alPlmFbNKrE.

76 MC Xuxú, "Mc Xuxú—Meus Desapegos (Clipe Oficial)," May 14, 2019, YouTube, 3:36, https://www.youtube.com/watch?v=Z2hQJ9QM08A.

77 MC Xuxú, "Mc Xuxú—Cuida do Seu," August 20, 2018, YouTube video, 2:46, https://www.youtube.com/watch?v=oFUhoV7-UL8.

78 Berenice Bento, *O que é transexualidade* (São Paulo, SP: Editora Brasiliense, 2017).

79 Garcia, "Identity."

80 MC Xuxú, "Mc Xuxú—Vingancinha (feat. Caetano Brasil) ÁUDIO OFICIAL," January 28, 2018, YouTube video, 2:37, https://www.youtube.com/watch?v=6dmJLhxkbPY.

81 Bernadette M. Calafell, "Pro(re-)claiming Loss: A Performance Pilgrimage in Search of Malintzin Tenépal," *Text and Performance Quarterly* 25, no. 1 (2005): 43–56.

82 Calafell, "Pro(re-)claiming Loss," 53.

83 José Esteban Muñoz, *Cruising Utopia: The Then and There of Queer Futurity* (New York, NY: New York University Press, 2009), 1.

84 Muñoz, *Cruising Utopia*, 1.

85 Muñoz, *Cruising Utopia*, 1.

86 Vergueiro, "Inflexões Decoloniais."

87 Fernando Luiz Cardoso, "The Relationship Between Sexual Orientation and Gender Identification Among Males in a Cross-Cultural Analysis in Brazil, Turkey and Thailand," *Sexuality & Culture* 17 (2013): 568–97.

88 Garcia, "Identity"; Severino Pereira and Eduardo Ayrosa, "Consumed Bodies: Gay Culture Consumption in Rio," *Organizações & Sociedade* 19, no. 61 (2012): 295–313.

89 Linn da Quebrada, "Mc Linn da Quebrada—Talento—clipe oficial," August, 23, 2016, YouTube video, 5:59, https://www.youtube.com/watch?v=hkAHuRPGgNk.

90 Linn da Quebrada, "MC Linn da Quebrada—Enviadescer—clipe oficial," May 25, 2016, YouTube video, 2:54, https://www.youtube.com/watch?v=saZywh0FuEY.

91 Garcia, "Identity," 615.

92 Linn da Quebrada, "Mc Linn da Quebrada—Bixa Preta," September 30, 2016, YouTube video, 4:28, https://www.youtube.com/watch?v=ZeMa942nYe4.

93 Chris Arsenault, "Evangelicalism Grows in Brazil's Favelas Amid Poverty and Violence," *Reuters*, April 10, 2017, https://www.reuters.com/article/us-brazil-religion-landrights/evangelicalism-grows-in-brazils-favelas-amid-poverty-and-violence-idUSKBN17C1H4.

94 Muñoz, *Disidentifications*, 5.

95 Eguchi and Asante, "Disidentifications Revisited," 174.

96 Vergueiro, "Despatologizar."

97 Muñoz, *Disidentifications*.

98 Vergueiro, "Despatologizar."

99 Vergueiro, "Despatologizar."

100 Charles Klein, " 'The Guetto Is Over, Darling': Emerging Gay Communities and Gender and Sexual Politics in Contemporary Brazil," *Culture, Health & Sexuality* 1, no. 3 (1999): 239–60.

101 Klein, "Guetto is Over."

102 Klein, "Guetto is Over."

103 Muñoz, *Disidentifications*, 71.

104 Muñoz, *Disidentifications*, 23.

105 Muñoz, *Disidentifications*, 195.

106 Dwight Conquergood, "Rethinking Ethnography: Towards a Critical Cultural Politics," *Communication Monographs* 58 (1991), 182.

107 D. Soyini Madison, *Critical Ethnography: Method, Ethics, and Performance* (Thousand Oaks: Sage, 2005).

Beyond Survival: Funkeiras, Embodied Politics, and the Future of Feminism

"My intention is to create femininities that are dangerous to the system," says Linn da Quebrada as we wrap up our interview. The Black travesti funkeira sums up nicely the kinds of femininities funkeiras create and perform—femininities that are persecuted and regulated but that, nonetheless, are in a constant state of reinvention. Over the ten years since I started to more attentively follow funkeiras, their performances have transformed and also stayed connected to the different cultural and political moments Brazil has been experiencing. Still, scholarly interest in them is yet to reflect their importance and contributions to favela funk in general. In fact, scholars need to work to undo some of the damage created by (white) feminist analyses that further pathologized favela funk and funkeiras. In this conclusion, I propose a few insights: first, contextualizing the changes funkeiras' work has experienced over the years, with special attention to the possibilities their performances enable, both challenges and contributes to a fresh perspective on embodied politics. Second, I contemplate the impact this book has on conceptions of feminism. I end the text with a reflection about the future—of funkeiras' work and the scholarship that is impacted by their complex existences and experiences.

Critical Ethnography and Reflections on Fieldwork

Ethnography, among other types of scholarly work, generates knowledge about others that in turn connects to the discourses produced about them.[1] In the case of funkeiras, the discursive production is still being constructed in academia, since there are so few works about them. In this study, I utilized critical ethnography to examine funkeiras' enactments of racialized femininities and to privilege knowledge production from their local culture, favela funk. As a method, critical ethnography is driven by the idea of a researcher's "ethical responsibility," which Madison explains as "a compelling sense of duty and commitment based on moral principles of human freedom and well-being."[2] In the process of producing discourses about the funkeiras, this study took into consideration the ethical implications of their impact on these marginalized artists.

The dynamics of the personal interactions I had with the funkeiras featured in this book is intriguing: while many of them experience structural marginalization, they are also artists and performers. Therefore, a lot of them carry a sense of confidence that complicates assumptions about researcher-interlocutor power relations. As a researcher, I always tried to be aware of my privileged position. But the reality is that, often, funkeiras were not bothered or intimidated by my presence. I was just a researcher—there was often a slight disappointment when I clarified that I was not a journalist working for a media outlet. Those moments functioned as an important reality check for me, as I grasped quickly that I needed them more than they needed me. That lesson, which I learned in 2013, persisted until the writing of this book in 2020. For instance, it took me a year of chatting with MC Xuxú on WhatsApp for her to make room in her agenda for our interview. However, not all funkeiras embody that sense of self-confidence. In the rare instances where I was regarded as the powerful person in the room, I had to consciously make an effort to let them know that, indeed, *I needed them* and that I was genuinely interested in their life story. Thus, my intention while interacting with funkeiras was to let them talk for as long as they wished, about any matter they considered relevant, even if not directly related to the topic of my research. By allowing them to lead our conversations, I was able to identify important issues that ultimately guided this study. These conversations contributed to the most important lesson I learned about researching in the field: self-reflexivity also means staying open to understanding shifting power relations and, consequently, being able to adapt to volatile, unplanned situations.

Throughout the book, I emphasized the significance of including performances and interviews instead of just analyzing lyrics. Part of the scholarly injustices done to funkeiras come from evaluation of lyrics that disregard their identities, their moving bodies, and the context in which their performances occur. Drawing on critical ethnography, I treated funkeiras as co-writers of their stories and struggles by privileging the experiences and knowledge created by them about their racialized, classed femininities. More than regarding funkeiras I interviewed as subjects "with agency, history, and[...][their] own idiosyncratic command of a story,"[3] I understand them as my co-creators.

As I established throughout this book, favela funk exists at the intersection of praise and condemnation in dominant culture. Like other cultural expressions that have emerged out of favelas, Rio's funk is simultaneously marginalized and regarded as immoral by the same mainstream media that welcomes, praises, and profits off it. This context of continuous marginalization makes the economic lives of the most vulnerable funkeiras even harder than they already are. In that sense, academic research has become one of the ways through which favela funk has been legitimized as a form of culture in some dimensions of the public sphere in Brazil and beyond. Scholars must be mindful, then, of their roles in furthering funkeiras' oppression. One of my motivations to write this book developed precisely from the need to correct both the invisibility of funkeiras in studies about favela funk in general and the few problematic studies that analyze lyrics while engaging in gender-first analyses.

This book, hopefully, made it evident that gender-first analysis perpetuates several issues: first, it erases the intersecting ways in which funkeiras are oppressed and, by default, are unable to correctly assess the political potentials and limitations of their performances. Second, it unreflectively maintains white feminism's supremacy. Previous studies investigating gender in favela funk have even suggested that those who enjoy bailes "lack" culture and education *because* of the way gender relations are represented in early 2000s lyrics.[4] Even works that provide more refined perspectives of funkeiras, such as Lopes's,[5] still somewhat fall into the trap of compartmentalized evaluations that, although considering other aspects of oppression like class and race, continue to have gender as their primary analytical lens. Along with a distinct, critical method for engaging funkeiras in both interviews and performances, I added mediated performances and news media interviews to the study when being physically present was not possible. Additionally, funkeiras' social media presence adds an exciting dimension to the analysis, as it provides another opportunity to reverberate their voices.

The Then and Now of Funkeiras

Funkeiras' first claims to fame happened in the early to the mid-2000s through performances that mostly fixated on sex and relationships. As this book shows, from the late 2000s on, different topics began to arise in their performances. One of these themes is financial independence, which slowly became more common and is now regularly performed among funkeiras. Exploring economic self-sufficiency in performances can be the result of a few tendencies: first, it may indicate funkeiras' emerging importance within the favela funk movement that, in turn, allows them to be more or less financially secure. If professional independence is often tied to personal autonomy in their narratives, then it makes sense that this newfound financial liberation would spill over into stage performances. These performances of financial autonomy, although perhaps context-bound and not yet enough to create generational wealth, may also be a sign of personal and professional liberation from abusive relationships with managers—both Valesca Popozuda and Pocah, who now regularly perform about bodily and financial autonomy, reported that their relationships with their partners-managers were indeed toxic. The material gains funkeiras have achieved, and their public performances about it, have propelled a discursive shift within male-dominated favela funk. Once one funkeira began to perform about it, others followed, and together, they are helping shift the culture in favela funk. Individually, funkeiras might not always have the ability to engage agency in the way white feminism proposes, as "self-making, self-determining" subjects;[6] however, these changes in favela funk point to an expression of communal agency. Together, these artists are able to build on each other's performances in order to drive significant changes in favela funk and beyond.

This book recognizes that favela funk is an industry that works within and against racist, sexist, classist, and heteronormative systems. Unsurprisingly, racist sexism within the movement operates in a similar manner as in Brazilian society at large: white and light-skinned brown women are favored over Black women. The consequences of sexist anti-Blackness are clear both through the perspectives of MC Dandara, MC Kátia, and Deize Tigrona, whose looks did not meet favela funk's standards of beauty in the early 2010s, and the fact that this standardized beauty meant that the muscular, light-skinned brown women with long, straight hair who embodied these features, like Valesca Popozuda, had the ability to more easily succeed and transition to mainstream success.

Despite the material barriers an anti-Black, sexist favela funk imposes on Black women and transfeminine folks, they are still able to negotiate and/or divert from those obstacles to achieve professional autonomy and some financial independence. Since Black funkeiras are less likely to be able to "whiten" their bodies and performances, an easier way to achieve mainstream popularity as favela funk performers, they have found distinct ways to enact femininities that reimagine the role of their bodies in performance. Black funkeiras like MC Carol, Tati Quebra Barraco, Deize Tigrona, and Linn da Quebrada were all able to succeed in different measures by performing Black femininities in varied ways; perhaps these performers embody well Linn da Quebrada's description of "furious femininities." More than other funkeiras, these artists mix anger, disdain, and sensuality to create a multifaceted and striking performative style. As Black funkeiras, however, their ability to reach mainstream, widespread fame is still limited by racist sexism and transphobia.

Funkeiras engage in a multifaceted assemblage of racialized, classed femininities and performance characters. The role of the stage, or the performance spotlight, is widely recognized by funkeiras as a space of visibility and power that allows them to experiment with diverse femininities. MC Carol feels seen and heard on stage, Deize Tigrona thinks she is courageous for doing whatever she wants on stage, and Linn da Quebrada claims the stage as a place of performative experimentation. Performances, whether live or recorded, present a space of possibility for funkeiras to enact various femininities, such as independent, assertive women and travestis; wives who cheat on their husbands; mistresses who make fun of faithful wives; people searching for casual sex; and independent beings, among others. As chapters three and four have showed, these performances are, indeed, acts of courage, as they make funkeiras' transgressions against normative white femininity public and visible. Finally, the performances are an expression of embodied politics: a communal performance of survival in which styles and purposes shift as context changes.

Because funkeiras' performances are not always in direct violation and disruption of normative white femininity, the contradictions in their performances are often misunderstood by both Brazilian academia and corporate media. The ambiguities that traverse their enactments of femininities cannot be explained with binaries such as active/passive and oppression/resistance. As Chapter Four has exposed, in the same live show, funkeiras may perform as faithful wives who incite violence against their partners' mistresses and then enact the role of single people who mock men's attempts to "trap" them in relationships. Transgression, thus, is provisionally a good framework through which to examine funkeiras' paradoxical performances. Many of funkeiras' performances, in fact, enact a "mixing of categories" that question "the boundaries" of said categories.[7] Binaries of masculinity/femininity and subordination/resistance are not equipped to explain, say, Deize Tigrona's performances about beating up another woman for sleeping with her man or about mocking a man for having a small penis that "even the mistresses don't want." This project's approach to funkeiras' performances hopefully illustrated the exciting and puzzling incongruities in their performances that disrupt monolithic, flattened meanings imposed on them as group.

Throughout the book, I have showed the specific, and often more perplexing, struggles Black funkeiras face in and outside of favela funk. Brazil's colonial history of anti-Blackness, racist sexism, and cisheteronormativity means that Black funkeiras' lives are harder than other light-skinned brown artists'. In the early years of favela funk, funkeiras for the most part did not openly engage or even directly acknowledge their race, per Lopes's assessment.[8] Later in 2013, my interviews with senior funkeiras Deize Tirgrona and MC Dandara show that these Black women were painfully aware of the material effects racism had in their lives. Perhaps they did not engage with the topic publicly out of fear of being further punished for bringing up racism in a context that suffocated these conversations. More recently, however, funkeiras like Tati Quebra Barraco and many others overtly discuss and construct their Black subjectivity and femininity through their music, media interviews, and social media presence. This fashioning of Black women/travestis identities includes the recognition of their subject positions as such, which was unthinkable in the early 2000s, when Tati Quebra Barraco first became famous. These Black artists affirm their subjectivities as strong, beautiful, and able to overcome struggles. They present their Black femininities as desirable and in tension with whiteness more broadly and with white femininity/white feminism in particular. Black funkeiras are engaged in an ongoing process of production of knowledge and practices about Blackness and Black femininity.

The analysis of Black travesti funkeiras in Chapter Six sheds light on the diverse iterations of travesti identity in favela funk. The three performers featured in the chapter—Lacraia, MC Xuxú, and Linn da Quebrada—illuminate the shifting nature of travesti identity within and beyond favela funk. My goal was to echo their voices in the process of trying to understand their relationship to each other and to the contexts that restrict or enable their performances. While it is still essential to focus on the obstacles travestis face, such as systemic and interpersonal violence and poverty, it is also important to shed light on the generative aspects of their performances and their knowledge.

Unlike Lacraia, who was silenced and exploited by a racist, transphobic mainstream media, MC Xuxú and Linn da Quebrada both engage in disidentificatory practices that enable them to work within and against dominant culture. Each artist performs Black travesti identity in distinct, idiosyncratic ways that transpire through their music and personal interviews. These artists use embodied politics to both dispute the political meanings of travesti femininity, Blackness, and working classness and to re-envision social relations from a travesti, nonbinary perspective.

The Funkeiras in Theory: Embodied Politics and Feminist Possibilities

Feminist theory and movements, in their devaluation of femininity through the unexamined focus on its white, normative version, have positioned all femininities in opposition to masculine agency, which disregards the agentic and transgressive potential of marginalized femininities for inciting structural change. Some scholars, like Lockford,[9] have made compelling arguments in favor of disrupting the supposed opposition between feminism and femininity by pointing out that the norms associated with femininity are difficult, if not impossible, to fully emulate. The connection between whiteness and this version of femininity Lockford criticizes is only assumed. Normative white femininity must not be feminism's invisible analytical center.

Like Serano[10] and Hoskin,[11] whose work advocates for marginalized femininities' visibility in all their potential, this book proposes something similar but with a greater focus on race and geography: femininities, especially those performed by working-class folks of color from the Global South, are the result of multiple, complex material and symbolic negotiations with normative systems of race, class, gender, and sexuality. Survival seems to be an important driving force for these performances, but it is certainly not the only outcome. The political potential that emerges out of these femininities is transgressive; it requires a constant navigation through and against the status quo, which in turn is constantly in flux in politically unstable areas such as Brazil.

Based on the postcolonial feminist concept of agency, which emphasizes the "capacity for action that historically specific relations of subordination enable and create,"[12] the chapters in this book show that funkeiras, through their performances of raced and classed femininities, certainly have agency: they navigate the intricate power relations in which favela funk is inserted, a context that often works in ways that puts them in positions of subordination as women and transfeminine people within and outside of the movement. In that way, a white, Western feminist approach to agency, which focuses on "an autonomous, self-making, self-determining subject,"[13] is not useful in apprehending the convoluted circumstances under which marginalized people have some kind of capacity for action. Similar to Mahmood,[14] Third World feminist Mohanty challenges white feminist conceptualizations of agency via Anzaldúa's *mestiza consciousness*.[15] In this case, agency is contingent on history, geography, and community more than on individuality. Therefore, the kind of agency that provides funkeiras' capacity for action is communal and context-dependent rather than based on liberal ideas like individuality and incremental progress.

One way to conceptualize this communal agency is through embodied politics. Fixmer and Wood have defined embodied politics as "personal acts that aim to provoke change by exercising and resisting power in local sites."[16] Although this definition is useful and important for feminist studies in communication, especially for Western third-wave feminism, its focus on "personal acts," ciswomen, and resistance does not quite capture the practices in which people like the funkeiras engage. Instead, I would like to propose embodied politics as performances (quotidian or staged) by feminine folks in the margins that possess transformational political capacities. Like Mohanty, I also believe that "everyday feminist, antiracist, anticapitalist practices are as important as larger, organized political movements."[17] People in vulnerable positions often rely on their bodies to survive. For those who are marginalized and are yet to experience significant structural changes, embodied politics can facilitate their fight against racism, classism, sexism, and transphobic misogyny in media, politics, and in their communities. Hence, embodied politics cannot be assumed to be simple matters of choice to exercise one's individual agency, like many in

Western third-wave feminism advocate. In the case of funkeiras, this book showed that their performances are collective, context-specific, and limited by oppressive structures.

Many of such vulnerable people are, indeed, coded as feminine in their cultures. As I mentioned earlier in this book, violence against women and transfeminine people in Brazil is alarmingly common, especially for those who are Black and indigenous. That means that they are also vulnerable to poverty, which is why marginalized feminine folks of all gender identities often feel like they must survive through their bodies. That is certainly the case with many funkeiras. Femininities, thus, are an important component of embodied politics for these artists. Drawing from funkeiras' performances and interviews analyzed in this book, along with Brazilian Black feminist and *transfeminista* scholarship, I have formulated five primary characteristics of funkeiras' embodied politics that could be useful for researchers in feminist, queer, and intercultural fields studying performances of marginalized feminine people in precarious contexts. These characteristics are not conclusive; instead, they are inductive and consequently subject to adjustments. Any formulation of embodied politics, however, must be firmly grounded on particular contexts and concrete performances of marginalized groups.

First of all, an understanding of funkeiras' embodied politics (and of others' in similar contexts) *must* de-center normative white femininity as a taken-for-granted analytical standpoint, and second, it should examine any kind of culturally specific construction of femininity vis-à-vis constructions of race and class. These categories—femininity, race, and class—should *not* be assumed either. The performance of racialized femininities via embodied politics must trace the contingent, historical roots of these classifications in order to critically assess their current shapes and future visions. Third, my understanding of funkeiras' embodied politics was shaped by Brazilian *transfeminismo*'s epistemological perspectives in order to question biological essentialism and essentialist constructions of "women" and femininity as inevitably attached to particular bodies. A *transfeminista* perspective suggests that those who perform racialized, subaltern femininities, no matter the body they inhabit, are often among the most susceptible to structural and relational violence. Fourth, funkeiras' embodied politics are not in themselves liberatory. Like Muñoz,[18] I understand that these performances—quotidian and staged—present both potential and limitations as vehicles for social change, especially in the case of funkeiras—artists inserted in capitalistic relations of labor. Scholars concerned with the material lives of marginalized people must pay attention to the distinct circumstances under which embodied politics take place. These contextual differences illuminate how and if contestations to oppressive structures are possible. Relatedly, fifth and finally, embodied politics are not always obviously disruptive or subversive; often this way of engaging with politics comes with public exposition that renders these performances risky. Thus, embodied politics are often transgressive and disidentificatory, which indicates marginalized folks' necessity to carefully navigate toxic, dangerous contexts.

Questions about agency and femininity are frequently attached to feminist theory and studies. Previous research about the funkeiras, for instance, posed the question "if they possess capacity for action, are these actions then feminist?" I have purposefully avoided this inquiry until now because my goal was to work inductively, just as I believe feminist work in general should. To the question about whether funkeiras are feminists, my answer is, it depends. Whose feminism are we talking about? As Chapter One shows, more than being inadequate to understand the performances of racialized, classed femininities from the Global South, white, Western feminism is possibly harmful to them as it further pathologizes and marginalizes those women and transfeminine people—Brazilian white feminists have suggested that favela funk is immoral and harmful toward women.[19] Before answering the "feminist question" posed in this paragraph, I would like to take a brief detour.

More than advocating for multiple feminisms, known in Brazil as "difference feminisms,"[20] it is essential that we disrupt the power and reach of feminism, in the *singular* form—the one that seems all-encompassing but is indeed Western, white, cisgender, middle-class, and more.[21] Feminisms, in the plural form, still function as peripheries to a center, namely "The" white, Western feminism. In our current neoliberal context, white feminism problematically has adopted (highjacked?) frameworks of "difference," such as intersectionality, to simply turn them into rhetorical modes that replace the analyses themselves.[22] In the case of intersectionality, Puar notes that, as it has been "mainstreamed" in feminist studies, intersectionality seems to indicate "difference from" white women—the essential center of gender identity: "many white feminists, although hailing intersectionality as [a] primary methodological rubric continue to take gender difference as foundational."[23] This movement happens in tandem with white feminist supremacy. Thus, is "diversifying" feminism really the answer to address the dominance of its white, Western center? I want to clarify that this does *not* apply to the theories and studies that directly contest and have been working tirelessly to hold white feminism accountable, such as Black feminism and Chicana feminism in the U.S. and Black, indigenous feminisms and *transfeminismo* in Brazil. The idea, rather, is to continue to shed light on the fact that white feminism—aided by other ideologies and systems like colonialism, white supremacy, and more recently neoliberalism—is still able to either ignore these challenges to its dominance or to co-opt the intellectual production of other feminisms. As is, there is little justification for the existence of (white) feminism. When we reflect on what kinds of feminist tenets should be prioritized in any version of it, the answers should include the ability to simultaneously account for *and* be molded by the most vulnerable persons under the most violent systems of oppression beyond the presumed foundation of sexism and misogyny. That requires a certain flexibility that Western thought usually squashes.

The most outspoken feminist funkeiras rarely qualify the type of feminism in which they engage. They regard themselves as feminists, period. What funkeiras deem feminist is contradictory, messy, fresh, and exciting. MC Carol, who tells me she is a feminist, often reacts to fatphobic social media comments by mocking the offender's appearance. Tati Quebra Barraco tells other women to both be financially independent and to take material advantage of men. MC Xuxú criticizes sexist, homophobic songs by cismen in favela funk but also tells me that she is no longer a feminist—"there are feminists who include me, and there are feminists who exclude me. If I'm not included, I'm not gonna claim [the label]." Linn da Quebrada not only refers to herself as a feminist, but she also explains that she is interested in "Black feminism, or a Black transfeminism" that understands "the places of other femininities, their specificities, acknowledging that we're very different, and that even though we are very different, maybe we have things in common, and these things we have in common are indeed very powerful." With teary eyes, I tell Linn, "Wow, that's so beautiful." Funkeiras, then, are feminists only insofar as feminism is truly fighting against its colonial, white supremacist, classist, and cisheteronormative bearings. Their version of it is also very much coalitional, as Linn's point indicates. Funkeiras' feminism definitely "fucks with the grays."[24]

Beyond Survival

The recent growing conservatism in Brazil culminated in the 2018 election of far-right conservative Christian Jair Bolsonaro for president. Waves of progressivism and conservativism speak to Latin America's clashes since colonial times.[25] As a consequence, political discourses and institutional violence around race, class, gender, and sexuality have deteriorated greatly in Brazil—Rio de Janeiro and São Paulo, who massively voted in favor of Bolsonaro and his local candidates, included.[26] Bolsonaro and his supporters, for instance, have adopted violent resistance to what Evangelical Christians across several countries term *"ideologia de gênero"* (gender ideology). This expression is used to refer to any modest efforts to promote discussions around gender identity and sexuality in educational settings.[27] Bolsonaro's appointed Secretary of Human Rights Damares Alves, who like the president is a conservative Christian and a fervent opponent of "gender ideology," stated that Brazil was entering a "new era" in her inauguration speech, one in which "boys wear blue and girls wear pink."[28] In terms of race, Black folks in Brazil are at a much greater risk of institutional violence, with Black women and travestis targeted more frequently than their non-Black counterparts.[29] On the local level, Rio de Janeiro registered the highest number ever of killings by police in 2019—1,810 victims—80% of whom were Black and *mestiços*.[30] The current violent right-wing landscape in Brazil reveals the historical and persistent systemic injustices

to which working-class Black feminine people—like the funkeiras—
are subjected, while also revealing the urgency and risk of their public
performances.

In this context of growing conservativism, favela funk continues to
occupy a liminal space of condemnation and popularity by corporate
media and governments at the federal and local levels. Case in point, a
47-year-old white, São Paulo-based web designer submitted a "legislative idea" in May 2017 proposing that favela funk should be criminalized. These suggestions by common citizens are subjected to a public
hearing by congress if they reach 20,000 signatures. This one received
over 21,985 supportive signatures.[31] The author of the proposal suggests
that favela funk is no more than a "recruitment tool for the organized
crime on social media," bailes are riddled with "orgies" and "pornog-
raphy," and the movement is "fake culture."[32] Even though the chair of
the Human Rights Commission dismissed the topic at the time, headlines about funk's possible official criminalization at the federal level
abounded. It is concerning that, under the current much-more conservative congress and presidency, if this suggestion gains visibility again,
it might pass. In a country as politically instable as Brazil, with a colonial history of anti-Blackness, there are no guarantees on favela funk's
legal status.

Funkeiras continue their struggle to survive in the midst of all
this persistent structural violence. However, from the performances
and interviews spotlighted in this book, it is clear that funkeiras today
want more than survival; they want a thriving future. Black funkeiras especially, both ciswomen and travestis, are in a public, communal process of subjectivity-building in which they concomitantly fight
against anti-Blackness, classism, misogyny, and transphobia and also
construct spaces of identity affirmation where they are able to become
Black women and travestis[33]—a revised version of the toxic identities
normative systems impose. Scholars should continue investigating the
intricacies of this process, especially via public platforms, such as social
media, in which Black feminine artists show support and solidarity for
each other.

It is difficult to envision a future when trying to survive because survival is infused with urgency; it is an immediate need. The temporality

of marginalized folks, then, is shaped by these urgencies and needs. That is why, according to Muñoz, queer culture, for instance, labors to materialize the future in the present —and a lot of that is concretized via art and performance. Indeed, art and culture possess an "anticipatory illumination:"[34] "Such illumination cuts through fragmenting darkness and allows us to see the politically enabling whole. Such illumination will provide us with access to a world that should be, that could be, and that will be."[35] For funkeira Linn da Quebrada, her art—live and mediated performances and social media photos—is the materialization and anticipation of something yet to exist widely. In her performances, Linn da Quebrada disrupts the cisgender masculine center to privilege, instead, queer and transfeminine people of color who dance freely and exchange affection in public, in broad daylight. These images are Linn's attempt to create "new networks of survival," according to our interview.

Linn da Quebrada's "vista" is in line with *transfeminismo*'s decolonial project. *Transfeminismo* sheds light on different systems of normativity— white supremacy, gender essentialism, gender hierarchy—that are integral aspects of Brazil's colonial legacy. Part of *transfeministas'* goal is then to underscore that cisnormativity intersects with other parts of colonialism in the Americas, which are "historically genocidal, white supremacist, and committed to myriad forms of subordination and biopolitical control."[36] A *transfeminista* decolonial perspective, thus, questions and destabilizes first and foremost the colonial logic of subordination, including the articulation of hierarchized binaries and ethnocentric medical discourses, to then reclaim indigenous and other non-Western perspectives around ways of being and relating.[37] *Transfeminista* scholar Vergueiro is explicitly committed to an intersectional decolonial effort that simultaneously foregrounds the colonial nature of cisnormativity while undoing the internalization of colonial forms of subjectivation.[38] Funkeiras like Linn are aiding in the materialization of these *transfeminista* decolonial goals.

Transfeministas focus on those who have been surviving and challenging coloniality, racism, and transphobia through their lived experiences in Latin America. It seems like a similar movement from scholars in intercultural communication and feminist studies could help address white, Western problem in these disciplines. In paying attention to how the funkeiras navigate and transgress systems of oppression—in many ways embodying an intersectional, *transfeminista* perspective—feminist and intercultural communication researchers could potentially help shift the pervasive Western-centric tendencies in both areas. This, in turn, could continue feminist and intercultural communication work in developing more nuanced understandings of power relations within context-specific structures, all while learning from the theoretical, political, and coalitional contributions from artists, activists, and scholars in the Global South. These possibilities fall perfectly in line with what critical scholars have demanded from both feminist studies and intercultural communication over the years.[39]

The funkeiras' performances and perspectives present many exciting scholarly possibilities. Their invisibility in research about favela funk is unacceptable. I hope this book encourages other scholars to take interest in the complexity funkeiras have to offer to diverse fields, such as feminist and queer studies, intercultural communication, and critical cultural studies. For now, my hope is that feminism, in the singular form, will continue to be challenged and transformed by folks like the funkeiras. Finally, I hope this book is perceived as an homage to the funkeiras. They have made me a better scholar and a better woman; they have made me hate feminism and become excited about it again. They have made me realize that social justice work needs beats and twerking.

Notes

1 John Fiske, "Writing Ethnographies: Contribution to a Dialogue," *Quarterly Journal of Speech* 77 (1991): 330–35.

2 D. Soyini Madison, *Critical Ethnography: Method, Ethics, and Performance* (Thousand Oaks: Sage, 2005), 5.

3 Madison, *Critical Ethnography*, 25.

4 Gabriel Adams Castelo Branco de Aragão, "O Discurso e a Construção da Imagem Feminina No Funk," *Cadernos de Pesquisana Graduação em Letras* 1, no. 1 (2011): 73–85.

5 Adriana Lopes, *Funk-se Quem Quiser: No Batidão Negro da Cidade Carioca* (Rio de Janeiro: Bom Texto, 2011).

6 Norma Alarcón, "The Theoretical Subject(s) of This Bridge Called My Back and Anglo-American Feminism," in *Criticism in the Borderlands: Studies in Chicano Literature, Culture, and Ideology*, 3rd ed., eds. Hector Calderón & José David Saldívar (Durham: Duke University Press, 1998): 29.

7 Chris Jenks, *Transgression* (London: Routledge, 2003), 9.

8 Lopes, *Funk-se*.

9 Lesa Lockford, *Performing Femininity: Rewriting Gender Identity* (Walnut Creek: Altamira Press, 2004).

10 Julia Serano, "Reclaiming Femininity" in *Transfeminist Perspectives in and Beyond Transgender and Gender Studies*, ed. Anne Enke (Philadelphia: Temple University Press, 2012): 170–83.

11 Rhea Ashley Hoskin, "Femme Interventions and the Proper Feminist Subject: Critical Approaches to Decolonizing Western Feminist Pedagogies," *Cogent Social Sciences* 3, no. 1276819 (January 2017): 1–16.

12 Saba Mahmood, "Feminist Theory, Embodiment, and the Docile Agent: Some Reflections on the Egyptian Islamic Revival," *Cultural Anthropology* 16, no. 2 (May 2001): 203.

13 Alarcón, "Theoretical Subject(s)."

14 Mahmood, "Feminist Theory."

15 Chandra Mohanty, *Feminism Without Borders* (Durham, NC: Duke University Press, 2003).

16 Natalie Fixmer and Julia T. Wood, "The Personal is *Still* Political: Embodied Politics in Third Wave Feminism," *Women's Studies in Communication* 28, no. 2 (Fall 2005): 237.

17 Mohanty, *Feminism*, 4.

18 José Esteban Muñoz, *Disidentifications: Queers of Color and the Performance of Politics* (Minneapolis: University of Minnesota Press, 1999).

19 Aragão, "Discurso"; Marcia Tiburi, "A Nova Moral do Funk," *Cult*, no. 163, November 2011, https://revistacult.uol.com.br/home/moral-funk/.

20 Heloísa Buarque de Hollanda, *Explosão Feminista: Arte, Cultura, Política e Universidade* (São Paulo: Editora Companhia das Letras, 2018), 252–72.

21 Mohanty, *Feminism*.

22 Sirma Bilge, "Intersectionality Undone: Saving Intersectionality from Feminist Intersectionality Studies," *Du Bois Review* 10, no. 2 (2013): 405–24; Brittney Cooper, "Intersectionality," in *The Oxford Handbook of Feminist Theory*, eds. Lisa Disch and Mary Hawkesworth (New York, NY: Oxford University Press, 2016), 1–15; Jaspir Puar, " 'I Would Rather Be a Cyborg Than a Goddess': Becoming Intersectional in Assemblage Theory," *PhiloSOPHIA* 2, no. 1 (2012): 49–66.

23 Puar, "I Would Rather," 53.

24 Joan Morgan, *When Chickenheads Come Home to Roost* (New York: Simon & Schuster, 1999), 59.

25 Jorge Contesse, "Conservative Governments and Latin America's Human Rights Landscape," *AJIL Unbound* 113 (2019), https://papers.ssrn.com/sol3/papers.cfm?abstract_id=3486444.

26 Amanda Rossi, "Eleições 2018: O Peso de Cada Região do Brasil na Votação para Presidente," *BBC*, October 8, 2018, https://www.bbc.com/portuguese/brasil-45780864.

27 Sérgio Rangel, "Bolsonaro pede disciplina e critica 'ideologia de gênero' em entrega de colégio da PM," *Folha de São Paulo*, December 17, 2018, https://www1.folha.uol.com.br/educacao/2018/12/bolsonaro-pede-disciplina-e-critica-ideologia-de-genero-em-entrega-de-colegio-da-pm.shtml; Paulo Saldaña, "Saiba como surgiu o termo 'ideologia de gênero,'" *Folha de São Paulo*, October 23, 2018, https://www1.folha.uol.com.br/cotidiano/2018/10/saiba-como-surgiu-o-termo-ideologia-de-genero.shtml.

28 Clarissa Pains, "'Menino veste azul e menina veste rosa', diz Damares Alves em video," *O Globo*, January 3, 2019, https://oglobo.globo.com/sociedade/menino-veste-azul-menina-veste-rosa-diz-damares-alves-em-video-23343024.

29 Paula A. Idoeta, "Atlas da Violência: Brasil Tem 13 Homicídios de Mulheres por Dia, e Maioria das Vítimas é Negra," *BBC Brazil*, June 5, 2019, https://www.bbc.com/portuguese/brasil-48521901.

30 Henrique Coelho and Felipe Grandin, "80% dos mortos por policiais no RJ no 1° semestre de 2019 eram negros e pardos, aponta levantamento," *G1*, February 8, 2020, https://g1.globo.com/rj/rio-de-janeiro/noticia/2020/02/08/80percent-dos-mortos-por-policiais-no-rj-no-1-semestre-de-2019-eram-negros-e-pardos-aponta-levantamento.ghtml.

31 e-Cidadania, "Criminalização do Funk Como Crime de Saúde Pública a Criança aos Adolescentes e a Família [sic]," *Senado Federal*, May 2017, https://www12.senado.leg.br/ecidadania/visualizacaoideia?id=65513.

32 e-Cidadania, "Criminalização."

33 Viviane Inês Weschenfelder and Elí Terezinha H. Fabris, "Becoming Black Woman: Self-Writing in an Intersectional Place," *Revista Estudos Feministas* 27, no. 3 (2019): 1–15.

34 José Estebán Muñoz, *Cruising Utopia: The Then and There of Queer Futurity* (New York, NY: New York University Press, 2009).

35 Muñoz, *Cruising Utopia*, 64.

36 Viviane Vergueiro, "Por Inflexões Decoloniais de Corpos e Identidades de Gênero Inconformes: Uma Análise Autoetnográfica da Cisgeneridade como Normatividade," *Repositório UFBA*, 2015, https://repositorio.ufba.br/ri/handle/ri/19685.

37 Vergueiro, "Inflexões Decoloniais."

38 Vergueiro, "Inflexões Decoloniais."

39 Bernadette M. Calafell, "The Future of Feminist Scholarship: Beyond the Politics of Inclusion," *Women's Studies in Communication*, 37 (2014): 266–70; Karma Chávez, "Pushing Boundaries: Queer Intercultural Communication," *Journal of International and Intercultural Communication* 6, no. 2 (2013): 83–95; Shinsuke Eguchi and Godfried Asante, "Disidentifications Revisited: Queer(y)ing Intercultural Communication Theory," *Communication Theory* 26 (2016): 171–89; Julia Johnson, "Cisgender Privilege, Intersectionality, and the Criminalization of CeCe McDonald: Why Intercultural Communication Needs Transgender Studies," *Journal of International and Intercultural Communication* 6, no. 2 (2013): 135–44; Gust Yep, "Toward the De-Subjugation of Racially Marked Knowledges in Communication," *Southern Communication Journal* 75, no. 2 (2010): 171–175.

Bibliography

Aguiar, Márcio M. "A Construção das Hierarquias Sociais: Classe, Raça, Gênero e Etnicidade." *Cadernos de Pesquisa do CDHIS* 36–37, no. 20 (2007): 83–8.

Alarcón, Norma. "The Theoretical Subject(s) of This Bridge Called My Back and Anglo-American Feminism." In *Criticism in the Borderlands: Studies in Chicano Literature, Culture, and Ideology*, 3rd ed., edited by Hector Calderón and José David Saldívar, 28–39. Durham: Duke University Press, 1998.

Amin, Tatiana. "Tati Quebra Barraco Agita Festival na Argentina." *O Fuxico*, November 21, 2006. https://www.ofuxico.com.br/noticias-sobre-famosos/tati-quebra-barraco-agita-festival-na-argentina/2006/11/21-53983.html.

"Anitta Se Pronuncia sobre Racismo após Ataques contra Ludmilla: 'A Justiça Vai Atrás de Você.'" *Extoína*, June 17, 2020. https://exitoina.uol.com.br/noticias/famo-sos/anitta-se-pronuncia-sobre-racismo-apos-ataques-contra-ludmilla-justica-vai-atras-de-voce.phtml.

Antunes, Anderson. "Could Brazil's Latest Music Sensation Anitta Be a Global Superstar in the Making?" *Forbes*, August 30, 2013. https://www.forbes.com/sites/andersonantunes/2013/08/30/could-brazils-latest-music-sensation-anitta-be-a-global-superstar-in-the-making/#3b316dc0432a.

Anzaldúa, Gloria. *Borderlands/La Frontera: The New Mestiza*, 3rd ed. San Francisco: Aunt Lute, 2007.

Aragão, Gabriel Adams Castelo Branco de. "O Discurso e a Construção da Imagem Feminina No Funk." *Cadernos de Pesquisa na Graduação em Letras* 1, no. 1 (2011): 73–85.

ArrebentaFunk. "MC Kátia—Froxona resposta Beyonce [clipe official]." October 9, 2012. YouTube video, 5:24. https://www.youtube.com/watch?v=3WM6k1lzzpI.

Arsenault, Chris. "Evangelicalism Grows in Brazil's Favelas Amid Poverty and Violence." *Reuters*, April 10, 2017. https://www.reuters.com/article/us-brazil-religion-landrights/evangelicalism-grows-in-brazils-favelas-amid-poverty-and-violence-idUSKBN17C1H4.

Arthurs, Jane, and Jean Grimshaw. *Women's Bodies: Discipline and Transgression.* London: Casell, 1999.

Auslander, Philip. "Live and Technologically Mediated Performance." In *The Cambridge Companion to Performance Studies*, edited by Tracy C. Davis, 107–19. Cambridge: Cambridge University Press, 2008.

Balloussier, Anna Virgínia. "Família de Marielle Reivindica Legado e Bissexualidade da Vereadora." *Folha de Pernambuco*, July 1, 2019. https://www.folhape.com.br/noticias/familia-de-marielle-reivindica-legado-e-bissexualidade-da-vereadora/109281/.

Baltazar, Thiago. " 'O Funk Me Deu Voz e Eu a Uso para Ajudar Mulheres', Diz Pocah." *Vogue*, November 10, 2019. https://vogue.globo.com/celebridade/noticia/2019/11/o-funk-me-deu-voz-e-eu-uso-para-ajudar-mulheres-diz-pocah.html.

Barbosa, Bernardo, and Cleber Souza. "Antes de Pisoteio e Mortes, PM Cercou Baile, Dizem Frequentadores." *UOL Cotidiano*, December 1, 2019. https://noticias.uol.com.br/cotidiano/ultimas-noticias/2019/12/01/antes-de-pisoteio-e-mortes-pm-cercou-baile-funk-dizem-frequentadores.htm.

Batista, Vera. "Na Periferia do Medo." In *Estudos Gerais da Psicanálise: Segundo Encontro Mundial.* Rio de Janeiro: Estudos Gerais da Psicanálise, October 30, 2003.

Belizario, Fernanda. "Gênero: Feminilidade Travesti." *Medium*, March 7, 2019. https://medium.com/@febelizario/g%C3%AAnero-feminilidade-travesti-aaffaf7fb386.

Bento, Berenice. *O Que é Transexualidade.* São Paulo, SP: Editora Brasiliense, 2017.

Bilge, Sirma. "Intersectionality Undone: Saving Intersectionality from Feminist Intersectionality Studies." *Du Bois Review* 10, no. 2 (2013): 405–24.

Butler, Judith. *Gender Trouble: Feminism and the Subversion of Identity.* New York: Routledge, 2006.

Caceres, Guillermo, Lucas Ferrari, and Carlos Palombini. "The Age of Lula/Tamborzão: Politics and Sonority." *Revista do Instituto de Estudos Brasileiros* 58 (2014): 157–207.

Calafell, Bernadette M. "Pro(re-)claiming Loss: A Performance Pilgrimage in Search of Malintzin Tenépal." *Text and Performance Quarterly* 25, no. 1 (2005): 43–56.

Calafell, Bernadette M. *Latina/o Communication Studies: Theorizing Performance.* New York: Peter Lang, 2007.

Calafell, Bernadette M. "The Future of Feminist Scholarship: Beyond the Politics of Inclusion." *Women's Studies in Communication* 37 (2014): 266–70.

Cardoso, Fernando Luiz. "The Relationship Between Sexual Orientation and Gender Identification Among Males in a Cross-Cultural Analysis in Brazil, Turkey and Thailand." *Sexuality & Culture* 17 (2013): 568–97.

Carneiro, Sueli. "Enegracer o Feminismo: A Situação da Mulher Negra na América Latina a Partir de uma Perspectiva de Gênero." *Geledés*, June 3, 2011. http://www.geledes.org.br/enegrecer-o-feminismo-situacao-da-mulher-negra-na-america-latina-partir-de-uma-perspectiva-de-genero/#gs.hB=CYyY.

Carvalho, Marcelle. "Valesca Popozuda: 'Bumbum Está no Seguro Porque É Meu Instrumento de Trabalho.' " *Extra*, February 2, 2012. https://extra.globo.com/tv-e-lazer/valesca-popozuda-bumbum-esta-no-seguro-porque-meu-instrumento-de-trabalho-3857097.html.

Ceratti, Mariana. "In Brazil, an Emergent Middle Class Takes Off." *The World Bank*, November 13, 2012. https://www.worldbank.org/en/news/feature/2012/11/13/middle-class-in-Brazil-Latin-America-report.

Chávez, Karma. "Pushing Boundaries: Queer Intercultural Communication." *Journal of International and Intercultural Communication* 6, no. 2 (2013): 83–95.

Coacci, Thiago. "Finding Brazilian Transfeminism: A Preliminary Mapping of a Rising Branch." *História Agora* 15 (2014): 134–61.

Coelho, Caia (@travestiviva). "THREAD, Lacraia era uma travesti e ficou conhecida nacionalmente em 2003 através do funk, eu tinha 11 anos …" Twitter, June 3, 2020, 5:20 p.m. https://twitter.com/travestiviva/status/1268306593441091590.

Coelho, Henrique, and Felipe Grandin. "80% dos Mortos por Policiais no RJ no 1° Semestre de 2019 Eram Negros e Pardos, Aponta Levantamento." *G1*, February 8, 2020. https://g1.globo.com/rj/rio-de-janeiro/noticia/2020/02/08/80percent-dos-mortos-por-policiais-no-rj-no-1-semestre-de-2019-eram-negros-e-pardos-aponta-levantamento.ghtml.

Cohen, Cathy. "Punks, Bulldaggers, and Welfare Queens: The Radical Potential of Queer Politics?" *GLQ: A Journal of Lesbian and Gay Studies* 3, no. 4 (1997): 437–65.

Collins, Patricia Hill. *Black Sexual Politics: African-Americans, Gender and the New Racism*. New York: Routledge, 2004.

Collins, Patricia Hill. *Black Feminist Thought: Knowledge, Consciousness, and the Politics of Empowerment*. New York: Routledge, 2009.

Conquergood, Dwight. "Rethinking Ethnography: Towards a Critical Cultural Politics." *Communication Monographs* 58 (1991): 179–94.

Contesse, Jorge. "Conservative Governments and Latin America's Human Rights Landscape." *AJIL Unbound* 113 (2019). https://papers.ssrn.com/sol3/papers.cfm?abstract_id=3486444.

Cooper, Brittney. "Intersectionality." In *The Oxford Handbook of Feminist Theory*, edited by Lisa Disch and Mary Hawkesworth, 1–15. New York, NY: Oxford University Press, 2016.

Côrrea, Mariza. "Sobre a Invenção da Mulata." *Cadernos Pagu* 6/7 (1996): 35–50.

Corrêa, Mariza. "Do Feminismo aos Estudos de Gênero no Brasil: Um Exemplo Pessoal." *Cadernos Pagu*, 16 (2001): 13–30.

Costa, Claudia de Lima. "Being Here and Writing There: Gender and the Politics of Translation in a Brazilian Landscape." *Signs* 25, no. 3 (2000): 727–60.

Costa, Sérgio. "A Construção Sociológica da Raça no Brasil." *Estudos Afro-Asiáticos* 24, no. 1 (2002): 35–61.

Coutinho, Reginaldo Aparecido. "The Acknowledgment of Funk Carioca as 'Patrimônio Cultural': Daily Life and Social and Political Clashes around the Law 5543/2009." *Antíteses* 8, no. 15 (2015): 520–41.

Crenshaw, Kimberlé. "Mapping the Margins: Intersectionality, Identity Politics, and Violence Against Women of Color." *Stanford Law Review* 43, no. 6 (1991): 1241–99.

da Quebrada, Linn. "MC Linn da Quebrada—Enviadescer—clipe official." May 25, 2016. YouTube video, 2:54. https://www.youtube.com/watch?v=saZywh0FuEY.

da Quebrada, Linn. "Mc Linn da Quebrada—Talento—Clipe official." August 23, 2016. YouTube video, 5:59. https://www.youtube.com/watch?v=hkAHuRPGgNk.

da Quebrada, Linn. "Mc Linn da Quebrada—Bixa Preta." September 30, 2016. YouTube video, 4:28. https://www.youtube.com/watch?v=ZeMa942nYe4.

da Quebrada, Linn (@linndaquebrada). "Baseado em carne viva e fatos reais, é o sangue dos meus que escorre pelas marginais …" Instagram photo, March 15, 2018. https://www.instagram.com/p/BgV1izBHArm/?igshid=pebho31qs3l1.

da Quebrada, Linn. "Linn da Quebrada—Coytada (Clipe Oficial)." September 17, 2018. YouTube video, 3:01. https://www.youtube.com/watch?v=IUq4WWJRngE.

da Quebrada, Linn (@linndaquebrada). "uma das coisas q mais tem me chamado atenção nesses protestos sobre o caso d Georg Floyd é o posicionamento da população branca, saindo da suposta neutralidade universal. isso eh mto importante e fundamental. principalmente pra nós. e pra aquelas aqui q se dizem anti-racistas." Twitter, May 29, 2020, 9:04 a.m. https://twitter.com/linndaquebrada/status/1266369778031013890.

da Quebrada, Linn. "[LIVE] Linn da Quebrada e Djamila Ribeiro: O que Vem Depois da Ocupação?" June 30, 2020. YouTube video, 1:19:39. https://www.youtube.com/watch?v=tYI4ZxZRGYc.

da Quebrada, Linn (@linndaquebrada). "tua pele és cura. faça de seu corpo seu patuá. faca amolada em mesa de cetim. corte profundo. amuleto & não muleta. mate & morra." Instagram photo, July 2, 2020. https://www.instagram.com/p/CCKE39MlaPz/.

Deliovsky, Kathy. "Normative White Femininity: Race, Gender and the Politics of Beauty." *Atlantis* 33, no. 1 (January 2008): 49–59.

Detona Funk. "Jessi—Boy machista (DJ Chileno)." June 5, 2018. YouTube, 3:00. https://www.youtube.com/watch?v=9SaOIZO7-gc.

Diamond, Elin. "Mimesis, Mimicry, and the 'True-Real.'" In *Acting Out: Feminist Performances,* edited by Lynda Hart and Peggy Phelan, 363–82. Ann Arbor: University of Michigan Press, 1993. Quoted in Deanna Shoemaker. "Queers, Monsters, Drag Queens, and Whiteness: Unruly Femininities in Women's Staged Performances." PhD diss., University of Texas at Austin, 2004. https://repositories.lib.utexas.edu/handle/2152/2202

Dow, Bonnie, and Julia T. Wood. "Repeating History and Learning from It: What Can SlutWalks Teach Us About Feminism?" *Women's Studies in Communication* 37, no. 1 (2014): 22–47.

Durham, Aisha, Brittney C. Cooper, and Susana M. Morris. "The Stage Hip-Hop Feminism Built: A New Directions Essay." *Signs* 38, no. 3 (2013): 721–37.

e-Cidadania. "Criminalização do Funk Como Crime de Saúde Pública a Criança aos Adolescentes e a Família [sic]." *Senado Federal*, May 2017. https://www12.senado.leg.br/ecidadania/visualizacaoideia?id=65513.

Eguchi, Shinsuke, and Godfried Asante. "Disidentifications Revisited: Queer(y)ing Intercultural Communication Theory." *Communication Theory* 26 (2016): 171–89.

Eguchi, Shinsuke, Bernadette M. Calafell, and Shadee Abdi. *De-Whitening Intersectionality: Race, Intercultural Communication, and Politics*. Lanham, MD: Rowman & Littlefield, 2020.

EliveltonMello FUNK. "Mc Pocahontas—Seu marido tá bancando." February 5, 2012. YouTube video, 2:14. https://www.youtube.com/watch?v=PrgXdNXg-CY.

Eng, David, Judith Halberstam, and José Muñoz. "Introduction: What's Queer About Queer Studies Now?" *Social Text* 23, no. 3–4 (2005): 15–7.

Essinger, Silvio. *Batidão: Uma História do Funk*. Rio de Janeiro, Editora Record, 2005.

Facina, Adriana. " 'Não Me Bate Doutor': Funk e Criminalização da Pobreza." *Encontro de Estudos Multidisciplinares em Cultura*, Salvador, May 27–29, 2009.

Facina, Adriana, Renan Moutinho, Dennis Novaes, and Carlos Palombini. "O Errado Que Deu Certo: *Deu Onda*, o Debate da Harmonia e a Construção da Batida Numa Produção Paulistana de Funk Carioca." *Opus* 24, no. 1 (2018): 222–63.

Falcheti, Fabrício. "Com 'Beijinho no Ombro', Cachê de Valesca Popozuda Passa para R$ 60 mil." *UOL*, February 24, 2014. https://natelinha.uol.com.br/celebridades/2014/02/24/com-beijinho-no-ombro-cache-de-valesca-popozuda-passa-para-r-60-mil-71861.php.

Fenske, Mindy. "The Aesthetic of the Unfinished: Ethics and Performance." *Text and Performance Quarterly* 24, no. 1 (2004): 1–19.

Fernandes, Nelito, and Alice Granato. "Mulherada de Respeito." *Época*, January 16, 2006. http://revistaepoca.globo.com/Revista/Epoca/0,,EDR72874-6011,00.html.

Fiske, John. "Writing Ethnographies: Contribution to a Dialogue." *Quarterly Journal of Speech* 77 (1991): 330–35.

Fixmer, Natalie, and Julia T. Wood. "The Personal is Still Political: Embodied Politics in Third Wave Feminism." *Women's Studies in Communication* 28, no. 2, (July 2005): 235–57.

FM Music BR. "MC Marcelly & Maikinho DVD—Duela rimeas na hora." January 30, 2012. YouTube video, 7:36. https://www.youtube.com/watch?v=A0NBwZmcxIo.

Foust, Christina. *Transgression as a Mode of Resistance: Rethinking Social Movement in an Era of Corporate Globalization*. Plymouth: Lexington Books, 2010.

Freire Filho, João, and Micael Herschmann. "Funk Carioca: Between Condemnation and Acclaim in the Media." *Eco-Pós* 6, no. 2 (2003): 60–72.

Funk Carioca. "MC Carol de Niterói:: Ao vivo em um video polêmico na roda de funk:: Especial." March 11, 2013. YouTube video, 6:39. https://www.youtube.com/watch?v=Eu-dsrtbuHE.

Funk Mídia. "MC Carol—Não foi Cabral." July 3, 2015. YouTube video, 3:17. https://www.youtube.com/watch?v=XchG_QRQ6Rc.

Furacão 2000. "DVD Furacão 2000 Tsunami I." January 11, 2011. YouTube video, 2:39. https://www.youtube.com/watch?v=gcOkX_CW1aQ.

Furacão 2000. "Twister Mc Katia Marido e meu." January 17, 2011. YouTube video, 1:57. https://www.youtube.com/watch?v=gVKj-EVIhYA.

Gagné, Patricia, and Deanna McGaughey. "Designing Women: Cultural Hegemony and the Exercise of Power Among Women Who Have Undergone Elective Mammoplasty." In *The Politics of Women's Bodies: Sexuality, Appearance and Behavior*, 3rd ed., edited by Rose Weitz, 192–213. New York: Oxford UP, 2010.

Gamson, Joshua. "Talking Freaks: Lesbian, Gay, Bisexual and Transgendered Families on Day-Time Talk TV." In *Queer Families, Queer Politics: Challenging Culture and the State*, edited by Mary Bernstein and Renate Reimann, 68–86. New York: Columbia University Press, May 2001.

Garcia, Denise. *Sou Feia, Mas Tô na Moda*. São Paulo: Imovision. Film, 2005.

Garcia, Marcos Roberto. "Identity as a 'Patchwork': Aspects of Identity Among Low-Income Brazilian Travestis." *Culture, Health & Sexuality* 11, no. 6 (July 2009): 611–23.

Gerrard, Jessica, and Jo Ball. "From Fuck Marry Kill to Snog Marry Avoid: Feminisms and the Excesses of Femininity." *Feminist Review* 105 (2013): 122–29.

Gill, Rosalind. "Postfeminist Media Culture: Elements of a Sensibility." *European Journal of Cultural Studies* 10, no. 2 (2007): 147–66.

Gill, Rosalind, and Christina Scharff, eds. *New Femininites: Postfeminism, Neoliberalism and Subjectivity*. New York: Palgrave Macmillan, 2011.

Gomes de Jesus, Jaqueline. "Gender Without Essentialism: Transgender Feminism as a Critique of Sex." *Universitas Humanística* 78 (June 2014): 241–57.

Gomes de Jesus, Jaqueline, and Haley Alves. "Transgender Feminism and Movements of Transsexual Women." *Cronos* 11, no. 2 (2012): 8–19.

Gomes, Mariana. "My Pussy é o Poder. Representação Feminina Através do Funk: Identidade, Feminismo e Indústria Cultural." Unpublished thesis, Federal Fluminense University, 2015.

Halualani, Rona Tamiko, Lily Mendoza, and Jolanta A. Drzewiecka. "'Critical' Junctures in Intercultural Communication Studies: A Review." *The Review of Communication* 9, no. 1 (2009): 17–35.

Heavy Baile. "Heavy Baile—BERRO (feat. Tati Quebra Barraco e Lia Clark)." December 1, 2017. YouTube video, 3:30. https://www.youtube.com/watch?v=NzILPU8PG2s.

Heavy Baile. "Heavy Baile, Tati Quebra Barraco & MC Carol—Mamãe da putaria (clipe oficial)." March 8, 2019. YouTube video, 3:35. https://www.youtube.com/watch?v=vw09YpI_QMQ.

Herschmann, Micael. *O Funk e o Hip-Hop Invadem a Cena*. Rio de Janeiro: Editora UFRJ, 2005.

Hill, Shonagh. "The Crossing of Boundaries: Transgression Enacted." *Theatre Research International* 36, no. 3 (2011): 278–82.

Hollanda, Heloísa Buarque de. *Explosão Feminista: Arte, Cultura, Política e Universidade.* São Paulo: Editora Companhia das Letras, 2018.

Holling, Michelle, and Bernadette Marie Calafell. "Tracing the Emergence of Latina/oVernaculars in Studies of Latin@ Communication." In *Latina/o Discourse in Vernacular Spaces: Somos de una Voz?* edited by Michelle Holling and Bernadette Marie Calafell, 17–29. Lanham: Lexington Press, 2011.

Hoskin, Rhea Ashley. "Femme Interventions and the Proper Feminist Subject: Critical Approaches to Decolonizing Western Feminist Pedagogies." *Cogent Social Sciences* 3, no. 1276819 (January 2017): 1–16.

Hoskin, Rhea Ashley. "Femme Theory: Refocusing the Intersectional Lens." *Atlantis* 38, no. 1 (June 2017): 95–109.

Hoskin, Rhea Ashley, and Allison Taylor. "Femme Resistance: The Fem(me)inine Art of Failure." *Psychology & Sexuality* (May 13, 2019): 1–20.

Idoeta, Paula A. "Atlas da Violência: Brasil Tem 13 Homicídios de Mulheres por Dia, e Maioria das Vítimas É Negra." *BBC Brazil*, June 5, 2019. https://www.bbc.com/portuguese/brasil-48521901.

Inovashow. "Tati Quebra Barraco—Tu quer ser eu (CD se liberta)." December 11, 2014. YouTube video, 2:15. https://www.youtube.com/watch?v=I_cMb4LA3-k.

Itaborahy, Lucas Paoli. "Pessoas LGBT Vivendo em Probreza no Rio de Janeiro." *Micro Rainbow International*, December 2014. https://mrifoundation.global/wp-content/uploads/2014/12/20141204-report-port.pdf.

Jenks, Chris. *Transgression.* London: Routledge, 2003.

Johnson, E. Patrick. ""Quare" Studies, or (Almost) Everything I Know About Queer Studies I Learned from My Grandmother." *Text and Performance Quarterly* 21, no. 1 (2001): 1–25.

Johnson, Julia. "Cisgender Privilege, Intersectionality, and the Criminalization of CeCe McDonald: Why Intercultural Communication Needs Transgender Studies." *Journal of International and Intercultural Communication* 6, no. 2 (2013): 135–44.

Kendall, Erica Nicole. "Female Athletes Often Face the Femininity Police—Especially Serena Williams." *The Guardian*, July 14, 2015. https://www.theguardian.com/commentisfree/2015/jul/14/serena-williams-female-athletes-femininity-police.

Klein, Charles. ""The Guetto Is Over, Darling": Emerging Gay Communities and Gender and Sexual Politics in Contemporary Brazil." *Culture, Health & Sexuality* 1, no. 3 (1999): 239–60.

Kulick, Don. *Travesti: Sex, Gender, and Culture Among Brazilian Transgendered Prostitutes.* Chicago: The University of Chicago Press, 1998.

Kulick, Don, and Charles Klein. "Scandalous Acts: The Politics of Shame Among Brazilian Travesti Prostitutes." In *Recognition Struggles and Social Movements: Contested Identities, Agency, and Power*, edited by Barbara Hobson, 215–38. New York, NY: Cambridge University Press, 2003.

Laignier, Pablo. "Towards a Political Economy of Funk Carioca: Notes on Postmodern Theory and Its Developments in Contemporary Popular Music." *Ciberlegenda* 2, no. 24 (2011): 61–76.

Laignier, Pablo. "Rodas de Funk: Remixando Música e Política com Alegria." In *Proceedings from XXXV Congresso Brasileiro de Ciências da Comunicação: Intercom— Sociedade Brasileira de Estudos Interdisciplinares da Comunicação.* Fortaleza: CE, Brazil, 2012.

Leander, Kevin M. "Toward a Connective Ethnography of Online/Offline Literacy Networks." In *Handbook of Research on New Literacies,* edited by Julie Coiro, Michele Knobel, Colin Lankshear, and Donald J. Leu. New York: Routledge, 2010.

Lee, Wenshu. "Kauering Queer Theory: My Autocritography and a Race-Conscious, Womanist, Transnational Turn." *Journal of Homosexuality* 45, no. 2/3/4 (2003): 147–70.

Lemke, Thomas. *Biopolitics: An Advanced Introduction.* New York: New York University Press, 2011.

Lippman, Alexandra. ""Law for Whom?": Responding to Sonic Illegality in Brazil's Funk Carioca." *Sound Studies* 5, no. 1 (2018): 1–15.

Lockford, Lesa. *Performing Femininity: Rewriting Gender Identity.* Walnut Creek: Altamira Press, 2004.

Londoño, Ernesto. "A Year After Her Killing, Marielle Franco Has Become a Rallying Cry in a Polarized Brazil." *The New York Times,* March 14, 2019. https://www.nytimes.com/2019/03/14/world/americas/marielle-year-death.html.

Lopes, Adriana. *Funk-se Quem Quiser: No Batidão Negro da Cidade Carioca.* Rio de Janeiro: Bom Texto, 2011.

Ludmilla (@Ludmilla). "É sobre isso." Twitter, July 3, 2020, 8:24 p.m. https://twitter.com/Ludmilla/status/1279224569098878976.

Ludmilla. "Ludmilla—Cobra Venenosa feat. DJ Will 22 (Official Music Video)." July 3, 2020. YouTube video, 2:44. https://www.youtube.com/watch?v=H9OCyYPQ7J8.

Ludmilla. "Ludmilla—Fala mal de mim." August 25, 2014. YouTube video, 3:30. https://www.youtube.com/watch?v=UKhdAumYKCc.

Lyra, Kate. "Eu Não Sou Cachorra Não. Não? Voz e Silêncio na Construção da Identidade Feminina no Rap e no Funk no Rio de Janeiro." In *Comunicação, Consumo e Espaço Urbano: Novas Sensibilidades nas Culturas Jovens,* edited by Everardo Rocha, Maria Isabel Mendes de Almeida, and Fernanda Eugenio, 175–95. Rio de Janeiro: Mauad Editora, 2006.

Madison, D. Soyini. *Critical Ethnography: Method, Ethics, and Performance.* Thousand Oaks: Sage, 2005.

Madison, D. Soyini. "Narrative Poetics and Performative Interventions." In *Handbook of Critical and Indigenous Methodologies,* edited by Norman Denzin, Yvonna Lincoln, and Linda Tuhiwai Smith, 392–421. Los Angeles: Sage, 2008.

Madison, D. Soyini, and Judith Hamera. *Handbook of Performance Studies.* Thousand Oaks, CA: Sage, 2006.

Mahmood, Saba. "Feminist Theory, Embodiment, and the Docile Agent: Some Reflections on the Egyptian Islamic Revival." *Cultural Anthropology* 16, no. 2 (May 2001): 202–36.

Malvino (@MalvinoIgor). "Se a gente atirar igual teu cirurgião plástico trabalha aí eu fico preocupado." Twitter, August 28, 2018, 11:06 a.m. https://twitter.com/MalvinoIgor/status/1034472222373629953.

Man Recordings. "Deize Tigrona Bandida Live." October 2, 2008. YouTube video, 3:29. https://www.youtube.com/watch?v=aLCt_Mby324.

Markowitz, Sally. "Pelvic Politics: Sexual Dimorphism and Racial Difference." *Signs* 26, no. 2 (Winter 2001): 389–414.

Marrow, Helen. "To Be or Not To Be (Hispanic or Latino): Brazilian Racial and Ethnic Identity in the United States." *Ethnicities* 3, no. 4 (2003): 427–64.

Martins, Helena. "Após Dois Anos da Marcha, Mulheres Negras Continuam Mobilizadas contra Racismo." *Agência Brasil*, November 18, 2017. https://agencia-brasil.ebc.com.br/direitos-humanos/noticia/2017-11/apos-dois-anos-da-marcha-mulheres-negras-continuam-mobilizadas-contra-racismo.

Maselli, Juliana. "Morre Dançarina de Funk Lacraia." *Ego*, May 10, 2011. http://ego.globo.com/Gente/Noticias/0,,MUL1661583-9798,00-MORRE+DANCARINA+DE+FUNK+LACRAIA.html.

Maxi, Diogo Santos. "Cachorra Solta—Tati Quebra Barraco." April 15, 2012. YouTube video, 2:22. https://www.youtube.com/watch?v=B1rL8OOSv4c&list=RDLj6Mk_1KHFQ&index=19.

Maxx, Matias. "A Funkeira Lacraia É um Ícone dos LGBTs no Brasil." *Kondzilla*, June 28, 2019. https://kondzilla.com/m/a-funkeira-lacraia-e-um-icone-dos-lgbts-no-brasil.

Mazenotti, Priscilla. "Mais de 800 Pessoas Participam de Marcha para Reivindicar Igualdade de Gênero." *Portal EBC*, June 18, 2011. http://memoria.ebc.com.br/agenciabrasil/noticia/2011-06-18/mais-de-800-pessoas-participam-de-marcha-para-reivindicar-igualdade-de-genero.

MC Carol (@mccaroldeniteroioficial). "Estou buscando palavras, pq eu só sinto ódio, só sinto raiva e mt medo, realmente, eu nao sei o que falar, mas do que nunca …" Instagram photo, March 15, 2018. https://www.instagram.com/p/BgVR76Hgy1A/.

MC Carol (@mccaroldeniteroioficial). "Photo of graffiti on a wall." Instagram photo, March 15, 2018. https://www.instagram.com/p/BgW6FSKAgk8.

MC Carol (@mccaroldeniteroioficial). "Alo mulheres gorda de pernão bundao … APRENDAM, não é você! É ELE! A maioria que rejeita é porque não tem pau. É mta areia pro caminhãozinho deles, é sério … Deus me livre de pau branco pequeno e fino." Instagram photo, September 17, 2018. https://www.instagram.com/p/Bn0OdtAnqfI/?igshid=d4ltolns6q5g.

MC Carol (@mc_caroloficial). "Ahhhh gente eu to tão feliz. Foram tantas palavras de carinhos, tantas pessoas pedindo adesivo e panfletos, eu não tinha noção dessa aceitação. Essa experiência está sendo tão importante em minha vida #ELENAO #mulheresunidascontrabolsonaro #mccarol 65100." Twitter, October 1, 2018, 12:53 a.m. https://twitter.com/mc_caroloficial/status/1046639339101466624.

MC Carol (@mc_caroloficial). "morto com um tiro na cabeça, o nome dele era Zé ele tinha 13 anos, ele era empacotador de mercado, estava descendo o morro e mataram ele, a cor do Zé era negra ..." Twitter, February 16, 2019, 9:21 p.m. https://twitter.com/mc_caroloficial/status/1096972904481411075.

MC Carol (@mc_caroloficial). "O que da vontade de fazer quando uma mulher branca rica privilegiada diz: 'Sou feminista MILITANTE mais essa Mc Carol não me representa.'" Twitter, April 23, 2019, 5:57 p.m. https://twitter.com/mc_caroloficial/status/1120823980875833345.

MC Carol (@mc_caroloficial). "Antes de eu saber meu gênero eu já apanhava DIARIAMENTE na escola por ser preta." Twitter, April 26, 2020, 12:10 a.m. https://twitter.com/mc_caroloficial/status/1254276615120605184.

MC Carol Oficial. "MC Carol & Karol Conka—100% feminista (prod. Leo Justi & Tropkillaz)." October 7, 2016. YouTube video, 3:19. https://www.youtube.com/watch?v=W05v0B59K5s.

MC Rebecca (@mcrebecca). "TRANÇAS♥ Penteados afros fazem parte da história do povo negro, e o nagô é um deles." Instagram photo, July 3, 2020. https://www.instagram.com/p/CCMmW8bp6UR/.

MC Xuxú. "Mc Xuxú—Um beijo (clipe official)." November 5, 2013. YouTube video, 2:34. https://www.youtube.com/watch?v=TZbyVY9slRo.

MC Xuxú. "Mc Xuxú—Eu fiz a Chuca." March 27, 2016. YouTube video, 3:10. https://www.youtube.com/watch?v=alPlmFbNKrE.

MC Xuxú. "Mc Xuxú—Kit Assume (feat. Mulher Pepita) ÁUDIO OFICIAL." January 28, 2018. YouTube video, 2:44. https://www.youtube.com/watch?v=EbJ4A9-R_z4.

MC Xuxú. "MC Xuxú—Senzala (feat. Ingoma) áudio official." January 28, 2018. YouTube video, 2:24. https://www.youtube.com/watch?v=NrvNrJ1ijvo.

MC Xuxú. "Mc Xuxú—Vingancinha (feat. Caetano Brasil) ÁUDIO OFICIAL." January 28, 2018. YouTube video, 2:37. https://www.youtube.com/watch?v=6dmJLhxkbPY.

MC Xuxú (@mcxuxu). "Olha pra ela, o brilho da senzala." Instagram photo, March 15, 2018. https://www.instagram.com/p/BgWU5WSHh6S/?igshid=1sh87v6ahekgk.

MC Xuxú. "Mc Xuxú—Cuida do Seu." August 20, 2018. YouTube video, 2:46. https://www.youtube.com/watch?v=oFUhoV7-UL8.

MC Xuxú. "Mc Xuxú—Meus Desapegos (Clipe Oficial)." May 14, 2019. YouTube video, 3:36. https://www.youtube.com/watch?v=Z2hQJ9QM08A.

MC Xuxú (@mcxuxu). "25 de julho, dia da Mulher Afro-Latina-Americana e Caribenha, uma data extremamente significativa para nós. Salve Tereza de Benguela!" Instagram photo, July 25, 2019. https://www.instagram.com/p/B0WuOFJllwR/?igshid=3di9zkbcikzt.

McNally, James. "Favela Chic: Diplo, *Funk Carioca*, and the Ethics and Aesthetics of the Global Remix." *Popular Music and Society* 40, no. 4 (2017): 434–52.

Medeiros, Janaina. *Funk Carioca: Crime ou Cultura? O Som Dá Medo. E Prazer.* São Paulo: Terceiro Nome, 2006.

Mendonça, Renata. "Valeska Popozuda, Que Canta o Tema de Rakelli, Posa Vestida de Barbie." *Ego*, August 8, 2008. http://ego.globo.com/Gente/Noticias/ 0,,MUL716947-9798, 00-VALESKA+POPOZUDA+ QUE+CANTA+O+TEMA+DE+ RAKELLI+POSA+VESTIDA+ DE+BARBIE.html.

MG2. "Cerca de 90% das Travestis e Transexuais do País Sobrevivem da Prostituição." *G1*, May 18, 2018. https://g1.globo.com/mg/minas-gerais/noticia/cerca-de-90-das-travestis-e-transexuais-do-pais-sobrevivem-da-prostituicao.ghtml.

Mishra, Raj K. "Postcolonial Feminism: Looking into Within-Beyond-to Difference." *International Journal of English and Literature* 4, no. 4 (2013): 129–34.

Mizrahi, Mylene. "Indumentária *Funk*: A Confrontação da Alteridade Colocando em Diálogo o Local e o Cosmopolita." *Horizontes Antropológicos* 13, no. 28 (2007): 232–62.

Mohanty, Chandra. *Feminism Without Borders*. Durham, NC: Duke University Press, 2003.

Moon, Dreama. "Concepts of Culture: Implications for Intercultural Communication Research." *Communication Quarterly* 44 (1996): 70–84.

Moon, Dreama G., and Michelle A. Holling. "A Politic of Disruption: Race(ing) Intercultural Communication." *Journal of International and Intercultural Communication* 8, no. 1 (2015): 1–6.

Moreira, Raquel. "Bitches Unleashed: Women in Rio's Funk Movement, Performances of Heterosexual Femininity, and Possibilities of Resistance." PhD diss., University of Denver, 2014.

Moreira, Raquel. " 'Now that I'm a Whore, Nobody Is Holding Me Back!': Women in Favela Funk and Embodied Politics." *Women's Studies in Communication* 40, no. 2 (April 2017): 172–89.

Moreira, Raquel. "Bicha Travesti Worldmaking: Linn da Quebrada's Disidentificatory Performances of Intersectional Queerness," *Queer Studies in Media & Popular Culture* 4, no. 3 (September 1, 2019): 303–18.

Moreira, Raquel. "De-Whitening Intersectionality Through *Transfeminismo*." In *De-Whitening Intersectionality: Race, Intercultural Communication, and Politics*, edited by Shinsuke Eguchi, Bernadette M. Calafell, and Shadee Abdi, 203–22. Lanham, MD: Rowman & Littlefield, 2020.

Moreman, Shane, and Dawn Marie McIntosh. "Brown Scriptings and Rescriptings: A Critical Performance Ethnography of Latina Drag Queens." *Communication and Critical/Cultural Studies* 7, no. 2 (2010): 115–35.

Moreno, Sayonara. "Brasil É o País que Mais Mata Pessoas Trans no Mundo." *Brasil de Fato*, January 30, 2018. https://www.brasildefato.com.br/2018/01/30/ brasil-e-o-pais-que-mais-mata-pessoas-trans-no-mundo.

Morgan, Joan. *When Chickenheads Come Home to Roost*. New York: Simon & Schuster, 1999.

Mr Bongo. "Tati Quebra Barraco—Se Marcar," June 6, 2013. YouTube video, 2:33. https://www.youtube.com/watch?v=55BN3EH2mfU.

Muñoz, José Esteban. *Disidentifications: Queers of Color and the Performance of Politics*. Minneapolis: University of Minnesota Press, 1999.

Muñoz, José Estebán. *Cruising Utopia: The Then and There of Queer Futurity.* New York, NY: New York University Press, 2009.

Nakayama, Tom, and Robert L. Krizek. "Whiteness: A Strategic Rhetoric." *Quarterly Journal of Speech* 81 (1995): 291–309.

Nolen, Stephanie. "Brazil Colour Bind." *The Globe and Mail,* July 31, 2015. https://www. theglobeandmail.com/news/world/brazils-colour-bind/article25779474/.

Novaes, Dennis. "Funk Proibidão: Música e Poder nas Favelas Cariocas." *Plataforma Sucupira,* 2006, https://sucupira.capes.gov.br/sucupira/public/consultas/ coleta/trabalhoConclusao/viewTrabalhoConclusao.jsf?popup=true&id_ trabalho=4374709.

Novaes, Marina. "MC Carol: 'Meu Namorado Não É Otário. Homem Tem que Dividir Tarefa.'" *El País,* August 9, 2015. http://brasil.elpais.com/brasil/2015/07/27/cultura/1438026091_663516.html.

Ochoa, Marcia. "Ciudadanía Perversa: Divas, Marginación y Participación en la 'Loca-Lización.'" In *Políticas de Ciudadanía y Sociedad Civil en Tiempos de Globalización,* edited by Daniel Mato, 239–56. Caracas: FACES, Universidad Central de Venezuela.

Oliveira, Anderson. "Gaiola das Popozudas Agora Virei Puta Larguei Meu Marido." January 19, 2009. YouTube video, 4:15. http://www.youtube.com/watch?v=u1XLx XNhgFo.

Oliveira, Edineia Aparecida Chaves de. "A Expressão da Identidade Feminina no Gênero Musical Funk." In *VI Semana Integrada das Licenciaturas,* 933–47. Tubarão, 2007.

Oliveira, Graziele. "Valesca Popozuda: 'Ser Vadia é Ser Livre.'" *Época,* April 11, 2014. http://epoca.globo.com/ideias/noticia/2014/04/bvalesca-popozudab-ser-vadia-e-ser-livre.html.

Ortega, Rodrigo. "Kondzilla Vira Maior Canal do YouTube no Brasil e Quer Dominar Funk Além de Clips." *G1,* April 11, 2017. https://g1.globo.com/musica/noticia/ kondzilla-vira-maior-canal-do-youtube-no-brasil-e-quer-dominar-funk-alem-de-clipes.ghtml.

Ortega, Rodrigo. "Kondzilla em Queda: Por Que o Canal de Funk Perdeu Audiência e a Liderança nas Paradas?" *G1,* June 4, 2019. https://g1.globo.com/pop-arte/ musica/noticia/2019/06/04/kondzilla-em-queda-por-que-o-canal-de-funk-perdeu-audiencia-e-a-lideranca-nas-paradas.ghtml.

Pains, Clarissa. "'Menino Veste Azul e Menina Veste Rosa', Diz Damares Alves em Vídeo." *O Globo,* January 3, 2019. https://oglobo.globo.com/sociedade/menino-veste-azul-menina-veste-rosa-diz-damares-alves-em-video-23343024.

Palombini, Carlos. "Proibidão em Tempo de Pacificação Armada." In *Patrimônio Musical Na Atualidade: Tradição, Memória, Discurso e Poder,* edited by Maria Alice Volpe, 215–36. Rio de Janeiro: Universidade Federal do Rio de Janeiro, 2013.

Parker, Richard. "Masculinity, Femininity, and Homosexuality: On the Anthropological Interpretation of Sexual Meanings in Brazil." *Journal of Homosexuality* 11, no. 3–4 (1986): 155–63.

Pasin, Lucas. "MC Carol Relembra Participação no Lollapalooza: 'Choro ao Ver Vídeos.'" *Ego*, March 16, 2016. http://ego.globo.com/lollapalooza/2016/noticia/2016/03/mc-carol-relembra-participacao-no-lollapalooza-choro-ao-ver-videos.html.

Passos, Pâmella, and Adriana Facina. "'Baile Modelo!': Reflexões sobre Práticas Funkeiras em Contexto de Pacificação." *Proceedings from the VI Seminário Internacional de Políticas Culturais: Fundação Casa de Rui Barbosa*. Rio de Janeiro: RJ, Brazil, 2015.

Pereira, Fabio Queiroz, and Jordhana M. C. Gomes. "Poverty and Gender: The Marginalization of Travestis and Transsexuals by the Law." *Revista Direitos Fundamentais e Democracia* 22, no. 2 (2017): 210–24.

Pereira, Márcia. "Funkeiras Cantam, Gritam e Armam Barracos em Novo Reality Show." *UOL*, May 25, 2015. http://noticiasdatv.uol.com.br/noticia/televisao/funkeiras-cantam-gritam-e-armam-barracos-em-novo-reality-show-7993.

Pereira, Severino, and Eduardo Ayrosa. "Consumed Bodies: Gay Culture Consumption in Rio." *Organizações & Sociedade* 19, no. 61 (2012): 295–313.

Pheeno TV. "Valesca Popozuda—Fiél é o caralho / caçadoras de piru @ The Week Rio—Pheeno TV." July 3, 2012. YouTube video, 2:25. https://www.youtube.com/watch?v=Jlitw9rlqg4.

Phillips, Dom. "Brazilian Queer Art Exhibition Cancelled After Campaign by Rightwing Protesters." *The Guardian*, September 12, 2017. https://www.theguardian.com/world/2017/sep/12/brazil-queer-art-show-cancelled-protest?CMP=share_btn_tw.

Philips, Dom. "Protests Held Across Brazil After Rio Councillor Shot Dead." *The Guardian*, March 15, 2018. https://www.theguardian.com/world/2018/mar/15/marielle-franco-shot-dead-targeted-killing-rio.

Pietsch, Nicole. "'I'm Not That Kind of Girl': White Femininity, the Other, and the Legal/Social Sanctioning of Sexual Violence Against Racialized Women." *Canadian Woman Studies* 28, no. 1 (January 2010): 136–40.

Piñero-Otero, Teresa, and Xabier Martínez-Rolán. "Memes in the Internet Feminist Activism. #ViajoSola as an Example of Transnational Mobilization." *Cuadernos. Info* 39 (2016): 17–37.

Pinho, Osmundo. "The 'Faithful', the 'Lover' and the 'Charming Young Male': Gender Subjects in a Racialized Periphery." *Saúde e Sociedade* 16, no. 2 (May/August 2007): 133–45.

Pinho, Patrícia de Santana. *Reinvenções da África na Bahia*. São Paulo: Annablume, 2004.

Pocah. "Pocah—Não sou obrigada (clipe official)." March 29, 2019. YouTube video, 2:51. https://www.youtube.com/watch?v=HutLSVbLWHM.

Pocah. "Pocah—Pode Chorar (Clipe Oficial)." August 23, 2019. YouTube video, 2:45. https://www.youtube.com/watch?v=6XRJXGes0Bc.

Popozuda, Valesca. "Valesca Popozuda—Beijinho no Ombro (official music video)." December 27, 2013. YouTube video, 7:34. https://www.youtube.com/watch?v=73sbW7gjBeo.

Popozuda, Valesca (@valescapopozuda). "Hoje o meu bom dia, não vem nada bom, #QuemMatouMarielleFranco Não vamos nos calar, não vão nos calar." Instagram photo, March 15, 2018. https://www.instagram.com/p/BgWFTx4nUcs/?igshid=r7qp6t270h2n.

Popozuda, Valesca (@ValescaOficial). "Só um aviso pra quem tem me ofendido por conta do #ELENao falar 'sua bunda é de silicone' não me ofende tá! Pq eu paguei caríssimo por ela … E falar 'Valesca tá velha e namora um homem novo' namoro mesmo, e sempre que posso eu dou todo dia pq isso é ótimo." Twitter, October 11, 2018, 11:19 a.m. https://twitter.com/ValescaOficial/status/1050420525200277504.

Puar, Jaspir. ""I Would Rather Be a Cyborg Than a Goddess": Becoming Intersectional in Assemblage Theory." PhiloSOPHIA 2, no. 1 (2012): 49–66.

Puff, Jefferson. "LBGTs Sofriam Torturas Mais Agressivas, Diz CNV." BBC, December 10, 2014. https://www.bbc.com/portuguese/noticias/2014/12/141210_gays_perseguicao_ditadura_rb.

Quak, Evert-jan, and Annemarie Vijsel. "Low Wages and Job Insecurity as a Destructive Global Standard." The Broker, November 26, 2014. https://www.thebrokeronline.eu/low-wages-and-job-insecurity-as-a-destructive-global-standard-d46/.

Quebra Barraco, Tati (@TatiQBOficial). "A pm tirou um pedaço de mim que jamais será preenchido A pm matou o meu filho Essa dor nunca irá se cicatrizar." Twitter, December 10, 2016, 10:40 p.m. https://twitter.com/TatiQBOficial/status/807807225012121600.

Quebra Barraco, Tati (@TatiQBOficial). "Seja piranha mas não se esqueça dos estudos. Seja uma piranha formada." Twitter, June 18, 2017, 11:28 a.m. https://twitter.com/TatiQBOficial/status/876476726792134656.

Quebra Barraco, Tati (@TatiQBOficial). "Discutir com pm é a maior causa de morte natural no RJ mesmo." Twitter, October 31, 2017, 7:21 p.m. https://twitter.com/TatiQBOficial/status/925518000459059200.

Quebra Barraco, Tati (@TatiQBOficial). "Marielle Presente!!!!" Twitter, June 8, 2018, 8:46 a.m. https://twitter.com/TatiQBOficial/status/1005083604630810624.

Quebra Barraco, Tati (@TatiQBOficial). "Privilégio branco é ter essa cara de mico e orelha de dumbo e ser chamado de lindo." Twitter, August 28, 2018, 2:32 p.m. https://twitter.com/TatiQBOficial/status/1034524050993938433.

Quebra Barraco, Tati (@TatiQBOficial). "Primeiramente: PARABENS PRA MIM Segundamente: ELENAO Terceiramente: SEGUNDAMENTE." Twitter, September 20, 2018, 11:07 p.m. https://twitter.com/TatiQBOficial/status/1042988667935936512.

Quebra Barraco, Tati (@TatiQBOficial). "Não visitem os meus tts de 2012/2013/2014. Eu era uma merda e meu pensamento era extremamente machista. Mas não irei apagar. Não vejo motivo de esconder que já fui uma merda um dia. Quem nunca né? Boa tarde." Twitter, November 12, 2018, 9:18 a.m. https://twitter.com/TatiQBOficial/status/1062001722955055104.

Quebra Barraco, Tati (@TatiQBOficial). "Ser mulher preta e favelada que venceu na vida através de músicas polêmicas não é fácil gente. Mas sigo resistindo. A putaria não pode acabar, fui feita dela." Twitter, January 21, 2019, 8:18 p.m. https://twitter.com/TatiQBOficial/status/1087535005797101568.

Quebra Barraco, Tati (@TatiQBOficial). "Não sabia de feminismo. A questão era, se os homens podem. Eu posso também e até mais." Twitter, June 24, 2020, 9:05 a.m. https://twitter.com/TatiQBOficial/status/1275792219136557057.

Radio Conexão Ultra Dgt. "MC Katia Olha a Malandragem {Os Brabos Produções}." February 8, 2013. YouTube video, 2:27. https://www.youtube.com/watch?v=0P9P9MxF8Yo.

Radio Conexão Ultra Dgt. "MC Katia—Mete Em Mim Piroção [Lançamento 2013] [Dj Ld De Realengo]." September 6, 2013. YouTube video, 3:04. https://www.youtube.com/watch?v=UX50w_PAgGU.

Rangel, Sérgio. "Bolsonaro Pede Disciplina e Critica 'Ideologia de Gênero' em Entrega de Colégio da PM." *Folha de São Paulo*, December 17, 2018. https://www1.folha.uol.com.br/educacao/2018/12/bolsonaro-pede-disciplina-e-critica-ideologia-de-genero-em-entrega-de-colegio-da-pm.shtml.

Rede Trans Brasil. "Diálogos Sobre Viver Trans—Monitoramento: Assassinatos e Violação de Direitos Humanos de Pessoas Trans no Brasil." *Brasil*, 2019. http://redetransbrasil.org.br/wp-content/uploads/2019/01/Dossi%C3%AA-Rede-Trans-Brasil-2018-Portugu%C3%AAs.pdf.

Renegar, Valerie, and Stacey Sowards. "Contradiction as Agency: Self-Determination, Transcendence, and Counter-Imagination in Third Wave Feminism." *Hypatia* 24, no. 2 (2009): 1–20.

Rezende, Cláudia Barcellos, and Márcia Lima. "Linking Gender, Class, and Race in Brazil," *Social Identities* 10, no. 6 (2004): 757–73.

Ribeiro, Djamilla. *Quem Tem Medo do Feminism Negro?* São Paulo: Companhia das Letras, 2018.

Ribeiro, Leonardo, and Ricardo Rigel. "Atriz em Clipe 'Cobra Venenosa' de Ludmilla Já Foi Apontada como Sósia de Anitta." *Extra*, July 3, 2020. https://extra.globo.com/tv-e-lazer/atriz-em-clipe-cobra-venenosa-de-ludmilla-ja-foi-apontada-como-sosia-de-anitta-24513824.html.

Ribeiro, Marcela. "Pocah Fala de Namoro com Ex de Anitta e Suposta Rixa: 'Tudo Certo.'" *Famosos UOL*, September 25, 2019. https://tvefamosos.uol.com.br/noticias/redacao/2019/09/25/pocah-fala-de-namoro-com-ex-de-anitta-e-rixa-com-a-cantora-tudo-certo.htm.

Ribeiro, Stephanie. "Quem Somos: Mulheres Negras no Plural, Nossa Existência É Pedagógica." In *Explosão Feminista: Arte, Cultura, Política e Universidade*, edited by Heloísa Buarque de Hollanda, 261–86. São Paulo: Companhia das Letras, 2018.

Ringrose, Jessica, and Valerie Walkerdine. "Regulating the Abject." *Feminist Media Studies* 8, no. 3 (September 2008): 227–46.

Rocha, Lucas. "Entrevista: Pocah Explica Novo Nome e Fase da Carreira, se Abre sobre Feminismo e Bissexualidade, e dá Detalhes de Namoro: 'Não Esperava que as Coisas Ficariam Sérias.'" *Hugo Gloss*, September 10, 2019. https://hugogloss.uol.com.br/entrevistas/entrevista-pocah-explica-novo-nome-e-fase-da-carreira-se-abre-sobre-feminismo-e-bissexualidade-e-da-detalhes-de-namoro-nao-esperava-que-as-coisas-ficariam-serias/.

"Rodrigo Faro se Transforma em Lacraia." *R7*, March 20, 2010. http://tv.r7.com/record-play/melhor-do-brasil/videos/rodrigo-faro-se-transforma-em-lacraia-21102015.

Rodrigues, Cristiane. "Maysa Abusada Vai Fazer Cirurgia em Janeiro para Retirar Prótese dos Glúteos." *Ego*, December 6, 2014. http://ego.globo.com/famosos/noticia/2014/12/maysa-abusada-vai-fazer-cirurgia-em-janeiro-para-retirar-protese-dos-gluteos.html.

Rossi, Amanda. "Eleições 2018: O Peso de Cada Região do Brasil na Votação para Presidente." *BBC*, October 8, 2018. https://www.bbc.com/portuguese/brasil-45780864.

Sá, Simone. "Funk Carioca: Música Electronica Popular Brasileira?" In *Proceedings from XVI Compós, Associação Nacional dos Programas de Pós-Graduação em Comuminação.* Curitiba: PR, Brazil, 2007.

Sábado Show. "As Abysolutas Interview." *Estilo Livre FM* 102,5 MHz, Rio de Janeiro, Brazil. July 27, 2013.

Saldaña, Paulo. "Saiba Como Surgiu o Termo 'Ideologia de Gênero.'" *Folha de São Paulo*, October 23, 2018. https://www1.folha.uol.com.br/cotidiano/2018/10/saiba-como-surgiu-o-termo-ideologia-de-genero.shtml.

Santiago, Haline. "A Adoção do Funk como Expressão de Subversão da Sexualidade na Cena Gay da Zona Sul Carioca." In *Proceedings from VI CONECO: Congresso de Estudantes de Pós-Graduação em Comunicação.* Rio de Janeiro: RJ, Brazil, 2013.

SBT do Brasil. "4/6—Os Opostos Se Atraem—Eliana—22/11/09." November 24, 2019. YouTube video, 7:21. https://www.youtube.com/watch?v=qkHj1Tk_htI.

Schwartzman, Simon. "Fora de Foco: Diversidade e Identidades Étnicas no Brasil." *Novos Estudos CEBRAP* 55 (November 1999): 83–96.

Serano, Julia. "Reclaiming Femininity." In *Transfeminist Perspectives in and Beyond Transgender and Gender Studies*, edited by Anne Enke: 170–83. Philadelphia: Temple University Press, 2012.

Shoemaker, Deanna. "Queer Punk Macha Femme: Leslie Mah's Musical Performance in Tribe 8." *Cultural Studies ↔ Critical Methodologies* 10, no. 4 (2010): 295–306.

Shome, Raka. "White Femininity and the Discourse of the Nation: Re/membering Princess Diana." *Feminist Media Studies* 1, no. 3 (December 2, 2001): 323–42.

Showlivre. "DJ Marlboro, MC Serginho e Lacraia no Nokia Trends—arquivo radar Showlivre 2004." June 12, 2009. YouTube video, 2:37. https://www.youtube.com/watch?v=BlvHaD9YuoU.

Shugart, Helene. "Parody as Subversive Performance: Denaturalizing Gender and Reconstituting Desire in Ellen." *Text and Performance Quarterly* 21, no. 2 (2001): 95–113.

Silva, Cidinha da. "De Onde Viemos: Aproximações de uma Memória." In *Explosão Feminista: Arte, Cultura, Política e Universidade*, edited by Helosia Buarque de Hollanda, 252–60. São Paulo: Companhia das Letras, 2018.

Silveira, Daniel, and Darlan Alvarenga. "Trabalho Informal Avança para 41,3% da População Ocupada e Atinge Nível Recorde, diz IBGE." *G1*, August 30, 2019. https://g1.globo.com/economia/noticia/2019/08/30/trabalho-informal-avanca-para-413percent-da-populacao-ocupada-e-atinge-nivel-recorde-diz-ibge.ghtml.

Silveira, Daniel. "Em Sete Anos, Aumenta em 32% a População que se Declara Preta no Brasil." *G1*, May 22, 2019. https://g1.globo.com/economia/noticia/2019/05/22/em-sete-anos-aumenta-em-32percent-a-populacao-que-se-declara-preta-no-brasil.ghtml.

Skeggs, Bev. "The Making of Class and Gender through Visualizing Moral Subject Formation." *Sociology* 39, no. 5 (December 2005): 974.

Snyder, R. Claire. "What is Third-Wave Feminism? A New Directions Essay." *Signs* 34, no. 1 (Autumn 2008): 175–96.

Soares, Rodrigo. "Com Visões Políticas Distintas, MC Carol e Antonia Fontenelle Trocam Farpas." *UOL Famosos*, October 1, 2018. https://tvefamosos.uol.com.br/noticias/redacao/2018/10/01/com-visoes-politicas-distintas-mc-carol-e-antonia-fontenelle-trocam-farpas.htm?cmpid=copiaecola .

Soihet, Rachel. "A Sensualidade em Festa: Representações do Corpo Feminino nas Festas Populares no Rio de Janeiro na Virada do Século XIX para o XX." In *O Corpo Feminino em Debate*, edited by Maria Izilda Matos and Rachel Soihet, 177–97. São Paulo: Unesp, 2003.

Soliva, Thiago Barcelos. "About the Talent of Being Fabulous: The 'Transvestite Shows' and the Invention of the 'Professional Transvestite.'" *Cadernos Pagu* 53 (2018): 1–40.

Tecidio, Luciana. "Mãe de Lacraia Conta Que o Filho Não Era Feliz: 'Sofreu Muito Preconceito.'" *Ego*, May 10, 2015. http://ego.globo.com/famosos/noticia/2015/05/mae-de-lacraia-conta-que-o-filho-nao-era-feliz-sofreu-muito-preconceito.html.

Thomas, Jim. *Doing Critical Ethnography*. Thousand Oaks: Sage, 1993.

Tiburi, Marcia. "A Nova Moral do Funk." *Cult*, no. 163, November 2011. https://revistacult.uol.com.br/home/moral-funk/.

Tigrona, Deize (@deizetigrona). "Quem não luta está morto. Hoje mesmo com essa quarentena vai ter um ato pela vida. #paremdenosmatar #vidasnegrasimportam." Instagram photo, May 31, 2020. https://www.instagram.com/p/CA24E9Rn1L6/.

Tincknell, Estella. "Scourging the Abject Body: Ten Years Younger and Fragmented Femininity Under Neoliberalisml." In *New Femininites: Postfeminism, Neoliberalism and Subjectivity*, edited by Rosalind Gill and Christina Scharff, 83–95. New York: Palgrave Macmillan, 2011.

Torres, Leonardo. "MC Pocahontas Assina Contrato com a Warner Music," *Terra Popline*, January 16, 2019. https://portalpopline.com.br/mc-pocahontas-assina-contrato-com-warner-music.

Torres, Livia. "Duas Pessoas Morrem em Tiroteio na Saída de Baile Funk na Zona Norte do Rio." *G1*, July 15, 2019. https://g1.globo.com/rj/rio-de-janeiro/noticia/2019/07/15/duas-pessoas-morrem-em-tiroteio-na-saida-de-baile-funk-na-zona-norte-do-rio.ghtml.

Trevizan, Karina. "36% das Mulheres Dizem Dividir com Marido as Tarefas de Casa Igualmente." *G1*, June 15, 2016. http://g1.globo.com/economia/concursos-e-emprego/noticia/2016/06/so-36-das-mulheres-dividem-tarefas-domesticas-com-marido-diz-pesquisa.html.

TV Onix. "Documentário Favela Gay completo." November 16, 2017. YouTube video, 1:11:45. https://www.youtube.com/watch?v=4gjjXLvhOXo.

Uchoa, Pablo. "Jair Bolsonaro: Why Brazilian Women Are Saying #NotHim." *BBC*, September 21, 2018. https://www.bbc.com/news/world-latin-america-45579635.

Uchoa, Tabata. "MC Marcelly Interpreta Vítima de Violência Doméstica em Clipe." *O Dia*, November 2, 2015. https://odia.ig.com.br/_conteudo/diversao/celebridades/2015-11-03/mc-marcelly-interpreta-vitima-de-violencia-domestica-em-clipe.html.

Universa. "Valesca Popozuda: 'Fico no Baile Até às 9h da manhã.'" October 5, 2018. YouTube video, 10:06. https://www.youtube.com/watch?v=BeuKVWsZulI.

Vartabedian, Julieta. *Brazilian Travesti Migrations*. New York: Palgrave Macmillan, 2018.

Vergueiro, Viviane. "Despatologizar é Descolonizar." *Global Action for Trans Equality*, October 26, 2015. https://transactivists.org/viviane-vergueiro-despatologizar-es-descolonizar/.

Vergueiro, Viviane. "Por Inflexões Decoloniais de Corpos e Identidades de Gênero Inconformes: Uma Análise Autoetnográfica da Cisgeneridade como Normatividade." *Repositório UFBA*, 2015, https://repositorio.ufba.br/ri/handle/ri/19685.

Viana, Iara Pires. "Funk Territory and Femininities: Subjectivities Built Between Power Relations, the Street and Violence." *Revista Brasileira de Estudos do Lazer* 3, no. 3 (2016): 118–35.

Vianna, Hermano. *O Mundo Funk Carioca*. Rio de Janeiro: Editora Jorge Zahar, 1998.

Vice Brasil. "Por dentro do Funk 150 BPM." December 3, 2018. YouTube video, 21:19. https://www.youtube.com/watch?v=1T7-6aWp7Hs.

Vieira, Helena. "Transfeminismo." In *Explosão Feminista: Arte, Cultura, Política e Universidade,* edited by H. Buarque de Hollanda, 343–78. Rio de Janeiro: Companhia das Letras, 2018.

Villela, Sumaia. "Na Luta contra a Pobreza, Mulheres Buscam Autnomia por Conta Própria." *Agência Brasil*, March 8, 2016. https://agenciabrasil.ebc.com.br/direitos-humanos/noticia/2016-03/na-luta-contra-pobreza-mulheres-buscam-autonomia-por-meio-do.

Weschenfelder, Viviane Inês, and Elí Terezinha H. Fabris. "Becoming Black Woman: Self-Writing in an Intersectional Place." *Revista Estudos Feministas* 27, no. 3 (2019): 1–15.

Windsor, Liliane C. "Deconstructing Racial Democracy: A Personal Quest to Understand Social Conditioning About Race Relations in Brazil." *Social Identities* 13, no. 4 (2007): 495–520.

Yep, Gust. "The Violence of Heteronormativity in Communication Studies: Notes on Injury, Healing, and Queer World-Making." *Journal of Homosexuality* 45, no. 2/3/4 (2003): 11–59.

Yep, Gust. "Toward the De-Subjugation of Racially Marked Knowledges in Communication." *Southern Communication Journal* 75, no. 2 (2010): 171–75.

Yep, Gust. "Queering/Quaring/Kauering/Crippin'/Transing 'Other Bodies' in Intercultural Communication." *Journal of International and Intercultural Communication* 6, no. 2 (2013): 118–26.

Index

Critical Intercultural Communication Studies

Thomas K. Nakayama and Bernadette Marie Calafell, General Editors

Critical approaches to the study of intercultural communication have arisen at the end of the twentieth century and are poised to flourish in the new millennium. As cultures come into contact—driven by migration, refugees, the internet, wars, media, transnational capitalism, cultural imperialism, and more—critical interrogations of the ways that cultures interact communicatively are needed to understand culture and communication. This series will interrogate—from a critical perspective—the role of communication in intercultural contact, in both domestic and international contexts. This series is open to studies in key areas such as postcolonialism, transnationalism, critical race theory, queer diaspora studies, and critical feminist approaches as they relate to intercultural communication, tuning into the complexities of power relations in intercultural communication. Proposals might focus on various contexts of intercultural communication such as international advertising, popular culture, language policies, hate crimes, ethnic cleansing and ethnic group conflicts, as well as engaging theoretical issues such as hybridity, displacement, multiplicity, identity, orientalism, and materialism. By creating a space for these critical approaches, this series will be at the forefront of this new wave in intercultural communication scholarship. Manuscripts and proposals are welcome that advance this new approach.

For additional information about this series or for the submission of manuscripts, please contact:

Thomas K. Nakayama, General Editor | *T.Nakayama@neu.edu*
Bernadette Marie Calafell, General Editor | *calafell@gonzaga.edu*

To order other books in this series, please contact our Customer Service Department at:

peterlang@presswarehouse.com (within the U.S.)
orders@peterlang.com (outside the U.S.)

or browse online by series: www.peterlang.com

www.ingramcontent.com/pod-product-compliance
Lightning Source LLC
Chambersburg PA
CBHW050637280326
41932CB00015B/2683